TRAVELING WEST
MARK TWAIN STYLE

By Dale H. Janssen
and
Janice J. Beaty

Janssen Education Enterprise, Inc.
Columbia, Missouri
1989

STAFFORD LIBRARY
COLUMBIA COLLEGE
1001 ROGERS STREET
COLUMBIA, MO 65216

Published by Janssen Education Enterprise, Inc.
P.O. Box 1601
Columbia, Missouri 65205

Printed by   General Printing Service
1910 North Providence
Columbia, Missouri 65202

Cover photo: Janice J. Beaty

Photo Credits: Janice J. Beaty, all photos except p. 22, James McCluskey

Copyright© 1989 by Dale H. Janssen. All rights reserved. No part of this book may be reproduced in any form, electronic or mechanical, including photocopy, recording, or any information storage and retrieval system, without permission in writing from the publisher.

First Edition 1989.

Although the authors and publisher have exhaustively researched all sources to ensure the accuracy and completeness of the information contained in this book, we assume no responsibility for errors, inaccuracies, omissions or any other inconsistency herein. Any slights against people or organizations are unintentional.

Library of Congress Catalog Card Number: 89-83658
International Standard Book Number: ISBN 0-9618217-2-8
Printed in the United States of America

To Cyril Clemens
who keeps alive
the Mark Twain heritage
of Samuel Clemens

PREFACE

"Go West, young man, go West, and grow up with the country" was advice that carried young men by the thousands across the Great Plains, the Rocky Mountains, and the Great American Desert in the 1850's and '60's. One of those travelers was Samuel Clemens who had not yet acquired his fame as Mark Twain. He and his brother Orion traveled west by stagecoach in the summer of 1861. Sam hoped to find silver in Nevada or gold in California, but he found something more valuable.

TRAVELING WEST MARK TWAIN STYLE relates this exciting adventure not only with the words of Mark Twain, but also from the pen of Dale Janssen and Janice Beaty as they too travel west in the summer of 1988, researching Mark Twain and transportation.

Historic stage stops, a herd of buffalo, a lively ghost town, and famous mining cabins marked their trail much in the manner of Clemens' trip in that long ago summer.

What was it like on the plains of Kansas, along the Platte River in Nebraska, through the mountains of Wyoming, and the deserts of Utah and Nevada in 1988 — as compared to 1861? The authors invite you to come along across the West as they found it to be in the summer of 1988 when they also traveled west Mark Twain style.

ACKNOWLEDGEMENTS

The authors express their thanks to the many individuals and organizations who gave their help and support in preparing this book: in New York State, Dr. Linda Pratt, Judy Clack, and Ben Otten of Elmira College; Mike Sheehe of B & C Photos; State Capitol office of the Lieutenant Governor, Albany; Seneca Army Depot, Romulus; in Missouri, Ralph Gregory of Marthasville; Gary Chilcote of St. Joseph; National Park Service, St. Louis; U.S. Navy Reserve Center, St. Louis; Becky Thatcher Bookstore, Hannibal; Holiday Inn Riverfront, St. Louis; Rodeway Inn and Niedermeyer Apts., Columbia. To the following libraries: Gannett-Tripp Learning Center, Elmira College; West Point Military Academy Library; The State Historical Museum of Missouri, Columbia; Columbia College Library; public libraries of Jamestown, Tennessee and Columbia, Kentucky; Harry S. Truman Library, Independence, Missouri; and high school library, Nelson, Nebraska. In addition: Union Pacific Railroad Offices, Omaha, Nebraska; Ken Martin of Marysville, Kansas; Ernst Enterprises, Unionville, Nevada; Julian Smith, Carson City, Nev.; State Capitol, Carson City, Nev., J.A. Schafer, Historic Territorial Enterprise Building, Virginia City, Nevada; Ted Laskin and Michael Paluszak, Angels Camp, California; and historic Old Sacramento, Sacramento, California. Also Noah's Ark Motor Inn, St. Charles, Missouri.

OTHER BOOKS BY THE SAME AUTHORS

MARK TWAIN WALKING AMERICA AGAIN

STORYTELLING MARK TWAIN STYLE

CONTENTS

CHAPTER 1, GO WEST, YOUNG MAN 3
   Introduction 3
   Mark Twain Goes West 3
   Janssen and Beaty Go West 5
   At Jamestown, Tennessee 8

CHAPTER 2, RIVERBOATS ACROSS MISSOURI 17
   Samuel Clemens in St. Louis 17
   Across Missouri by Riverboat 18
   Missouri Riverboats in the 1850's and '60's 20
   Riverboating Today 20
   Janssen and Beaty in St. Louis 21
   In St. Charles 23
   The "Spirit of St. Charles" 25
   Historic St. Charles 26
   A "Mark Twain alias Dale Janssen" Appearance 26
   Historic St. Joseph 29
   Janssen and Beaty in St. Joseph 29

CHAPTER 3, STAGE STOPS IN KANSAS 37
   The Clemenses in St. Jo 37
   Janssen and Beaty at the Patee House 38
   Central Overland California Trail 38
   Across Kansas 39
   Marysville Home Station 41
   On the Trail 43
   Bremen 45
   Hollenberg Station 47

CHAPTER 4, STAGE STOPS IN NEBRASKA 53
   Historic Rock Creek Station 53
   Rock Creek Station Today 54
   Wheel Ruts 54
   A Stagecoach 55
   Fellow Travelers 57
   Valley of the Little Blue River 57
   Stage Station Buildings 59
   Fort Kearny 61
   The Authors at Fort Kearny 61
   Stories from the Early Days 62

CHAPTER 5, ON THE PLATTE RIVER TRAIL ... 69
- The Trails ... 69
- The Travelers ... 70
- The Dangers ... 71
- Janssen and Beaty at Cozad and Gothenberg ... 74
- Janssen at Gothenberg ... 76
- On to North Platte, Nebraska ... 76
- The Buffalo Bill Connection ... 77

CHAPTER 6, THE BUFFALO BILL CONNECTION ... 81
- Scout's Rest Ranch ... 81
- Buffalo Stew Cookout ... 82
- Other Parallels ... 82
- The Pony Express ... 83
- Buffalo Bill, a Pony Rider ... 84
- On the Buffalo Bill Trail ... 87
- Across the Sandhills of Nebraska ... 89
- At Cody, Wyoming ... 95

CHAPTER 7, LANDMARKS ON THE TRAIL ... 101
- Courthouse Rock and Jail Rock ... 101
- Chimney Rock ... 104
- Scotts Bluff ... 105
- Horse Creek Station ... 109
- Independence Rock ... 112
- Devil's Gate ... 113
- Ice House Slough ... 113
- South Pass ... 113
- Janssen and Beaty on the Road ... 115
- Breakfast at Fort Bridger ... 116

CHAPTER 8, A GOLDEN SPIKE IN UTAH ... 121
- Echo Canyon, Utah ... 121
- Sunsets and Rainbows ... 121
- The Great Salt Lake Desert ... 122
- Mark Twain on the Great Salt Lake Desert ... 123
- Winds of Change ... 125
- Mark Twain and Railroads ... 127
- Janssen and Railroads ... 129
- To Promontory ... 130
- Janssen and Beaty at Promontory ... 131
- Ten Miles of Track ... 133
- The Golden Spike ... 135

Another Rainbow 137

CHAPTER 9, CARSON CITY, NEVADA 141
Across Nevada 141
The "Passenger" at Ragtown 142
Janssen's "Horace Greeley and the Stagecoach" Story 143
At Carson City 145
The "Washoe Zephyr" 147
The Modern City 149
The 1861 Town 149
A Place to Live 150
A Horse to Ride 152
Janssen's Horse Story 155
Orion's House 157

CHAPTER 10, MARK TWAIN'S NEVADA CABIN 161
News of the Cabin 161
Back Across the Desert 161
At Unionville 163
Mark Twain's Cabin 163
Samuel Clemens' Unionville 168
Mining 169
Unionville Rock Shop 173

CHAPTER 11, VIRGINIA CITY, NEVADA 177
Virginia City Today 177
Mark Twain's Mark 177
Mark Twain's Name 178
Janssen's Version of the Pen Name 178
Mark Twain's Hoaxes 180
Janssen and Beaty in Virginia City 181
Mark Twain's Robbery 183
Piper's Opera House 185
Territorial Enterprise 185

CHAPTER 12, CALIFORNIA GOLD 189
Placerville/Sacramento 189
Clemens in San Francisco 190
Jackass Hill 191
Pocket Mining 192
A Lunar Rainbow 193
Back to the Cabin 195

CHAPTER 13, THE CELEBRATED JUMPING FROG 203
To Angels Camp 203
The Jumping Frog 204
The Story 209
Janssen and Beaty at Angels Camp 210
Frogtown 210
The Cabin on Jackass Hill 212

DALE'S TALES

"I Was Born Excitedly"..................................12

"In the Beginning"....................................19

"The Wild Missouri River"..............................25

"An Island Known as Catfish Island"....................27

"Hogs Under the Church"................................27

"Acorn on the Tree Stump"..............................43

"I'm Concerned About These Railroads".................127

"The Train with the Cowcatcher".......................129

"Horace Greeley and the Stagecoach"...................143

"A Horse in Honolulu".................................157

"My Pen Name Mark Twain"..............................179

"Stupid Story"..181

"Leaving Town in a Hurry".............................185

"Left-handed Pool Player".............................191

TWAIN'S TALES

"I Remember the Departure" 7
"I Envied My Brother" 17
"St. Louis to St. Joe" 19
"She Has Two Tall Fancy-topped Chimneys" 21
"Twenty-five Pounds of Baggage" 37
"We Jumped into the Stage" 39
"A Woman Got In" 44
"A Great Swinging and Swaying Stage" 55
"Our Party Inside Got Mixed Somewhat" 56
"The Station Buildings Were Long, Low Huts" 59
"The Shallow, Muddy South Platte" 63
"The Thoroughbrace Is Broke" 71
"The Indian Mail Robbery and Massacre" 73
"A Consuming Desire to See a Pony-Rider" 83
"This Desperado Slade" 84
"We Sat Down to Breakfast" 86
"When the Buffalo Climbed the Tree" 90
"Buffalo Bill's Horse" 96
"Horace Greeley's Stagecoach Ride" 104, 107, 110, 117
"Alkali Water" 106
"Mormon Wagon Train" 109
"South Pass City" 114
"A Vast Waveless Ocean" 124
"The 'Passenger' at Ragtown" 142
"The Washoe Zephyr" 147
"The Tarantulas is Loose" 150
"A Genuine Mexican Plug" 152
"Discovery of a Brand-new Mining Region" 164
"Falling Down the Chimney" 165
"All that Glitters" 169
"The 'City' of Virginia" 181
"We Lived in a Small Cabin" 191
"Pocket Hunting" 192
"Tom Quartz, Gold Mine Cat" 195
"Jim Smiley and his Jumping Frog" 205

LIST OF PHOTOGRAPHS

Janssen at back of stagecoach (Courtesy Mo. Dept. of Natural Resources)	cover
Janssen aboard *Mississippi Queen* riverboat at St. Louis Gateway Arch	2
Rail locomotive at Kearney, Nebraska	4
Janssen and *Missouri Queen* riverboat at St. Charles, Mo.	6
Co-author at Mark Twain Spring, Jamestown, Tenn.	9
Gateway Arch over historic Courthouse, St. Louis riverfront	16
Janssen alias Mark Twain & *Julia Belle Swain* riverboat at St. Charles, Mo.	22
Spirit of St. Charles riverboat & Janssen alias Mark Twain on bank of Missouri River	24
Spirit of St. Joseph riverboat reflected in Missouri River	30
Janssen framed by cottonwood trees looking across Missouri River toward Kansas	32
At Patee House Museum, St. Joseph, Mo.	36
At Pony Express Home Station, Marysville, Kansas	40
Pony Express statue, Marysville, Kansas	42
At Hollenberg Station near Hanover, Kansas	46
Ox wagon at Rock Creek Station, Fairbury, Nebraska	52
Little Blue River at Oak, Nebraska	58
Adobe building at Fort Kearny, Nebraska	60
Platte River at North Platte, Nebraska	64
Covered wagon on Nebraska trail	68
Janssen and stagecoach	72
At Pony Express Station, Gothenberg, Nebraska	75
Janssen in horse barn at Buffalo Bill's Scouts Rest Ranch, North Platte, Nebraska	80
Missouri foxtrotter filly *Lindy's Star* (with halter) and *Lindy*	85
Buffalo Bill's Irma Hotel, Cody, Wyoming	94
Scotts Bluff National Monument in Nebraska	100

Janssen looking at Courthouse & Jail Rocks outside Bridgeport, Nebraska	102
Janssen at Horse Creek, Wyoming	108
At Independence Rock, Wyoming	111
Beaty at Golden Spike National Historic Site, Promontory, Utah	120
Historic Hannibal & St. Joseph Railroad engine, Patee House Museum, St. Joseph, Missouri	126
Modern Union Pacific locomotive at Winnemucca, Nevada	128
Historic roadbed of Central Pacific Railroad, Promontory, Utah	132
At Golden Spike rail site where East met West, Promontory, Utah	136
Janssen at site of historic Desert Well Stage Station, Nev.	140
Janssen alias Mark Twain telling stage coach story	144
Mark Twain Avenue on road to Carson City, Nevada	146
Nevada State Capitol, Carson City	148
Janssen's Missouri foxtrotter colt, *J.J.'s Calloway Squire*	154
Orion Clemens' house, Carson City, Nevada	156
Mark Twain's cabin, Unionville, Nevada	160
Beaty at Mark Twain's cabin, Unionville, Nev.	162
Historic mode of early transportation	166
Territorial Enterprise newspaper building across C Street, Virginia City, Nevada	176
Site of infamous robbery, Virginia City, Nevada	182
Piper's Opera House, Virginia City, Nevada	184
Mark Twain cabin at Jackass Hill near Angels Camp, Calif.	188
Interior of cabin at Jackass Hill	194
Janssen outside Angels Hotel, site of Jumping Frog story, Angels Camp, Calif.	202
Mark Twain cabin at Jackass Hill	211
Janssen and Mark Twain statue, town park, Angels Camp, Calif.	213

TRAVELING WEST MARK TWAIN STYLE

Dale H. Janssen
Janice J. Beaty

CHAPTER 1
"GO WEST, YOUNG MAN"

INTRODUCTION

Americans have always had a "westering urge", it seems. The pull of new lands, of wide-open spaces, and of a continent to be explored have drawn pioneers, explorers, and emigrants from the beginning. To make a new start in life, to discover gold, to stake out a homestead, or just plain "for the adventure of it," were reasons enough to start west in the early days.

Today it is different — and yet the same. We are still a restless people, we Americans. Our country is settled now from coast to coast, and still we are a nation of travelers, moving from job to job, visiting friends and relatives, or vacationing further and further afield.

Sometimes we go by jet. Sometimes by bus. Less frequently by train because there are so few of them for passengers nowadays. More often we travel by car across the ranging miles of interstate highways. But whatever the means, we go. And the one direction we choose most frequently is WEST.

Horace Greeley, the famous newspaper editor of the *New York Tribune* first caught the attention of the nation in 1851 by quoting John Soule's "Go west, young man, go west, and grow up with the country," in his *Advice to Aspiring Young Men*. Thousands of young men took him up on it.

MARK TWAIN GOES WEST

One of those young men was twenty-five-year-old Samuel L. Clemens who had yet to acquire his fame as Mark Twain. While we know that Mark Twain was an inveterate traveler, we usually associate

his travel with riverboats on the Mississippi River going in a north and south direction. When did Mark Twain ever go west?

He not only traveled across the West from St. Louis, Missouri to Carson City, Nevada, but he also made his journey during the exciting but dangerous summer of 1861 when the Civil War was at full tilt, when Indians were on the western warpath, and when the first overland stagecoaches and early pony express riders made their debut from St. Joseph, Missouri. Not only did he experience the excitement that all western travelers have known, but he recorded his adventures for posterity in his travel book ROUGHING IT.

What was it really like for a western traveler during that long ago summer? Through the windows of Samuel Clemens' stagecoach and the pen of Mark Twain, we are able to visualize the vast sweep of plains, the majesty of mountains, and the difficulties of rivers to be forded or deserts to be crossed.

But it can't be like that today, we counter. Or can it? What is it really like to follow the trail Mark Twain traveled? Has the West been so totally tamed that "the deer and the antelope" no longer "play" where Clemens saw them in Nebraska and Wyoming? Has the pony express rider that Mark Twain so excitedly watched from his stagecoach been completely forgotten? (*"Wanted: Young, skinny, wiry fellows, not over eighteen. Must be expert riders, willing to risk death daily. Orphans preferred. Wages $25 per week. Apply Pony Express Stables, St. Joseph, Missouri,"* read the 1860 ad). If we get off the super highways and look for the things that Mark Twain saw, will we be able to find any of his images in the West today?

JANSSEN AND BEATY GO WEST

That is the question Dale Janssen asked himself in the summer of 1988. He had been traveling the Mark Twain trail (often unknowingly) in Missouri, Illinois and Iowa, up and down the Mississippi River, as well as over to New York and Connecticut since 1983. He and his co-author, Twain researcher Janice Beaty, had recorded his experiences in their book MARK TWAIN WALKING AMERICA AGAIN. Now Janssen was eager to turn west. While Beaty's focus was on Samuel Clemens' early experiences, Janssen's focus also included early transportation in America. What was it like traveling on the early riverboats, stagecoaches, and railroads? His background as a transportation consultant and transportation law "practitioner" gave

Janssen an added impetus to follow the development of transportation in our country during Samuel Clemens' day.

Where should they start? St. Joseph, Missouri seemed to be the proper "jumping-off place" for people bound west both in Samuel Clemens' day and today. Preliminary research indicated that Clemens had indeed boarded the overland stage in St. Joseph for his trip to Carson City. But he, like the other stage and wagon train travelers of his day, did not actually begin his journey at that western edge of Missouri. Most of them first traveled by steamboat up the Missouri River from St. Louis to St. Joseph.

Janssen was familiar with Missouri River riverboats. He was pleased to think that the several boats he had traveled on would find a place in this new literary venture. Let St. Louis be their starting place, then.

But what brought Samuel Clemens to St. Louis, in the first place, Janssen wondered? Could it have been his boyhood dreams back in the Mississippi River town of Hannibal? Most of us connect Mark Twain's dreams with the river itself and his longing to become a steamboat pilot on the river. After all, he told us about it himself in his book LIFE ON THE MISSISSIPPI, didn't he?

That was certainly true as far as it went. Clemens had, in fact, become the pilot of his dreams even before his western adventure began. But Clemens had other longings, as well. He mentions in his AUTOBIOGRAPHY how excited he was back in his boyhood days when his friend George RoBard's little brother John went west from Hannibal in 1849:

"I Remember the Departure"

> When he was twelve years old he crossed the plains with his father amid the rush of the gold seekers of '49; and I remember the departure of the cavalcade when it spurred westward. We were all there to see and to envy. And I can still see that proud little chap sailing by on a great horse, with his long locks streaming out behind. We were all on hand to gaze and envy when he returned two years later in unimaginable glory — *for he had traveled!* None of us had ever been forty miles from home. But he had crossed the continent. He had been in the gold mines, that fairyland of our imagination. (Neider, 1959)

*****

Did that mean Janssen should start his western trip at Hannibal, Twain's boyhood home? Or maybe at Florida, Missouri, Samuel Clemens' birthplace? It was evident that the more Janssen and Beaty delved into the real beginnings of Mark Twain's "travel bug," the further back it would take them. Well, why not? Why not start at the real beginning of it all. What was it that began all the traveling that carried the Clemens family west in the first place? Or rather, who was it? Research eventually revealed that the originator of the "westering urge" in the Clemens family was Mark Twain's father, John Marshall Clemens. And his western movement began in Jamestown, Tennessee where he had settled early in his marriage to Jane Lampton of Columbia, Kentucky.

AT JAMESTOWN, TENNESSEE

So that is where the authors found themselves driving one misty Saturday morning in July. Halfway between Knoxville and Nashville they turned north onto Rte. 127 and followed it up and up to the level top of the Cumberland Plateau. Behind them was the "knob" country of Tennessee, where mountaintop-like protuberances covered the landscape. But this was a pleasant rural country with pastures, corn, and horses. Many homes along the road showed orangish native stone in their walls and tin on their roofs. Would Jamestown be like this?

It is always exciting to visit a new "Mark Twain location." Would it have any resemblance to the olden days? Might a building or other historical remains be preserved? Might there be any evidence of early transportation? And what about the people — would they recall and willingly share their town's Mark Twain heritage? Would they have anecdotes to relate or stories to tell about the Clemens family? This was the type of "oral research" the authors were seeking.

A drive down the main street revealed a pleasant town of tree-shaded houses and a handsome stone courthouse in the middle of the business section, (the first one was designed by John M. Clemens, it turned out). And, yes, they did remember Mark Twain! Across the street was a Mark Twain Cafe. Just down the block was the town park labeled "Mark Twain Park" and flanked by a historical marker that informed the visitors:

MARK TWAIN SPRING

This historical landmark of Fentress County was named for

Samuel Langhorne Clemens, known worldwide as Mark Twain. It was the source of water for early settlers of Jamestown, including Clemens' parents who settled on adjoining property to the north, where they lived from 1827-1832. In the spring of 1835 they left for Missouri, where Clemens was born that November.

As Janssen took notes about the historical marker, Beaty explored the sand spring at the edge of the park and the wooden head of Mark Twain carved by a local chainsaw artist from an immense tree trunk. They had not been in the park more than five minutes when suddenly, from across the street came an excited man with a camera around his neck and a pad and pencil in his hand. He turned out to be the editor of the local paper, the *Fentress Courier*, and he wanted to do a story! Now where had he come from?

What a coincidence that the local editor should be passing by just at that instant, one would ordinarily exclaim. Not Janssen. Coincidences like this had become a part of his life since 1983 when he was accidently discoverd as a Mark Twain look-alike while stopping at a Hannibal, Missouri nursing home to play harmonica music. (See book MARK TWAIN WALKING AMERICA AGAIN).

Now he was beginning another summer of exploring, traveling, and following the Twain and the transportation trails wherever they would lead. What an auspicious beginning!

A few days later the *Fentress Courier* ran a front page fully illustrated article on the visitors:

"MARK TWAIN" MAKES VISIT TO COUNTY
By Bill Bowden

Driving through the downtown Jamestown area Saturday morning, while passing the Mark Twain Sand Spring Park, I did a double-take, for standing looking at the park's sign was a real-life Mark Twain.

After making sure that my eyes weren't playing tricks on me, since I wasn't wearing my glasses at the time, I stopped and introduced myself to this Mark Twain character, who introduced himself to me as Dale H. Janssen of Columbia, Missouri, and introduced a colleague of his Dr. Janice J. Beaty of Elmira, New York.

The couple explained that they are researching Mark Twain's heritage, and more particularly, seeking information concerning Mark Twain's father, John M. Clemens, who, after living in Fentress County near the Sand Spring Park for several years, took his family west, leaving Fentress County in the spring of 1835 before his youngest son, Samuel Langhorne Clemens, later known as Mark Twain, was born in the fall . . .

John Marshall Clemens was the Clerk of the Circuit Court as well as a farmer and storekeeper during his five years at Jamestown. But in his heart of hearts, he was a pioneer — always searching for new lands to claim, new riches to discover. When his wife's relatives and his own called for him to come out where they had settled in an even richer frontier country, he could not resist. He packed up his three youngest children in his two-horse barouche, with two more horses for his oldest boy, Orion and the house-girl, Jennie. Then off they rode north for a brief visit to his wife's home in Columbia, Kentucky, and on up to Louisville where they boarded a steamer for the trip west to St. Louis; then overland to St. Charles on the Missouri River. After a rest stop for the mother-with-child, they struck out overland on the Salt River Trail to the tiny village of Florida, Missouri — the "Far West" — the rich frontier land where Samuel Langhorne Clemens would be born November 30, 1835.

But Clemens, the father, never gave up on his Tennessee dream. Before he left for Missouri he invested in 75,000 acres of land-grant property — enough to provide for his family in later years when the country was sure to open up for timber, coal, iron, and vineyards. John Marshall Clemens never lived to see it happen. He died of pneumonia contracted while riding from a circuit court hearing in Palmyra, Missouri to his home in Hannibal, when his son Samuel was eleven years old. But his "westering" dream did not die. His sons Orion and Samuel, ever on the move, were to follow the western trail across the continent in the summer of 1861. And his son Samuel as Mark Twain would eventually travel west around the entire world to the greatest acclaim ever awarded an American author in 1895.

Dale Janssen knew the John Marshall Clemens story. Now he filled out his knowledge with an awareness of the country Clemens had settled in and helped to develop; with an acquaintance of the people of Jamestown and a knowledge of their continued interest in the Mark

Twain heritage. Janssen's monologue of Mark Twain's birth seemed more realistic than ever, next time he delivered it as Mark Twain to an entranced audience:

"I Was Born Excitedly"

My mother and my father, John Marshall Clemens lived in the State of Tennessee. I don't remember when, because I wasn't born — I was postponed. There was this new and unknown State of Missouri that wanted to be better known, so my parents postponed having me until after they had moved to Florida, Missouri. And that's where I was born November 30, 1835 as Samuel Clemens.

I was born excitedly they tell me. One reason I was born excitedly was that Halley's Comet was streaking across the skies. Another reason I was born excitedly was that I wasn't expected. I came two months early.

There were one hundred people living there in this small town of Florida, Missouri when my folks arrived. When I was born the population increased to one hundred and one, or you could say I increased the population of my home town by one percent. I could have done it for any other town had I chosen, but I'm glad it happened right there in Florida, Missouri. (Janssen and Beaty, MARK TWAIN WALKING AMERICA AGAIN, 1987).

* * * * *

Now that they had found the source of Mark Twain's "travel bug" the authors were ready to start on their own adventure west, as well. They invite you to come along — across the west as Mark Twain described it from 1861, and as Janssen and Beaty found it to be in the summer of 1988 when they also traveled west, Mark Twain Style.

* * * * *

REFERENCES

Bartlett, John, FAMILIAR QUOTATIONS, Boston: Little, Brown & Co., 1955.

Bowden, Bill, " 'Mark Twain' Makes Visit to County," *Fentress Courier*, July 27, 1988.

Henderson, Roswell P. and Ralph Gregory, "Judge John Marshall Clemens," *Bulletin of the Missouri Historical Society*, Oct., 1964, pp. 25-30.

Janssen, Dale H., and Janice J. Beaty, MARK TWAIN WALKING AMERICA AGAIN, Columbia, Missouri: Janssen Education Enterprise, Inc., 1987.

MARK TWAIN REMEMBERS (Videotape with Dale Janssen as Mark Twain), Elmira, New York: Three-to-Five, P.O. Box 3213, 1986.

Neider, Charles (ed), THE AUTOBIOGRAPHY OF MARK TWAIN, New York: Harper & Row Publishers, 1959.

Paine, Albert Bigelow, MARK TWAIN A BIOGRAPHY, New York: Harper and Row, 1912.

Twain, Mark, ROUGHING IT, New York: Harper & Brothers Publishers, 1913.

CHAPTER 2
RIVERBOATS ACROSS MISSOURI

SAMUEL CLEMENS IN ST. LOUIS

So there stood the young Sam Clemens looking out the window of his sister Pamela's home in St. Louis that summer of 1861, trying to surpress the excitement that rose in his throat at the very thought of his upcoming trip across the continent to Nevada. His older brother Orion had been appointed by President Lincoln to be the Secretary of the Territory of Nevada; or as Sam described it in ROUGHING IT:

"I Envied My Brother"

. . . an office of such majesty that it concentrated in itself the duties and dignities of Treasurer, Comptroller, Secretary of State, and Acting Governor in the Governer's absence. A salary of eighteen hundred dollars a year and the title of "Mr. Secretary," gave to the great position an air of wild and imposing grandeur. I was young and ignorant, and I envied my brother. I coveted his distinction and his financial splendor, but particularly and especially the long, strange journey he was going to make, and the curious new world he was going to explore. He was going to travel! I never had been away from home, and that word "travel" had a seductive charm for me. Pretty soon he would be hundreds and hundreds of miles away on the great plains and deserts, and among the mountains of the Far West, and would see buffaloes and Indians, and prairie-dogs, and antelopes, and have all kinds of adventures, and maybe get hanged or scalped, and have ever such a fine time, and write home and tell us all about it, and be a hero. And he would see the gold-mines and the silver-mines, and maybe go about of an afternoon when his work was done, and pick up two or three pailfuls of shining slugs and nuggets of gold and silver on the hillside. And by and by he would become very rich, and return home by sea, and be able to talk as calmly about San Francisco and the ocean and "the isthmus" as if it was nothing of any consequence to have seen those marvels face to face. (Twain, ROUGHING IT, 1913).

*****

Samuel Clemens had actually done a bit of traveling himself before he wrote those words. He had gone east from St. Louis by rail and riverboat to New York City, then to Philadelphia, then Washington, D.C., and back again to St. Louis and finally Keokuk, Iowa where his brother lived. Then he had traveled up the Ohio River to Cincinnati, back down to St. Louis, and clear to New Orleans and back, as a cub pilot learning to navigate the Mississippi River. Once he had his pilot's license, he had served as a steamboat pilot between St. Louis and New Orleans for two years until 1861 when the outbreak of the Civil War closed the river to civilian steamboating for the duration.

Now, what Sam had in that long ago summer of 1861 when he stood looking out of his sister's window, was not only envy for his brother's position and for his prospective trip West, he also had a pocket full of money saved from his pilot's salary — enough money to pay the way across the West for himself and his brother, and enough left over to give himself a start in the new territory. Orion, who was strapped for cash, quickly accepted Sam's offer and purchased steamboat tickets for the two of them to travel from St. Louis up the Missouri River to the end of the line in St. Joseph where the "real" West began. Said Sam:

> . . . when he offered me, in cold blood, the sublime position of private secretary under him, it appeared to me that the heavens and earth passed away, and the firmament was rolled together as a scroll! I had nothing more to desire. My contentment was complete. At the end of an hour or two I was ready for the journey. (Twain, ROUGHING IT, 1913)

ACROSS MISSOURI BY RIVERBOAT

The two of them loaded a trunk and a valise aboard the steamboat *Souix City* down at the St. Louis waterfront, and then began their trip up the Mississippi to the confluence of the Missouri River fifteen miles north, and then their weeklong excursion across the entire state on the Missouri River for 385 miles to St. Joseph where the stagecoach line began.

The Missouri River was surely a study in contrasts for Sam, a

Mississippi steamboat pilot. It was by no means a calm and placid river rolling along toward the sea like the Mississippi he knew. Even at its junction with the Mississippi, the Missouri River impressed its character upon the landscape. Its flow was swifter, more turbulent, and muddier. Its gush of chocolate water poured into the Mississippi with such force that the two rivers did not mix their waters for many miles downstream, and thereafter the Mississippi's color was "Missouri brown."

The nickname "Big Muddy" was an apt one for this river that could not decide whether it was land or water. In flood times a canoe paddle would disappear from sight less than an inch underwater.

Dale Janssen enjoyed telling the following tale about its creation:

"In the Beginning"

In the beginning God created heaven and earth. And he was proud. He realized however, after He had created the lands and the forests and the rivers and the oceans, that He had left over a bucket of muddy water. And wanting to complete His work, He emptied out the bucket of muddy water across the land, and that became the Missouri River: too thick to drink, too thin to plow!

* * * * *

To travel upstream against the Missouri's flow took more steampower than the Mississippi boats required. Sidewheel paddleboats were preferred to sternwheelers in Mark Twain's day because they handled more easily in the swift but crooked Missouri channels.

Sam was anxious to move on across his native state, and annoyed that they did not make better time. Perhaps he had forgotten that this river was characterized by large s-shaped bends known as "meanders" that seemed to carry them as far north or south as they did west. Then there were the snags and sawyers, the sand bars and mud bars, the eddies and boils, and the collapsing river banks complete with trees! In ROUGHING IT he complained:

"St. Louis to St. Joe"

We were six days going from St. Louis to "St. Joe" — a trip that was so dull, and sleepy, and eventless that it has left no more impression on my memory than if its duration had been six minutes instead of that many days. No record is left in my mind, now, concerning it, but a confused jumble of savage-looking snags, which we deliberately walked over with one wheel or the other; and of reefs which we butted and butted, and then retired from and climbed over in some softer place; and of sand-bars which we roosted on occasionally, and rested, and then got out our crutches and sparred over. In fact, the boat might almost as well have gone to St. Joe by land, for she was walking most of the time, anyhow — climbing over reefs and clambering over snags patiently and laboriously all day long. The captain said she was a "bully" boat, and all she wanted was more "shear" and a bigger wheel. I thought she wanted a pair of stilts, but I had the deep sagacity not to say so. (Twain, ROUGHING IT, 1913)

* * * * *

MISSOURI RIVERBOATS IN THE 1850'S AND '60'S

The 1850's saw steamboating on the Missouri reach its peak. By the mid-1860's the Civil War and the building of railroads across the state had taken their toll. Samuel Clemens' river trip in 1861 was almost a "last hurrah."

The passenger boats of his day were like floating palaces: double engines, a battery of boilers, several decks of cabins, staterooms, and ornate saloons. The first deck housed the boilers, firewood, cargo, and deck passengers. The second or "cabin" deck housed staterooms and the saloon. Above that was the "hurricane deck" with its "texas" near the front where the officers were housed. Over the texas was the glass-enclosed pilothouse, giving the steersman a clear view of snags and river obstructions. He needed to keep a sharp eye for suspicious ripples marking underwater snags that could rip out the wooden bottom of his boat, allowing river water to reach the boilers and blow them up. From 1834 to 1872 eighty-one steamboats on the Missouri River exploded their boilers, causing over four thousand deaths. (Griffith, THE MISSOURI RIVER, 1974)

RIVERBOATING TODAY

The thrill of riverboating is still with us today. River towns across America are realizing the lure of the past. Oshkosh, Wisconsin;

Cincinnatti, Ohio; Albany, New York; Sacramento, California; New Orleans, Louisiana; and of course, St. Louis, to name a few, all have their riverboats for cruises or charters, dinners and shows. The thrill of old time riverboating as Mark Twain knew it is still around, but the danger is gone. Rivers have been tamed with dams, locks, and navigation signals; the boats themselves are mainly steel-hulled diesels with the latest safety devices. Each year sees more new riverboats joining the throng. And each year sees more Americans succumbing to the pull of the past, the thrill of the old time "steamboat" as Mark Twain described it in LIFE ON THE MISSISSIPPI:

"She Has Two Tall, Fancy-topped Chimneys"

. . . she has two tall, fancy-topped chimneys, with a gilded device of some kind swung between them; a fanciful pilot-house, all glass and "gingerbread" perched on top of the "texas" deck behind them; the paddle-boxes are gorgeous with a picture or with gilded rays above the boat's name; the boiler-deck, the hurricane deck, and the texas deck are fenced and ornamented with clean white railings; there is a flag gallantly flying from the jack-staff; the furnace doors are open and the fire glaring bravely; the upper decks are black with passengers; the captain stands by the big bell, calm, imposing, the envy of all; great volumes of the blackest smoke are rolling and tumbling out of the chimneys — a husbanded grandeur created with a bit of pitch-pine just before arriving at a town; the crew are grouped on the forecastle; the broad stage is run far out over the port bow, and an envied deck-hand stands picturesquely on the end of it with a coil of rope in his hand; the pent steam is screaming through the gauge-cocks; the captain lifts his hand, a bell rings, the wheels stop; then they turn back, churning the water to foam, and the steamer is at rest. (Twain, 1917)

* * * * *

JANSSEN AND BEATY IN ST. LOUIS

Janssen and Beaty stood at the soaring steel Gateway Arch in the riverfront park gazing east at the array of paddlewheelers still lining the St. Louis levee. Moored boats included the *Goldenrod Showboat*

with its dinner theatre, the three-deck sidewheeler Burger King boat *Spirit of the River*, the large sternwheel *Lt. Robert E. Lee* restaurant boat, and the McDonald's Restaurant paddlewheeler. Excursion boats included smaller paddlewheelers the *Huck Finn, Tom Sawyer,* and *Becky Thatcher* riverboats; then in summer and fall, the largest excursion vessel on the Mississippi, the *President*, docked at St. Louis.

Historic steamboats, the *Delta Queen* and the *Mississippi Queen* also made St. Louis a port of call on their longer overnight cruises from New Orleans up the Mississippi, Ohio, Tennessee, and Cumberland Rivers.

The authors realized that they could no longer board a riverboat at St. Louis to journey up the Missouri River to St. Joseph as Samuel Clemens had done in 1861. But they could ride a passenger tram up a leg of the Gateway Arch to an observation room on top where the northward trip up to the confluence of the Missouri River was almost visible on a clear day. Or they could tour the underground Museum of Westward Expansion at the base of the Arch where films, live programs, and artifacts illustrated the "westering urge" of thousands of Americans out from St. Louis in ever widening circles. But to experience the actual thrill of riverboating on the Missouri, the authors had to go northwest like the Clemenses, to St. Charles, the first port on the Missouri River.

IN ST. CHARLES

St. Charles was familiar to both authors. Janssen had lived there earlier during his career as a transportation manager of agricultural products that were shipped to and from St. Louis by rail, truck, and river barge lines. More recently he had renewed his acquaintance with St. Charles in his research on the John Marshall Clemens family. But his most recent contact with St. Charles involved riverboats.

He knew them all: the *Julia Belle Swain* that had started the river cruise business by "testing the waters" at St. Charles in 1985 with trips to Pere Marquette State Park on the Illinois River; the *Missouri River Queen* on its late fall "tramping" cruise from port to port down the Missouri River from Kansas City to its winter berth; and finally the present *Spirit of St. Charles* riverboat domiciled at St. Charles on the Missouri River. (See MARK TWAIN WALKING AMERICA AGAIN).

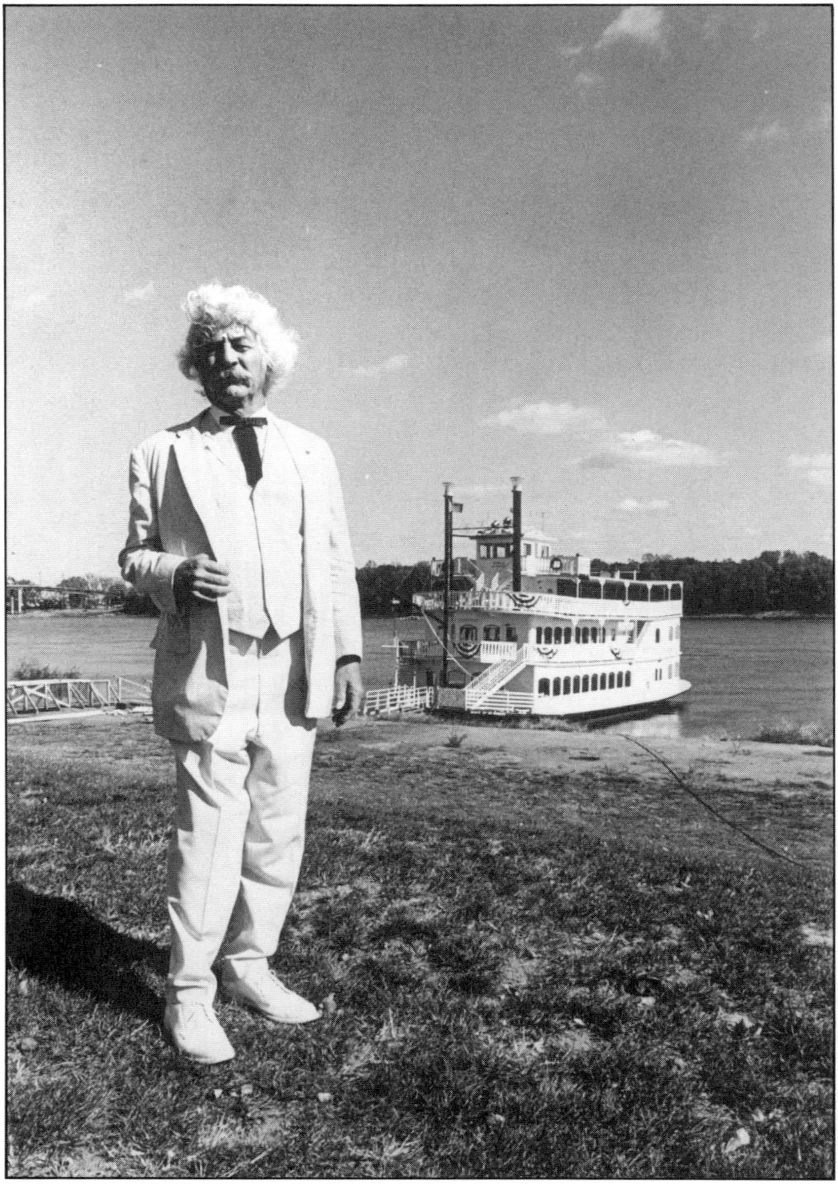

THE "SPIRIT OF ST. CHARLES"

Only the *Spirit of St. Charles* remained in 1988, owned and captained by David Flaven. The *Julia Belle Swain* had moved on up the Mississippi. The *Missouri River Queen* remained at Kansas City, but stopped by St. Charles occasionally on the way to its winter berth.

Both Janssen and Beaty enjoyed cruising on the *Spirit of St. Charles* with its daytime excursions, dinner entertainment cruises, moonlight excursions, Sunday brunch cruises, gospel entertainment cruises and "three river" historic cruises on the Missouri, Mississippi, and Illinois Rivers. A feature of the season was sometimes a riverboat race between the *Spirit of St. Charles* and the *Missouri River Queen*. Both of these sister ships were authentic replicas of Victorian-era, three-deck paddlewheelers.

When Janssen appeared as Mark Twain on the *Spirit of St. Charles*, he couldn't help but include in his repertoire of Twain stories, this one:

"The Wild Missouri River"

My brother Orion and I booked passage on a riverboat in 1861 at St. Louis, Missouri, and traveled up the Missouri River all the way to St. Jo, Missouri. That was the Western frontier in those days. I'd been a pilot on the Mississippi River — a highly respectable job — and here I was a lowly passenger coming up this muddy Missouri River. This Missouri River was WILD! It had mud bars and sand bars, and sometimes difficulty of getting on up the river caused us to be on that riverboat for over a week! I remember the pilot and the captain saying: "Well, if we just had more water, or if we were only on a larger river, or if we only had a larger paddlewheel, or larger steam boilers, we could travel much faster." I thought really what they needed was a pair of STILTS for the riverboat. Then we could sort of WIG-WAG our way up the river over those brush piles and mud bars. Arrived in St. Jo a week later. Most uneventful trip. (Janssen and Beaty, STORYTELLING MARK TWAIN STYLE, 1988, p. 96)

*****

HISTORIC ST. CHARLES

But St. Charles was more than riverboats. The authors had only to look around at the restored Historic District paralleling the river to realize that this first city on the Missouri River had more history packed into its boundaries than almost any other location in the state. They knew that the John Marshall Clemens family had stopped in St. Charles on their way from Jamestown, Tennessee to the village of Florida, Missouri. But so had hundreds of thousands of other emigrants, from Daniel Boone and his family to the flood of Germans who had settled the valley from the 1830's to the 1870's. St. Charles was surely the original gateway to the West, thought Janssen. He found that it was also the rendezvous point for the beginning and ending of the Lewis and Clark expedition, the Zebulon Pike Expedition, and the Boone's Lick Trail, and drafting of the Santa Fe Trail.

Begun by a French fur trader in 1769, St. Charles was formerly organized as an American village on October 13, 1809 — an auspicious date, thought Janssen, another October 13th celebrant. St. Charles was also chosen to house the First Capitol of Missouri from 1820-1826, today a handsome restoration of three adjoining brick buildings with a log cabin "dog-trot" down toward the river. Outfitting shops, brick kilns, grist mills, and tan yards served the early river travelers; just as the restored brick antique shops, craftsmen's galleries, and restaurants attract the modern touring public. Blanchette/Chouteau Mill, now a restaurant and the oldest building in St. Charles, was once a major wagon train stop. St. Charles' French, Spanish, American, and German influences still blended well in this fast-growing modern city that remembered its heritage. The Festival of the Little Hills, Mardi Gras, Oktoberfest, and Lewis and Clark Rendezvous were annual celebrations that brought the traveling public once again to this gateway city. And now a riverboat once more graced its riverfront park, completing the cycle.

Once a necessity for travel — for rivers were the only highways — now a luxury for the touring public, the *Spirit of St. Charles* riverboat carried not only passengers for pleasure but also memories of the past and reminders for the future. Or as Dale Janssen expressed it: "One of the greatest benefits of learning about the past, is as a guide for the future."

A "MARK TWAIN ALIAS DALE JANSSEN" APPEARANCE

Janssen's life was dedicated to sharing that past with present generations who would carry this heritage into the future. Thus when four schools of St. Charles asked him to appear as Mark Twain at a combined assembly of fourth graders, he was delighted. As with all of his Mark Twain appearances, Janssen conferred first with teachers to identify subject material and presentation methodologies he might use. Then he tailored his appearance to the audience. (See STORYTELLING MARK TWAIN STYLE)

As Dale Janssen himself, he first told the "tall tale" that rivermen still spin about Catfish Island just upstream from the city, and how it got its name:

"An Island Known as Catfish Island"

A short distance up the Missouri River from St. Charles is an island known as Catfish Island. It has this name because of the BIG catfish that lived just off the island. Many people tried to catch that catfish but it always broke their lines. Finally two farmers decided that they would catch that fish. They had a blacksmith make this HUGE fishhook. It was so big that they baited their hook with a COW. Then they tied the hook to this big cottonwood tree on the island with riverboat mooring lines.

The next morning it became known that at last this big catfish had been caught, because he had pulled the island three miles down the Missouri River. He had skinned the bark and broken the branches off the big cottonwood tree. And when the two farmers pulled him in they realized that they would never be able to tell how big he was because no tape measure was long enough to measure him from his head to his tail. So they measured the distance across his head from one eye to the other. It was seven feet and eleven inches.

*****

Next Janssen returned to the stage in "Mark Twain's" white suit to tell them about "his" memories of the past.

"Hogs Under the Church"

My father, John Marshall Clemens practiced the law. He was also a farmer and a merchant. He left St. Charles, Missouri and traveled overland on the Salt River Trail up to this small town of Florida, Missouri where I was born as Samuel Clemens in 1835. I remember this small town of Florida having a number of lanes going in different directions — livestock would travel on, and horses and wagons. Well, two of these lanes were called "streets." These streets, when it had been raining, were paved with the same kind of material. It was a chocolate covered material — stick to the bottom of your shoes. That was called Missouri MUD. Well, when it had been dry for a long time, these two same streets were covered with a different kind of material — you could kick around with your shoes — a powdery kind of material. That was called DUST.

I well remember that under this log church that was hoisted two or three feet up off the ground there was a considerable amount of this dust. And under the church in this dust and in the shade was where the HOGS stayed. Sometimes on Sunday when the preacher was preaching the DOGS would find those HOGS and there'd be such a commotion under there that the preacher would have to stop. Sometimes we'd get to go home early.

This small town of Florida, Missouri did not develop the way that my father thought that it would. Being there on the Salt River, my father thought that riverboats would come up there, and also that railroads would be built. This did not happen, and some years later people started moving away. Well, some people moved clear over on the other side of the Mississippi River to Quincy, Illinois. Some moved to Palmyra, Missouri. But my folks, we moved to Hannibal, and it was there at Hannibal, Missouri where I enjoyed many years. (See *Mark Twain Remembers*)

* * * * *

The St. Charles fourth graders were spellbound. They knew the words were true because there was the evidence before their very eyes — "Mark Twain" himself. No one could convince them afterwards that Mark Twain had not been to their school, telling them what it was like when he was a boy. Because of his extreme Mark Twain look-alike, act-alike appearance, Janssen has that affect on people. He realized this in St. Charles even more so, when such a large audience of children hung on every word he said — in complete silence.

Therefore he knew his decision to keep moving west, researching as he went, was the right one, so that future appearances would be based as close as he could make them on the factual material of Samuel Clemens' life.

His own personal interests, however, were broader than that of Samuel Clemens' life. Being in the transportation field for much of his own life, Janssen was anxious to research the origins and modes of transportation in our country in the mid-1800's: of riverboats, stagecoaches, and railroads. What better way to do this than to travel west, Mark Twain style.

HISTORIC ST. JOSEPH

St. Joseph, Missouri was the "jumping off place" for traveling west in the early days. It was here that the first railroad across Missouri, the *Hannibal and St. Joseph Railroad*, had its terminus. It was here that the Central Overland California Trail began. It was here that the Pony Express began carrying the mail 1800 miles across to Sacramento, California. And it was here that numerous steamboats from St. Louis had their terminus during the middle and late 1800's.

Any way you looked at it, St. Joseph was a transportation magnet during the 1860's. The role St. Charles had served during the 1820's and '30's belonged to St. Joseph at mid-century. Emigrants poured into town, outfitted themselves for the journey west, and ferried across the Missouri River to begin it. Samuel Clemens and his brother Orion were among them.

JANSSEN AND BEATY IN ST. JOSEPH

The authors soon recognized this renewal of interest, this refocusing of attention on early travel, when they visited St. Joseph in the spring of 1988. True, St. Joseph had never forgotten its heritage or its place in history in the settling of the West. Some called St. Joseph a "city of museums" because of the eight such institutions it featured: Pony Express Museum, Patee House Museum, St. Joseph Historical Museum, Doll Museum, Albrecht Art Museum, Jesse James Home, St. Joseph State Hospital Psychiatric Museum, and Robidoux Row (the original settlement).

But Janssen and Beaty were more interested in searching out living history — people and places with stories to tell about the old times, with activities to share about their heritage. They found them in

SPIRIT OF ST. JOSEPH
ROBIDOUX RIVER BOAT COMPANY
DINING
CHARTERS
SIGHTSEEING
SPIRIT OF ST. JOSEPH

St. Jo, for the riverboat had just arrived! Everyone in town was talking about it: museum people, newspaper reporters, waitresses in restaurants, motel desk clerks, people on the streets. When the citizens of St. Jo encountered a natural Mark Twain look-alike in Dale Janssen, it was the first question they asked him: "Have you seen our riverboat?" "Have you been out on the riverboat yet?"

The authors hurried down to the riverfront to see this new phenomenon. There it was: tied to the river bank adjacent to the cottonwood trees, with its stage (gangplank) fastened to the framework of a new docking area — a triple deck paddleboat, *The Spirit of St. Joseph!* They later learned that the boat had beat the construction crew, arriving before the facilities were in the tiptop condition they would present before the end of the summer. It didn't matter. Boat trips had already begun and St. Joseph was all agog at the thought of a riverboat of its own. Kansas City, Missouri (downstream) had its *Missouri River Queen*. Brownsville, Nebraska (upstream) had its *Belle*. But St. Joseph, the old gateway to the West, was once again coming into its own with a riverboat! Twenty riverboats a day, the city had experienced in the 1850's. Now they had one back again. It was a summer to celebrate, for sure!

Janssen was surprised to hear his name being called out from the pilot house. He and Beaty went aboard to see what that could mean. The pilot knew him! Had met him aboard the *Missouri River Queen* three years before! Oh, no, not another Mark Twain coincidence, thought Beaty. But she too had the funny feeling that all of this was strangely familiar. Somehow she too had been here before. How could that be? But it was. She later discovered that this very boat had originally plied the waters of Biscayne Bay at Miami Beach, Florida, and that she had indeed been aboard — on a dinner cruise for a national conference.

The two of them of course took a day cruise up the Missouri River to the turn-around buoy, and back. They tried to visualize what Samuel Clemens and Orion might have seen those many summers ago. The river banks were still high, of mud, and lined with cottonwoods. But this channel was deep and its surface swirls indicated swift currents rather than snags. Channel markers helped the pilot keep the boat in midstream where it belonged, and "wing dams" jutting out from the banks kept the channel where it belonged, too.

On the eastern shore stood St. Joseph, its soaring highway "skyways" paralleling the river in airborne layers of concrete. On the

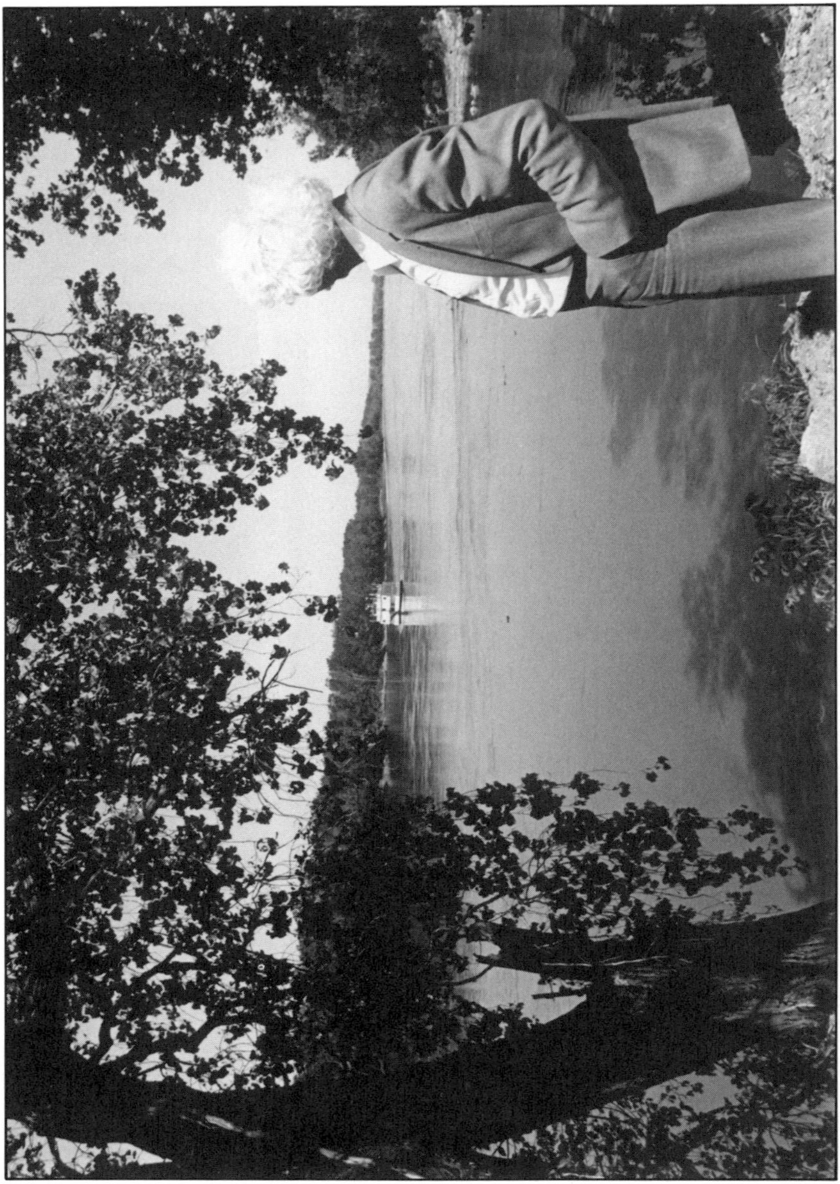

western shore was the State of Kansas hidden in the river thickets. That was where the emigrants landed in 1861 for their journey west. That was where the authors would follow the Clemens' "westering urge". What would they find? Only tomorrow would tell.

* * * * *

REFERENCES

Everhart, William C., "So Long, St. Louis, We're Heading West," *National Geographic Magazine,* Nov., 1965, pp. 643-669.

Griffith, Cecil R., THE MISSOURI RIVER, Leawood, Kansas: Kenneth R. Canfield and Richard L. Sutton, Jr., 1974.

Janssen, Dale H. and Janice J. Beaty, MARK TWAIN WALKING AMERICA AGAIN, Columbia, Missouri: Janssen Education Enterprise, Inc., 1987.

Janssen, Dale H. and Janice J. Beaty, STORYTELLING MARK TWAIN STYLE, Columbia, Missouri: Janssen Education Enterprise, Inc., 1988.

Jordan, Robert Paul and Bruce Dale, "St. Louis: New Spirit Soars in a Proud Old City," *National Geographic Magazine,* Nov., 1965, pp. 605-641.

MARK TWAIN REMEMBERS (Videotape with Dale Janssen as Mark Twain), Elmira, N.Y.: Three-to-Five, P.O. Box 3213, 1986.

Pierce, Don, EXPLORING MISSOURI RIVER COUNTRY, Missouri Dept. of Natural Resources, Division of Parks and Historic Preservation, No Date.

Twain, Mark, LIFE ON THE MISSISSIPPI, New York: Harper and Brothers, Publishers, 1917.

Twain, Mark, ROUGHING IT, New York: Harper and Brothers, Publishers, 1913.

Works Project Administration (Writers' Project), MISSOURI: A GUIDE TO THE "SHOW ME" STATE, New York: Duell, Sloan and Pearce, 1941.

Young, Gordon and David Hiser, "The Dammed Missouri River," *National Geographic Magazine,* Sept., 1971, pp. 297-413.

* * * * *

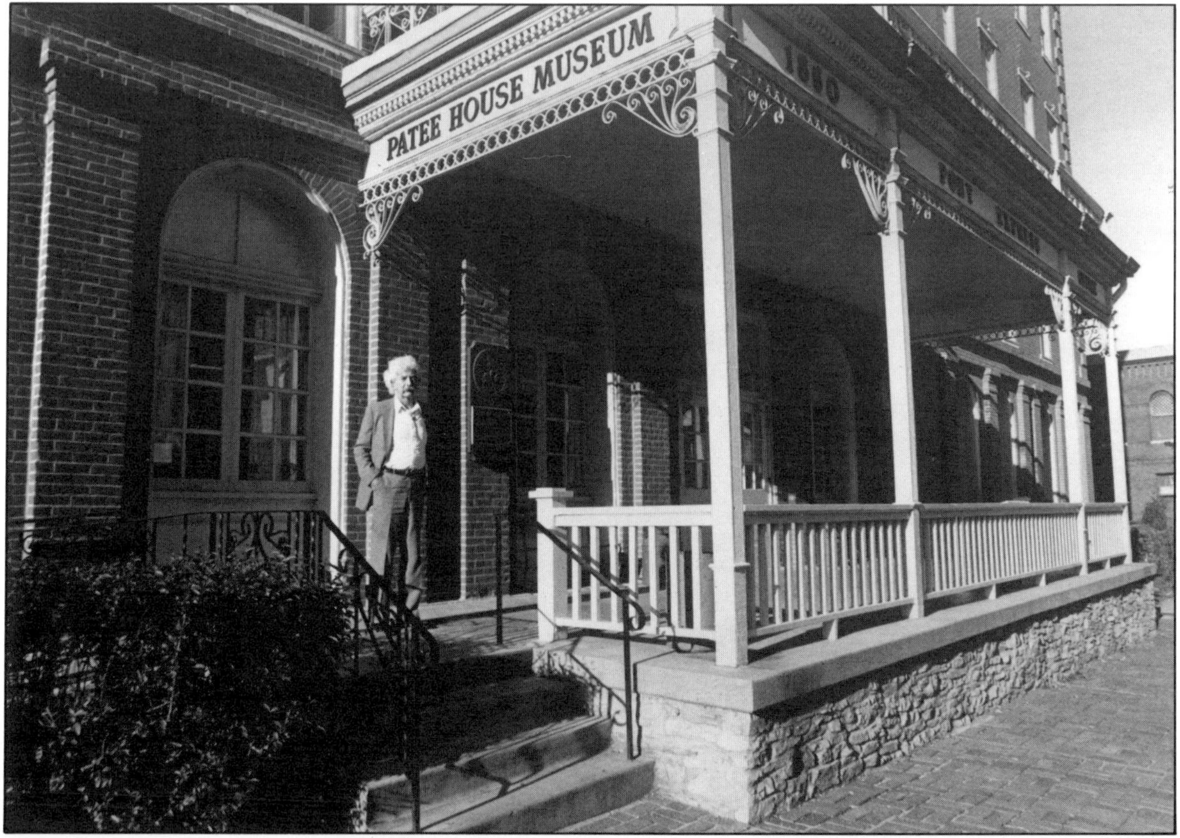
PATEE HOUSE MUSEUM

CHAPTER 3
STAGE STOPS IN KANSAS

THE CLEMENSES IN ST. JO

The records indicate that Samuel Clemens and his brother Orion remained in St. Joseph from July 24 to July 26, 1861. Where they stayed, there is no record. The grand new hotel, the Patee House, had been opened by John Patee three years earlier, and still stands today as a living museum to the past. The present staff would like to believe that the Clemens boys stayed there. Perhaps they did. The building was and is an imposing one — four stories tall, covering an immense block, of ornate brick and floor-length windows. It stood on the high ground, on the bluffs above the river plain looking down in 1861 on a congested mass of horses, mules, oxen, wagons, tents, and a flood of humanity on the river banks, straining to push west. Since the Patee House housed the stage station, it is almost certain that the Clemenses visited those offices. According to Mark Twain in ROUGHING IT:

"Twenty-five Pounds of Baggage"

The first thing we did on that glad evening that landed us at St. Joseph was to hunt up the stage-office, and pay a hundred and fifty dollars apiece per overland coach to Carson City, Nevada.

The next morning, bright and early, we took a hasty breakfast, and hurried to the starting-place. Then an inconvenience presented itself which we had not properly appreciated before, namely, that one cannot make a heavy traveling trunk stand for twenty-five pounds of baggage — because it weighs a good deal more. But that was all we could take — twenty-five pounds each. So we had to snatch our trunks open, and make a selection in a good deal of a hurry. We put our lawful twenty-five pounds apiece all in one valise, and shipped the trunks back to St. Louis again. . . . Each of us put on a rough, heavy suit of clothing, woolen army shirt and "stogy" boots included; and into the valise we crowded a few white shirts, some under clothing and such things. My brother, the Secretary, took along about four pounds of United States statutes and six pounds of Unabridged Dictionary . . . (Twain, ROUGHING IT, 1913)

* * * * *

JANSSEN AND BEATY AT THE PATEE HOUSE

Dale Janssen and Janice Beaty also enjoyed the hospitality of the Patee House, but not as a hotel or stage office. As a living history museum, the immense building housed a complete train depot with a historic steam locomotive and mail car of the *Hannibal and St. Joseph Railroad*, the first railroad built across Missouri. The authors were excited to learn that Samuel Clemens' father, John Marshall Clemens, had hosted the original railroad planning meeting in his Hannibal office in 1846. Even his son Sam was surprised to find this out about his father's support of early railroads when the information turned up later in Samuel Clemens' life. Here was yet another example of western transportation development as envisioned by John M. Clemens. What other important contributions might this visionary pioneer have made, had he lived, wondered the authors?

Another unusual "first" was the mail car that had been invented by this same Hannibal railroad in order to save time by sorting the eastern mail en route, and thus having it ready for the St. Joseph Pony Express rider to carry west to Sacramento, California. Later their idea of a "mail car" was adopted universally by all the railroads.

Now in this summer of 1988, St. Joseph was prepared to welcome both a re-enactment of the Pony Express ride to and from California, and also a convention of members of the Oregon-California Trails Association (OCTA) — history and "trail" buffs who enjoyed researching and following the old trails across the West.

CENTRAL OVERLAND CALIFORNIA TRAIL

Janssen and Beaty wished them all well as the authors began their own trek west. Two trails originated in St. Jo: the Pony Express Trail to Sacramento and the Central Overland California Trail that shared much of the same route as the Pony Express. When the Civil War closed down the southwestern Santa Fe Trail (another Missouri trail), a new stagecoach line was opened for travelers to California and goldrushers to Pike's Peak: the *Central Overland California and Pike's Peak Express Company*. Originally established as a freight line, by

1861 its coaches were also carrying both passengers and the mail over 1800 miles of plains, mountains, and deserts — and did it in twenty days! Even this wasn't fast enough, as it turned out, so the company hired horse riders to relay the mail even faster — ten days to Sacramento on the Pony Express.

From the Pike's Peak Stables in St. Jo, (now the Pony Express Museum) the stagecoaches and their passengers, the horses and their riders, rode down to the levee, and ferried across the Missouri River into Kansas Territory to begin their long gallop west. A series of stage stations ten to fifteen miles apart supplied fresh horses, food, and water. It was from here that Samuel Clemens and his brother started for Carson City July 26, 1861:

> "We Jumped into the Stage"
>
> By eight o'clock everything was ready, and we were on the other side of the river. We jumped into the stage, the driver cracked his whip, and we bowled away and left "the States" behind us. It was a superb summer morning, and all the landscape was brilliant with sunshine . . . We were spinning along through Kansas, and in the course of an hour and a half we were fairly abroad on the great Plains. Just here the land was rolling — a grand sweep of regular elevations and depressions as far as the eye could reach — like the stately heave and swell of the ocean's bosom after a storm. And everywhere were corn-fields, accenting with squares of deeper green this limitless expanse of grassy land . . . (Twain, ROUGHING IT, 1913)

*****

ACROSS KANSAS

Janssen and Beaty found it just as scenic in 1988. They crossed the Missouri River by bridge of course, and were soon rolling through Kansas themselves on US36 — Janssen at the wheel, Beaty reading from ROUGHING IT and taking notes. "Rolling land with cornfields and pastures stretching to the horizon," she wrote: "trees dividing fields or at low spots," (that was something the Clemens boys had not seen: trees!) "road perfectly straight and smooth; alfalfa, milo; here and there a farm complex with barns and silos; a grain elevator in the distance; vision unlimited clear to the horizon!" This was the West that

BARN MUSEUM
OPEN TO VISITORS
ORIGINAL PONY EXPRESS
HOME STAT N NO.1
MARYSVILLE

Beaty, an easterner, looked forward to seeing. But this Kansas, she noted, was prosperous farmland and not the wild Great Plains of 1861. Mark Twain's "limitless expanse of grassy land" had been put into production by some of those energetic emigrants from St. Jo, she guessed.

Janssen, a westerner, was familiar with northeast Kansas. What he looked for now were signs of early transportation. He found them in the stagecoach stations. In 1861 relay stations were located every ten or fifteen miles along the stagecoach and Pony Express route. The stages stopped only long enough to change horses (as little as four minutes), and then they were off again, bowling along to the next relay station. Stagecoach drivers would blow a bugle even before the station was in sight to alert the stock tender to harness a fresh team and have it ready to go. Every 50 miles or so was a "home station" where the drivers would also change and the passengers could alight for a brief rest stop and food if they wanted it. But they did their sleeping on the stage, and never disembarked permanently until their final destination.

Beaty spread out a Kansas highway map and marked the stage stations on the route they were following. Books such as SADDLES AND SPURS: THE PONY EXPRESS SAGA and HISTORIC SITES ALONG THE OREGON TRAIL (see references) helped them plan their stops. They soon realized, however, that unplanned, venturesome stops were equally exciting. Only a few of the actual stage stations still remained intact. Of the rest, there was little left but a historical marker or the words recorded by travelers such as Mark Twain in ROUGHING IT.

MARYSVILLE HOME STATION

Driving down the main street of Marysville, Kansas, Janssen noted a sign and turned left as indicated to the Pony Express Barn Museum, a large stone building that once housed the stables and home station for both the Pony Express and the Overland Stage. It was exciting to think that Samuel Clemens and Orion had actually been there 127 years earlier! People in Marysville were clued into the Pony Express. In fact, the Pony Express national offices were located there. It was evident that the community was very much focused on the preservation of its historical heritage.

Handsome Victorian buildings of brick, stone or wood dotted the community: the Historic Courthouse (1891) on Broadway, the Koester House Museum (1876), the South Koester House (1904) now a fine

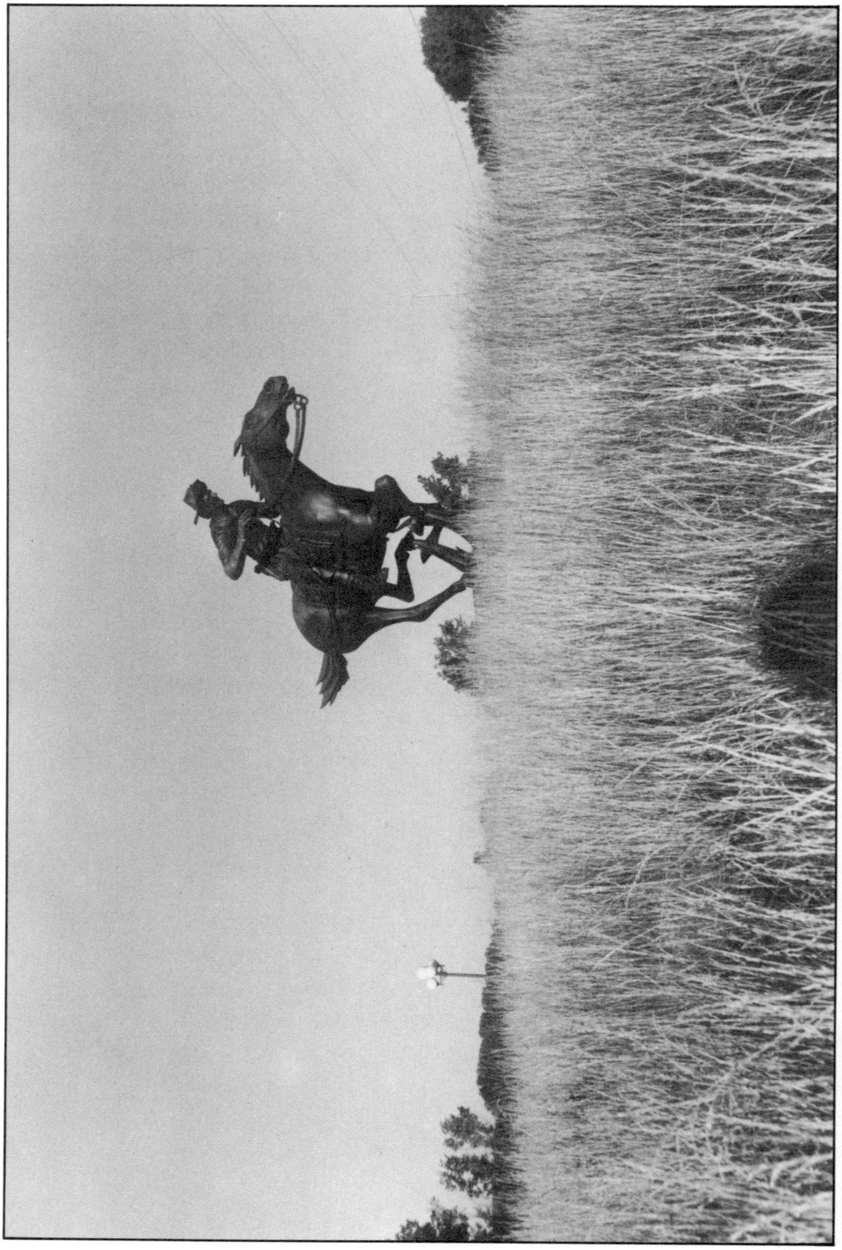

restaurant, and the Hutchinson House (1872) were among the more elegant. The city park featured yet other historic treasures: a sod house, a little red schoolhouse, a railroad depot from 1870, and a steam locomotive from 1901.

And what about those strange-looking *black* squirrels running around in the park? Legend has it that a boy who did not like to see animals caged, turned loose a cage full of them on exhibit at a carnival in the early 1900's. Today the town bills itself as: "Marysville, Kansas, home of the black squirrel." Evidently the surrounding Kansas prairies kept squirrels, at least, from migrating west!

Janssen had something to say about squirrels. The Marysville squirrels seemed to jog his memory, or was it the crossing of the Big Blue River just up ahead. Another "tall tale" soon emerged:

"Acorn on the Tree Stump"

This bass fisherman in his boat was moving quietly along the edge of the water when all of a sudden under some of the trees just ahead, he saw a tree stump jutting out of the water about two feet. And on it was an acorn. He heard a rustling in the trees and looked up. Climbing down a tree limb directly overhead was a squirrel, attempting to reach that acorn on the tree stump. KERPLOP! When that squirrel picked up that acorn, a BIG bass jumped right out of the water and gobbled up the squirrel and the acorn! That fisherman thought he was seeing things. But then he really couldn't believe his eyes when this same BIG bass emerged quietly from the water and placed the acorn back on the stump in hopes of catching another squirrel!

*****

It was evident that traveling west Mark Twain style was becoming just as much fun for the authors as it had for those original travelers in Samuel Clemens' stagecoach.

ON THE TRAIL

A handsome lifesize bronze Pony Express horse and rider "gallops" through a platform of real wild prairie grass just west of Marysville. The authors turned their vehicle in this direction also, as they headed out of town on Route 36 across the Big Blue River and through the cultivated "prairies" to the west. Just outside of Marysville the Pony Express/stagecoach trail from St. Joseph had joined the Oregon Trail up from Independence, Missouri in the early days. The two trails had then turned northwest along the valley of the Little Blue River and on up to the Platte River Trail across Nebraska, prompting the authors to turn northwest also — or rather north, since modern Kansas roads are squared off as boundaries to land sections. There were numerous unmarked boundary roads. Which one to take up to Hollenberg, the next station on the trail?

The authors got so caught up in Mark Twain's stagecoaching adventures along the route, that they missed their turn. His narrative in ROUGHING IT related:

"A Woman Got In"

We changed horses every ten miles, all day long, and fairly flew over the hard, level road. We jumped out and stretched our legs every time the coach stopped, and so the night found us still vivacious and unfatigued.

After supper a woman got in, who lived about fifty miles further on, and we three had to take turns at sitting outside with the driver and conductor. Apparently she was not a talkative woman. She would sit there in the gathering twilight and fasten her steadfast eyes on a mosquito rooting into her arm, and slowly she would raise her other hand till she had got his range, and then she would launch a slap at him that would have jolted a cow; and after that she would sit and contemplate the corpse with tranquil satisfaction — for she never missed her mosquito; she was a dead shot at short range. She never removed a carcass, but left them there for bait. I sat by this grim Sphinx and watched her kill thirty or forty mosquitoes — watched her, and waited for her to say something, but she never did. So I finally opened the conversation myself. I said:

"The mosquitoes are pretty bad, about here, madam."
"You bet!"
"What did I understand you to say, madam?"
"You BET!"

Then she cheered up, and faced around and said:

"Danged if I didn't begin to think you fellers was deef and dumb. I did, b'gosh. Here I've sot, and sot, and sot, a-bustin' muskeeters and wonderin' what was ailin' ye. Fust I thot you was deef and dumb, then I thot you was sick or crazy, or suthin', and then by and by I begin to reckon you was a passel of sickly fools that couldn't think of nothing to say. Where'd ye come from?"

The Sphinx was a Sphinx no more! The fountains of her great deep were broken up, and she rained the nine parts of speech forty days and forty nights, metaphorically speaking, and buried us under a desolating deluge of trivial gossip that left not a crag or pinnacle of rejoinder projecting above the tossing waste of dislocated grammar and decomposed pronunciation!

How we suffered, suffered, suffered! She went on, hour after hour, till I was sorry I ever opened the mosquito question and gave her a start. She never did stop again until she got to her journey's end toward daylight; and then she stirred us up as she was leaving the stage (for we were nodding, by that time), and said:

"Now you git out at Cottonwood, you fellers, and lay over a couple o' days, and I'll be along some time to-night, and if I can do ye any good by edgin' in a word now and then, I'm right thar. Folks'll tell you't I've always ben kind o' offish and partic'lar for a gal that's raised in the woods, and I *am*, with the ragtag and bobtail, and a gal *has* to be, if she wants to be anything, but when people comes along which is my equals, I reckon I'm a pretty sociable heifer after all."

We resolved not to "lay by at Cottonwood." (Twain, ROUGHING IT, 1913)

* * * * *

Was there really such a woman? Who can say? Readers of ROUGHING IT need to be aware that Mark Twain inserted a whole series of imaginary stagecoach passengers into his book purely for "comic relief"!

BREMEN

"Still vivacious and unfatigued" like Samuel Clemens, the authors

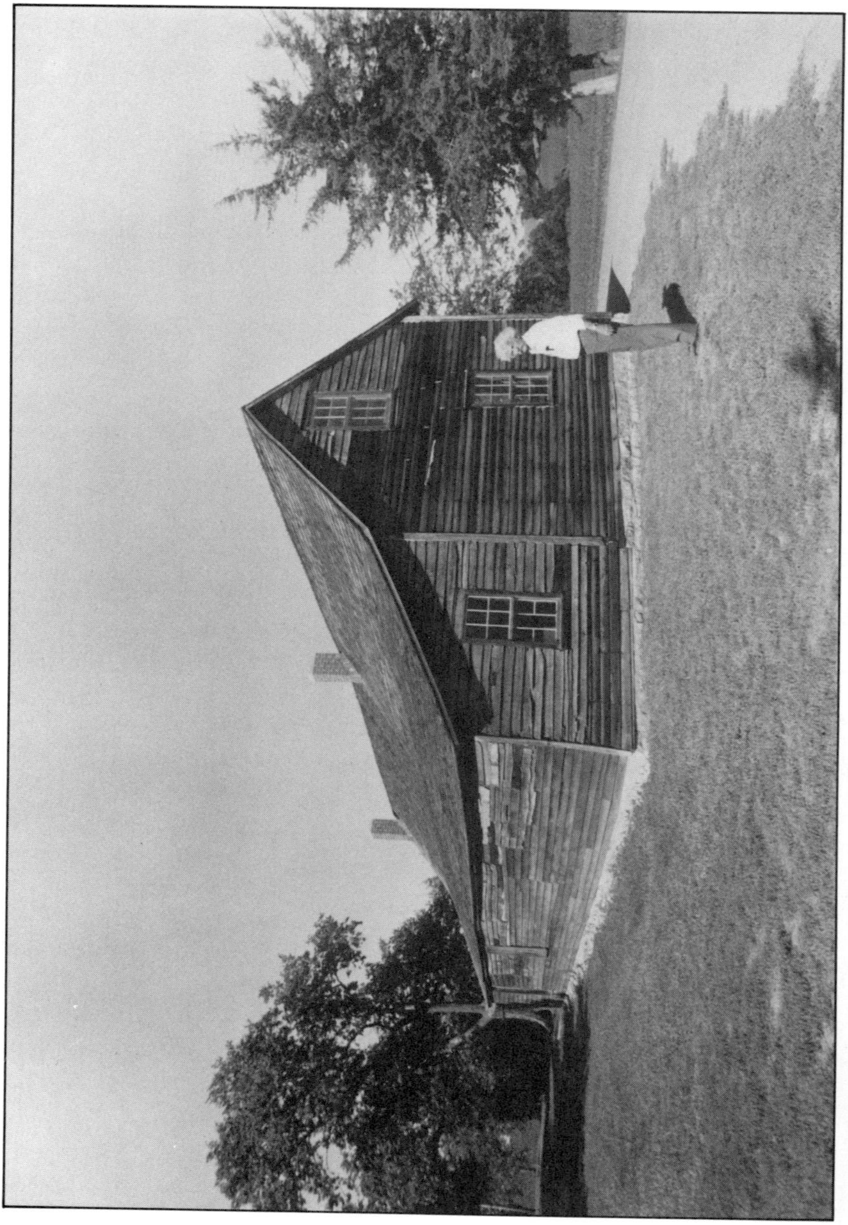

journeyed north and then west alongside the corn and milo fields of northeast Kansas looking for Hollenberg (originally "Cottonwood") Station. They found Bremen instead: a tiny two-street town on the rail line, with a grain elevator, a few stores and houses, and an open dug *well* right in the middle of the two main cross streets!

Water is precious in Kansas. It *was* during the drought summer of 1988. It *was* during Samuel Clemens' trip west in 1861. It has been from first to last in rural Kansas. Stories abound about pioneer women who hauled water by hand up to their homes from a distant well while their men were at work in the fields. What made this particular well stand out in 1988, was not only that it stood in the middle of the two main streets, but that it was straddled by a spindly derrick, like an oil well, with a bell halfway up.

Two weighted fire buckets dangled from either end of a long well rope, and the townsfolks claimed that the water deep down below was still sweet and pure. Furthermore, they said that every new bride in the community directly after the wedding ceremony, had to climb up that derrick and ring the bell, with the community around the well looking on! Mark Twain would have something to say about that, Janssen decided. Beaty's admiration was for the climbing skill of the brides.

HOLLENBERG STATION

The authors eventually found Hollenberg Station (1½ miles from Hanover on Rte. 243), also known in Mark Twain's day as Cottonwood Station because of its proximity to Cottonwood Creek. Located on a slight rise above the rolling farm land, above a grove of old cottonwood trees, the well-preserved frame building was once the ranch house of Gerat H. Hollenberg who built it in 1857 or '58 for the express purpose of serving the Oregon/California/Pike's Peak Trail travelers who passed by his front door. Modern tourist information tags it as "the only unaltered Pony Express station which remains in its original location."

It served all at the same time as a family home, a store, a tavern, an unofficial post office, and the stage station for the Central Overland California and Pike's Peak Express Company, as well as for the Pony Express. Larger than most stage stations, the long frame structure contained two ground-floor rooms housing the grocery store, post office, and tavern, and four family rooms. Upstairs was a loft the length of the house, used as common sleeping quarters for the Pony Express and stage employees. Built of native lumber, it was the first frame house in the county. Restored in 1963, it is truly a gem of mid-nineteenth century ranch-house architecture. Today it houses a museum of pioneer artifacts.

Hollenberg was wise to place his station where he did. Nearby the travelers had to cross Cottonwood Creek, a tributary of the Blue River that they were following up to the Platte. His invitingly cool grove of cottonwoods was just the place for a picnic — still is today! The Independence and St. Joseph Trails had already merged before they reached Cottonwood. Now travelers from both locations could stop to rest while they fed their livestock or bought supplies.

Here was truly one of the most heavily traveled trails in the West in the late 1850's and early '60's. The hoards of modern vacationers we are used to encountering in every tourist location today, have nothing on the early travelers. Janssen and Beaty were astonished to learn that 15,000 west-bound travelers stopped at the Hollenberg station in 1859! The "westering urge" was truly not a new one! It was a common sight for the Hollenberg family to look out over a hundred or more wagons encamped in the cottonwood bottoms below their house during those peak years!

Below the station house was once a long stable for horses and oxen, a corral for loose animals, and several cribs for grain and ricks of hay. It brought home to us modern travelers the reason for the location of the early trails. We had asked ourselves, why did the trail across Kansas suddenly veer northwest and go up to Nebraska and the Platte River? Why didn't it simply go straight across Kansas like the modern highway does?

Hollenberg Station gave us the answer. This most westerly stage station on the Overland Trail in Kansas sat on a river crossing. Travelers in the 1800's depended literally on "horse power" and "ox power" and "mule power." And these animals could only be "refueled" with water and grass or grain. Early travelers could not just strike out across the dry plains. They had to follow the rivers — not for ease of traveling, as we had originally thought, but for "refueling" their animal-power. Rivers were the gas stations of the early tourists, and stage stations were the rest stops.

*****

REFERENCES

"The First Railroad Built in 1857," *The Mark Twain Pilot House, Monroe County Appeal,* Paris, Missouri, June 23, 1988, p. 2.

Haines, Aubrey L. HISTORIC SITES ALONG THE OREGON TRAIL, Gerald, Missouri: The Patrice Press, 1981.

Paine, Albert Bigelow, MARK TWAIN A BIOGRAPHY, New York: Harper and Brothers, 1912.

Ruetti, Oretha, *The Marysville Advocate*, Marysville, Kansas: June 30, 1988.

Settle, Raymond W. and Mary Lund Settle, SADDLES AND SPURS, THE PONY EXPRESS SAGA, Lincoln, Nebraska: University of Nebraska Press, 1955.

Twain, Mark, ROUGHING IT, New York: Harper and Brothers, Publishers, 1913.

*****

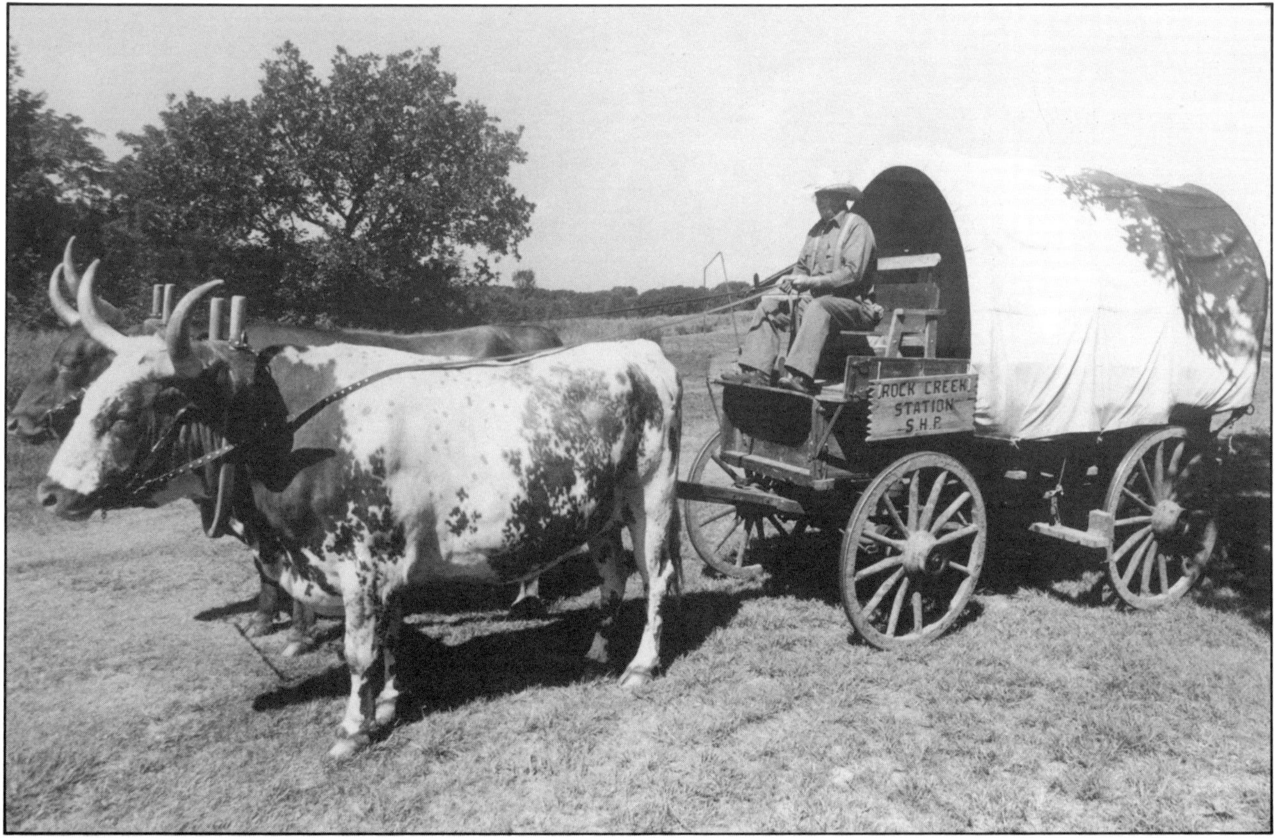
ROCK CREEK
STATION
S.H.P.

CHAPTER 4
STAGE STOPS IN NEBRASKA

HISTORIC ROCK CREEK STATION

Rock Creek Station was the next stage stop on the Overland Trail. Just over the border in Nebraska, the station straddled both banks of the deep and narrow Rock Creek ford in Samuel Clemens' day. But by then a toll bridge had been built so that Clemens' stage rolled high and dry above the creek without the difficult hauling that so many early emigrants had experienced. It was an entire day's work for many of the travelers, letting their wagons down the steep-sloping banks of the creek and then hauling them up the other side. Boulders in the creek bed and swift water during flood time were added woes.

But when David McCanles from North Carolina bought Rock Creek Station in 1859 along with its cabin and barn on the west bank, he decided to add a log cabin, stables, and corral on the east bank, as well, since the primary travel direction was east-to-west. Then he also dug a well and built a toll bridge across the creek. Stagecoaches, freight wagons, and covered wagons paid a toll of 10-to-50 cents, depending on their load and their ability to pay.

McCanles did a brisk business in his first year of operation, with stages coming and going, and wagon trains following one another up this "feeder trail" to the great "Platte River Road" across Nebraska. Like Hollenberg, McCanles was known as a "road rancher" who catered to the freight lines, mail lines, and emigrant traffic. Business was so good he added a 20-by-18-foot lean-to on one side of his cabin where hay, grain, and supplies could be bought, sold or traded. His wife and children from North Carolina soon joined him, and his brother's family came along, as well.

When the Pony Express Company began operating in 1860 they rented the McCanles' road ranch at first, and later bought him out entirely, hiring their own men to run the operation. "Wild Bill" Hickok was one of them. But somehow McCanles never got paid for his property. His demands were eventually met with gun fire by Hickok with support from the station agent, killing McCanles and two of his friends from ambush. The two killers were acquitted during the ensuing trial on the grounds of "self-defense," even though McCanles and his friends were unarmed.

This infamous and controversial "McCanles Massacre" was pounced upon by the Eastern press who glorified "Wild Bill Hickok" as a hero, emerging triumphant from a fight in which he gunned down ten armed men of the dreaded "McCanles' Gang." History has finally got the facts straight, but the stage station itself soon faded from view with the coming of the railroad in the late 1860's. The McCanles name, however, is still a proud one among American pioneers, the current famous family member being astronaut Bruce "McCandles" Jr., great-great-grandson of David, and the first American astronaut to accomplish a "space walk" without a lifeline from the space shuttle "Challenger" in 1984.

ROCK CREEK STATION TODAY

Bruce must have been proud that the State of Nebraska Game and Parks Commission began development of his great-great-grandfather's Rock Creek Station State Historical Park in that very same year of 1984. State archeologists had labored since 1980 digging, scraping, and sifting for evidence of the early station on the deserted site. With a grant from the Burlington Northern Railroad Foundation, they were now able to construct a modern Visitors Center (with museum and theater), a campground, and replicas of the West Ranch and East Ranch log buildings with a bridge between them over Rock Creek.

As Janssen and Beaty drove into the park, six miles southeast of Fairbury, Nebraska, off Highway 8, they were at once struck with the sight of prairie grass preserved as the pioneer "trail trekkers" once saw it (more than 70 species of wildflowers and native grasses are identified); and of the deep indentations in the earth that the authors would come to know across the West as "wheel ruts."

WHEEL RUTS

Here at Rock Creek Station they saw their first of many wheel ruts. Countless stage and wagon wheels — hundreds, thousands of them had rolled across the prairies and up the banks of streams — leaving behind their indelible evidence: deep wheel ruts on the land like a dug out road bed. Nothing would ever completely obliterate the evidence of their passing. And nothing more exciting would ever stir the blood of the modern "trail buffs" than the sight of these "wheel ruts." It was the true signature of the pioneer, the adventurer, the homesteader, the goldrusher, the American who got up and followed his "westering urge" clear across the vastness of the continent with his pioneer wheels.

The authors felt a lump in their throats too, at the sight of these impressive depressions in the prairie sod, marking the path of the stagecoaches and wagons up from the difficult crossing of Rock Creek and out into the western unknown. How did Samuel Clemens feel, they wondered? Little did he realize that the wheels of his Overland Stage would soon be leaving their own indelible mark upon America: a "Mark Twain mark" with the publication of ROUGHING IT, as well as leaving a true "pioneer trail mark" that Janssen and Beaty or anyone else could follow across the West in the years to come.

Rock Creek Station would also be a memorable site for the authors because of its element of "living history." How about a ride in a real covered wagon pulled by a team of oxen? Or what about watching an outdoor blacksmith with hammer and tongs ply his trade beside his covered supply wagon?

A STAGECOACH

But first of all, Janssen and Beaty made a beeline for . . . . yes, an authentic western stagecoach standing beside a log cabin at the West Ranch! Not all that many stagecoaches are left today, they realized, and those that remain intact are usually in museums. To see a real stagecoach actually standing on the open prairie next to "trail ruts" was mind-boggling for the authors! They hurried up to this one excitedly and peered inside. There were leather seats "fore and aft," windows with curtains that could be rolled down to dim the prairie sun or diminish its winds, compartments at the outside rear and under the driver's feet called "boots," for storing luggage.

They could imagine the driver cracking his whip and urging his team up the incline from the Rock Creek crossing. And they found out what Samuel Clemens thought about such travel, for his words in ROUGHING IT expressed it all:

"A Great Swinging and Swaying Stage"

Our coach was a great swinging and swaying stage, of the most sumptuous description — an imposing cradle on wheels. It was drawn by six handsome horses, and by the side of the driver sat the "conductor," the legitimate captain of the craft; for it was his business to take charge and care of the mails, baggage, express matter, and passengers. We three were the only passengers, this trip. We sat on the back seat, inside. About all the rest of the coach was full of mail-bags — for we had three days' delayed mails with us. Almost touching our knees, a perpendicular wall of mail matter rose up to the roof. There was a great pile of it strapped on top of the stage, and both the fore and hind boots were full . . .

The stage whirled along at a spanking gait, the breeze flapping curtains and suspended coats in a most exhilerating way; the cradle swayed and swung luxuriously, the pattering of the horses' hoofs, the cracking of the driver's whip, and his "Hi-yi! g'lang!" were music; the spinning ground and the waltzing trees appeared to give us a mute hurrah as we went by, and then slack up and look after us with interest, or envy, or something; and as we lay and smoked the pipe of peace and compared all this luxury with the years of tiresome city life that had gone before it, we felt that there was only one complete and satisfying happiness in the world, and we had found it.

* * * * *

Samuel Clemens and his traveling companions also experienced the crossing of steep-sided streams without bridges in Nebraska. In ROUGHING IT he tells:

"Our Party Inside Got Mixed Somewhat"

We began to get into country, now, threaded here and there with little streams. These had high, steep banks on each side, and every time we flew down one bank and scrambled up the other, our party inside got mixed somewhat. First we would all be down in a pile at the forward end of the stage, nearly in a sitting posture, and in a second we would shoot to the other end, and stand on our heads. And we would sprawl and kick, too, and ward off ends and corners of mailbags that came lumbering over us and about us; and as the dust rose from the tumult, we would all sneeze in chorus, and the majority of us would grumble, and probably say some hasty thing, like: "Take your elbow out of my ribs! — can't you quit crowding?"

Every time we avalanched from one end of the stage to the other, the Unabridged Dictionary would come too; and every time it came it damaged somebody. One trip it "barked" the Secretary's elbow; the next trip it hurt me in the stomach . . .

Still, all things considered, it was a very comfortable night. It gradually wore away, and when at last a cold gray light was visible through the puckers and chinks in the curtains, we yawned and stretched with satisfaction, shed our cocoons, and felt that we had slept as much as was necessary . . . Five minutes afterwards the driver sent the weird music of his bugle winding over the grassy solitudes, and presently we detected a low hut or two in the distance. Then the rattling of the coach, the clatter of our six horses' hoofs, and the driver's crisp commands, awoke to a louder and stronger emphasis, and we went sweeping down on the station at our smartest speed . . .

*****

FELLOW TRAVELERS

Wherever the authors went on this summer's travels, they met fascinating people, as well: the man with the black squirrel story in Marysville, the woman with the "well" story in Bremen. Now at Rock Creek Museum was a man from California who was tracing historic trails, and couldn't believe his eyes meeting "Mark Twain" walking up the path from the creek crossing below. It did little good for Janssen to try to explain from a Twentieth Century perspective. This man knew about Mark Twain's travels. And unlike most people the authors met, this man knew all about Mark Twain traveling west: in his museum in California he had on exhibit Mark Twain's trunk!

VALLEY OF THE LITTLE BLUE RIVER

Once this valley teemed with animal life: buffalo, turkeys, and even wild horses. But by the 1860's most of it was gone: driven away by the swarms of emigrants and hunters who shot the game to satisfy their needs as they traveled. Mark Twain mentions but one, the jackrabbit. He called it the "jackass rabbit," and says: "he is well named. He is

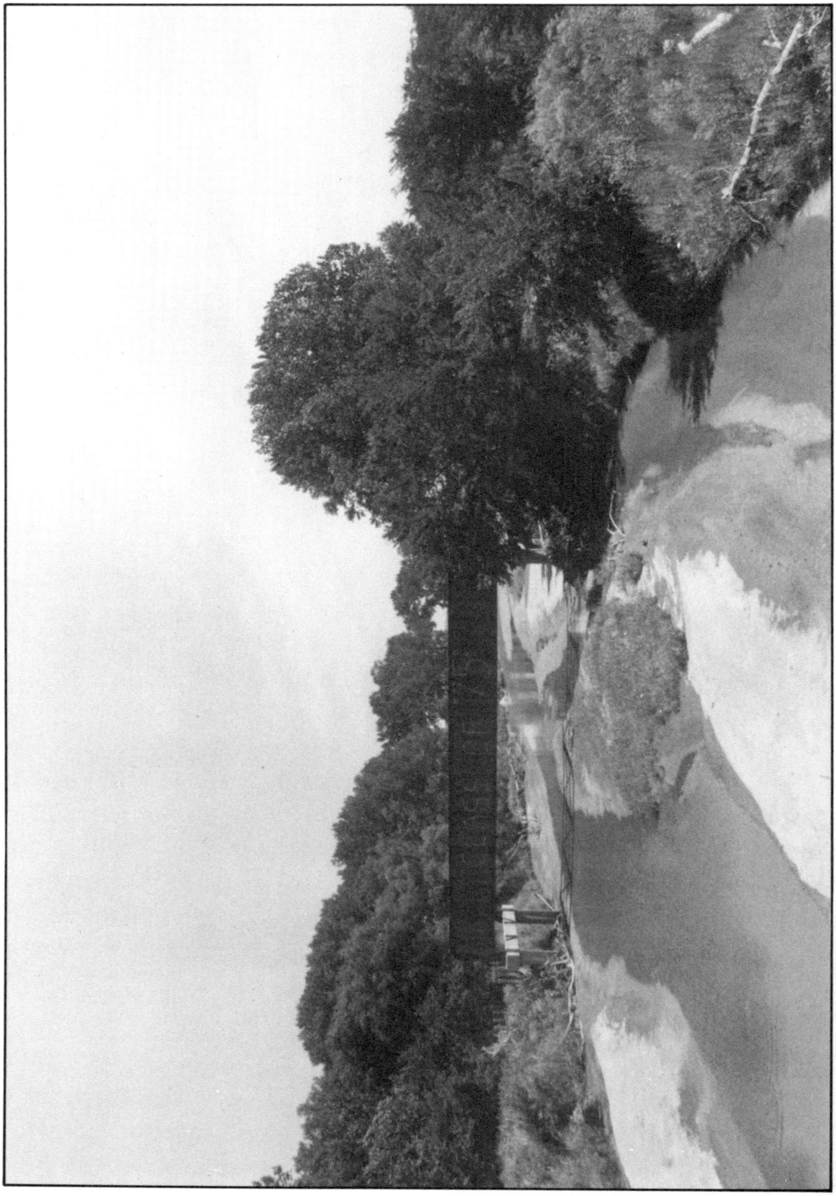

just like any other rabbit except that he is from one-third to twice as large, has longer legs in proportion to his size, and has the most preposterous ears that ever were mounted on any creature *but* a jackass. When he is sitting quiet, thinking about his sins, or is absent-minded or unapprehensive of danger, his majestic ears project above him conspicuously; but the breaking of a twig will scare him nearly to death, and then he tilts his ears back gently and starts for home." (Twain, ROUGHING IT, 1913).

By 1988 the animals and birds too had once again repopulated the Valley of the Little Blue. Historical sites like Rock Creek Station were protected nesting grounds for prairie and woodland species. Northern and orchard orioles nested in the woods along the creek. Red-headed, downy, and hairy woodpeckers abounded. The calls of the dickcissel, meadowlark, grasshopper sparrow, and kingbird resounded from the grasslands these days.

STAGE STATION BUILDINGS

Most of the stage stations that Janssen and Beaty encountered in 1988 were of wood or stone: cabins of barked and squared logs, frame buildings like Hollenberg's, or native stone buildings like the Marysville station. Mark Twain, on the other hand, remembered the typical stage station in Nebraska as being of adobe and sod:

"The Station Buildings Were Long, Low Huts"

The station buildings were long, low huts, made of sun-dried, mud-colored bricks, laid up without mortar (*adobes*, the Spaniards called these bricks, and Americans shortened it to *dobies*). The roofs, which had no slant to them worth speaking of, were thatched and then sodded or covered with a thick layer of earth, and from this sprung a pretty rank growth of weeds and grass. It was the first time we had ever seen a man's front yard on top of his house. The buildings consisted of barns, stable-room for twelve or fifteen horses, and a hut for an eating-room for passengers. This latter had bunks in it for the station-keeper and a hostler or two. You could rest your elbow on its eaves, and you had to bend in order to get in at the door. In place of a window there was a square hole about large enough for a man to crawl through, but this had no glass in it. There was

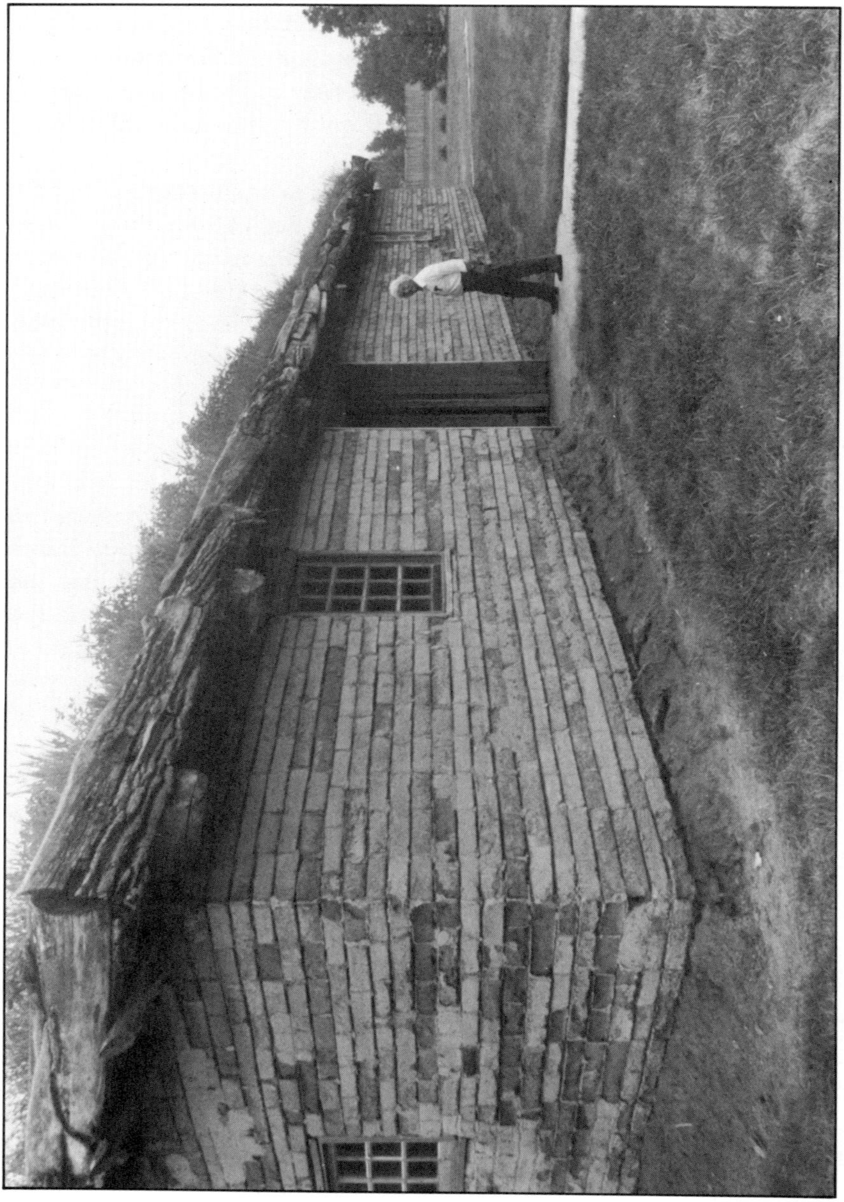

no flooring, but the ground was packed hard. There was no stove, but the fireplace served all needful purposes. There were no shelves, no cupboards, no closets. In a corner stood an open sack of flour, and nestling against its base were a couple of black and venerable tin coffee-pots, a tin teapot, a little bag of salt, and a side of bacon. (Twain, ROUGHING IT, 1913)

*****

FORT KEARNY

Fort Kearny on the Platte River had twenty-four such long, low adobe buildings in Samuel Clemens' day, along with five frame buildings, two- and three stories tall. Located at the junction of the Independence-St. Jo Trail and the Platte River Trail, the fort served as a home station for the stage and Pony Express, an outfitting depot for western troops and wagon trains, and the headquarters of both military and civilian government for the recently-formed Nebraska Territory. Fort Kearny was the first of a chain of military forts from Missouri to the Rockies built to protect travelers on the trails.

They needed protection in the beginning. At first the Pawnees and later the other Plains Indian tribes attacked wagon trains, Mormons, gold-rushers, and homesteaders along the trails. Samuel Clemens was fortunate to make his crossing when he did in 1861. By the next year the Sioux, Cheyenne, and Arapaho began attacks in the Platte Valley that would crescendo to a rampage by the summer of 1864, because so many of the western troops had been recalled east to fight in the Civil War. The fort was manned in those days by volunteers, including a number of former Confederate soldiers called "Galvanized Yankees", and by peaceful Pawnees who were enlisted to help control their enemies, the Sioux.

Then by 1871, the transcontinental railroad had "tamed" the West, depriving the old fort of its usefulness. It was eventually abandoned and dismantled, leaving nothing behind but crumbling earthwork fortifications and huge cottonwood trees around the parade grounds.

THE AUTHORS AT FORT KEARNY

Luckily for the modern traveler, the State of Nebraska recognized the historic value of the old fort, and had carefully reconstructed yet another "living history" museum. The authors eyed with excitement the low building that seemed to have grass growing out of its roof. Could it be? Yes! Wonderful! It was a rebuilt adobe blacksmith-carpenter's shop with a sod roof: their first! They felt just like Samuel Clemens witnessing "a man's front yard growing on his roof"! Snug and comfortable inside and out, it was hard to believe the walls were made of earth blocks rather than real bricks. Inside were shop furnishings in workable condition ready for demonstration by the blacksmith.

STORIES FROM THE EARLY DAYS

Outside were other workable historic items: two canons from the early days, for instance. They were being readied for demonstration firing by a real army sergeant (retired) who would soon reappear in regulation uniform of the 1860's. But first he told stories about the old fort as if he had witnessed them himself: about the nearby wooden stockade that was originally built for the protection of animals, not people; about the cottonwood trees that were first planted around the parade grounds for the comfort of the military wives, and those two gnarled old giants nearby that were all that was left of the original cottonwoods; finally, about the flagpole in the center of the grounds — see it? — that was the tallest object in the county in the early days, and all property was measured out from this survey point.

The grounds were immense then: ten square miles in area, the same size as the District of Columbia — and that was yet another story. It seems that one of the fort's more colorful characters was Moses Henry Syndenham, its postmaster from 1858-1871. In 1862 he began publishing the *Kearney Herald* "to herald the advent of Christian civilization, material and spiritual, in the 'great American desert,' and show forth the then latent possibilities for humanity yet to come." (Wilson, FORT KEARNY ON THE PLATTE, p. 185)

That was just the beginning. In 1870 he began publication of the *Central Star* to support his plan to move the nation's capital from Washington, D.C. to Fort Kearny, Nebraska, to be renamed "New Washington." This energetic supporter of Nebraska toured the entire country on his crusade to bring the nation's capital to the center of the nation, Nebraska, thus binding up the wounds created by the Civil War, developing the frontier more effectively, and keeping the capital forever safe from coastal enemy attack. His plan was eventually rejected by a congressional committee — unfortunately, say many

Nebraskans!

Meanwhile, out on the plains, the Clemens boys saw their first Indians 75 miles from Fort Kearny, according to Orion's letter to his wife. They had buffalo skin wigwams "the hide dressed on both sides, and put up on poles, sugar loaf shape. Here we found Buffalo robes at three to six dollars, beautifully dressed, and some of them wonderfully large. This is the Buffalo region, and robes are higher as you go further, either east or west." (Twain, ROUGHING IT, 1972, p. 547)

The authors, on the other hand, saw no wigwams or Indians outside of Fort Kearny in the summer of 1988. As a matter of fact, they did not even see the plains. All the land in sight was thickly covered with agricultural products: corn, milo, alfalfa, and beans with fields irrigated by pipe, pivot or gravity. "Agribusiness" you could call it.

But beyond the fields there was something else to see; something the emigrants and pioneers longed to see, yet loathed to see when they came face to face with it: the flat water itself — the Platte River. As Orion told his wife: "The Platte is a muddy, shallow stream, full of sand bars. This was the South Platte. In places it is skirted by timber but generally it meanders through the plains like a ribbon, without a tree or shrub on its banks." (Twain, ROUGHING IT, p. 547)

Samuel Clemens, the grand Mississippi River pilot, the man whose name would later be synonymous with rivers, of course had vigorous words to describe this strange river of the plains:

"The Shallow, Muddy South Platte"

We came to the shallow, yellow, muddy South Platte, with its low banks and its scattering flat sand-bars and pygmy islands — a melancholy stream straggling through the center of the enormous flat plain, and only saved from being impossible to find with the naked eye by its sentinel rank of scattering trees standing on either bank. The Platte was "up," they said — which made me wish I could see it down, if it could look any sicker and sorrier. They said it was a dangerous stream to cross, now because its quicksands were liable to swallow up horses, coach, and passengers if an attempt was made to ford it. But the mails had to go, and we made the attempt. Once or twice in midstream the wheels sunk into the yielding sands so threateningly that we half believed we had dreaded and avoided the sea all our lives to be shipwrecked in a "mud-

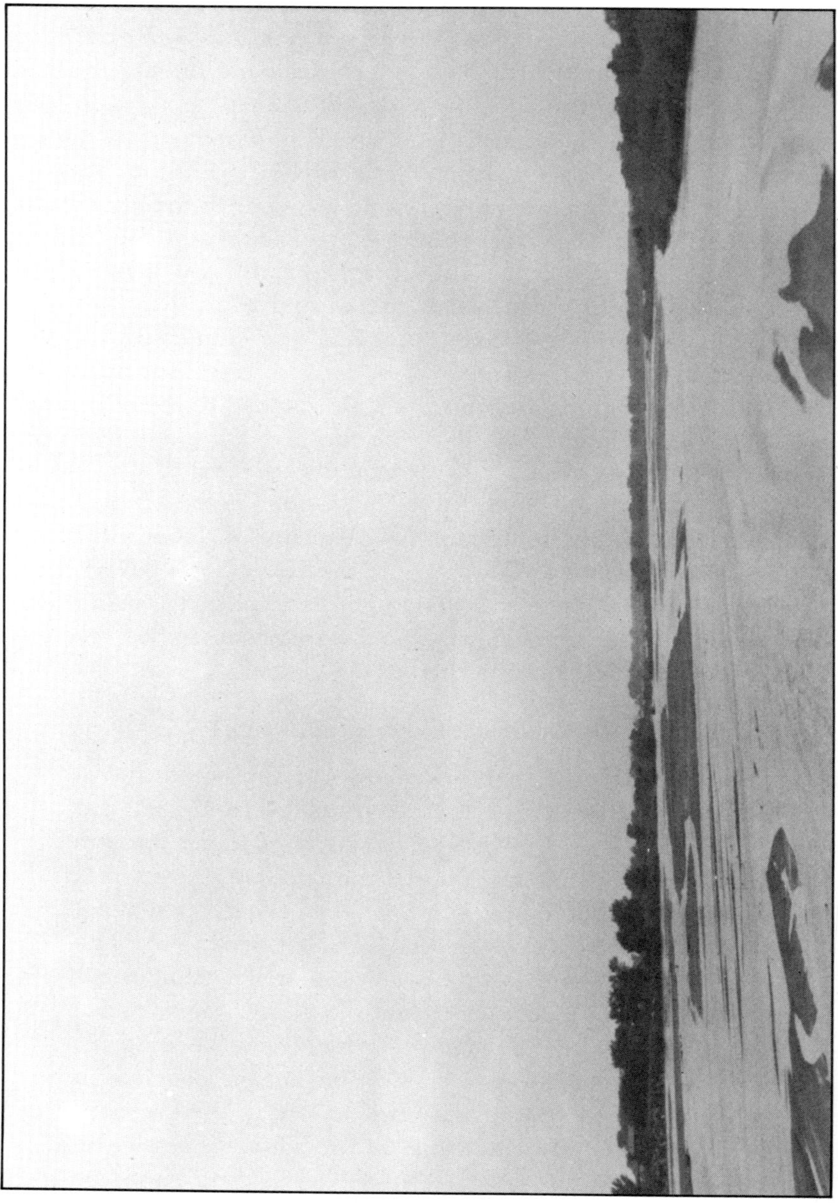

wagon" in the middle of a desert at last. But we dragged through and sped away toward the setting sun. (Twain, ROUGHING IT, 1913)

*****

Janssen and Beaty looked forward to their own encounter with the Platte River. They would not have to ford it in 1988. But would its presence somehow influence their own journey west?

*****

REFERENCES

Federal Writers' Project, NEBRASKA, A GUIDE TO THE CORNHUSKER STATE, Lincoln, Nebraska: University of Nebraska Press, 1979.

"Rock Creek Station, State Historical Park," Lincoln, Nebraska: Nebraska Game & Parks Commission, No Date.

Twain, Mark, ROUGHING IT, Berkeley, California: University of California Press, 1972.

Twain, Mark, ROUGHING IT, New York: Harper and Brothers, Publishers, 1913.

Wilson, D. Ray, FORT KEARNY ON THE PLATTE, Dundee, Illinois: Crossroads Communications, 1980.

*****

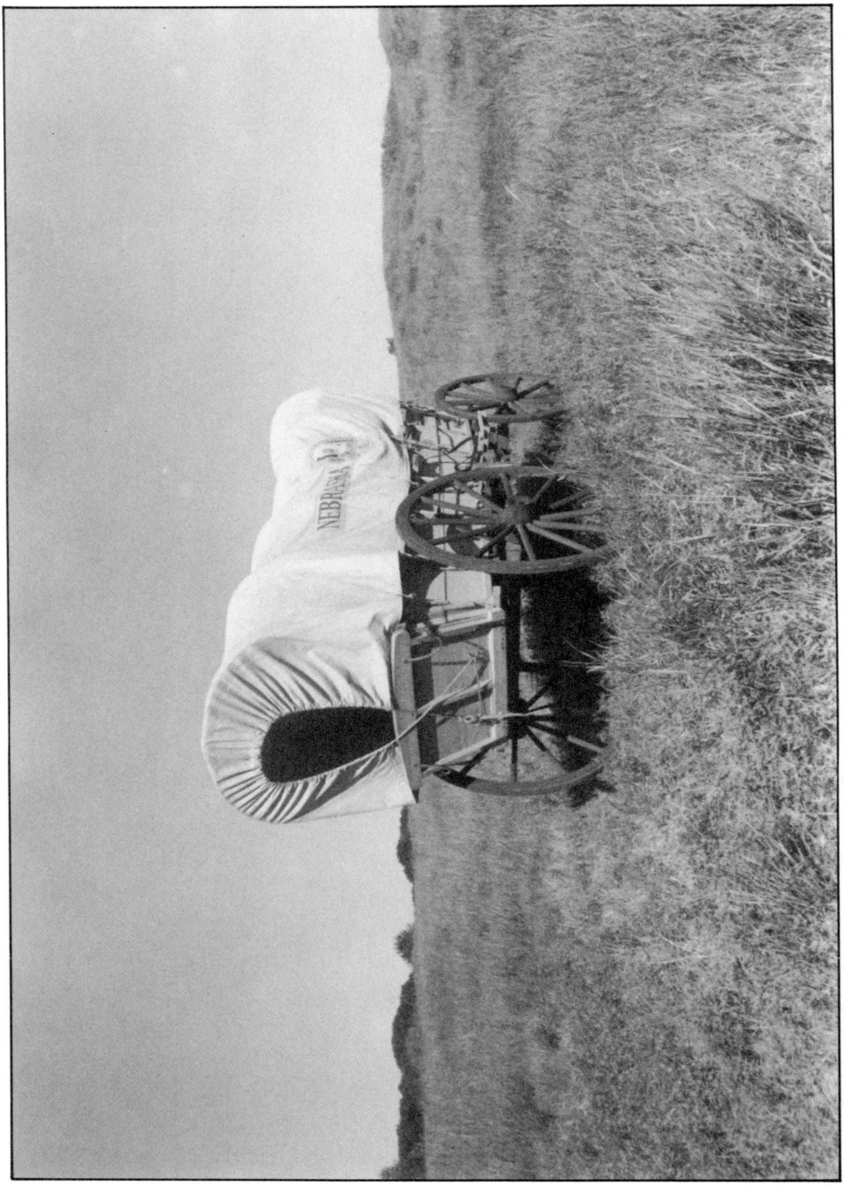

CHAPTER 5

ON THE PLATTE RIVER TRAIL

THE TRAILS

Whether or not the presence of the Platte River would influence Janssen and Beaty's trek across the West in 1988 remained to be seen. But there was no doubt that the Platte's influence on Nineteenth Century Americans traveling east to west was profound. The greatest migration corridor in American history followed the Platte, the South Platte, and the North Platte Rivers across Nebraska. Surprisingly, this passage was discovered not by Lewis and Clark or explorers from the east, but by Robert Stuart, one of the early "Astorians" (John Jacob Astor's men who settled Oregon). Stuart led a company of men back east across the continent to New York in 1812 by way of a new central route that later became known as the "Oregon Trail."

Missionaries, adventurers, and fur-traders who followed this trail west in the 1830's, "jumped off" the Missouri River at Independence, and then cut across northeastern Kansas, up the Blue River to Fort Kearny (as Samuel Clemens did), and then along the south side of the Platte River and South Platte River, which they eventually forded. The trail then led north across plateau lands to the valley of the North Platte River which they followed to Wyoming. Here they picked up the Sweetwater River, following it to the South Pass of the Rocky Mountains. Thousands of Oregon settlers trekked this trail in waves of migration during the 1840's.

Mormon Pioneers in 1847 created their own "Mormon Trail" on the north side of the Platte and North Platte Rivers, after "jumping off" the Missouri River at Council Bluffs. Their northside trail paralleled the more heavily traveled Oregon Trail south of the river, but avoided the South Platte and its notorious ford altogether.

The California gold rush of 1849 sparked another surge of emigrants over the Oregon Trail. So many, in fact, that it eventually became known as the "California-Oregon Trail," or the "Oregon-California Trail" (depending on who was talking). This was the trail that the Pony Express riders followed from St. Joseph, Missouri during their brief but spectacular dashes across the West and back from 1860-1861. Samuel Clemens' *Central Overland California and Pike's Peak Express* stagecoach followed this same trail. So did silver-rushers to the

Comstock Lode in Nevada and gold-rushers to Pike's Peak in Colorado during the 1850's and 1860's.

When would it all end, the American public probably wondered? The answer was: America's "westering urge" would never end, as even today's traveling public can attest to. But trail travel across the West came to a sputtering halt in 1869 with the pounding in of a golden spike on a lonely railroad line at Promontory, Utah, and the linking of America by the first transcontinental railroad.

THE TRAVELERS

Altogether over 250,000 men, women, and children traveled the trails from east to west by covered wagon, ox-cart, horseback, handcart, stagecoach, or on foot. They were trappers, adventurers, furtraders, soldiers, gold-rushers, missionaries, farmers, storekeepers, stockmen, millmen, craftsmen, newsmen, teachers, dancers, housewives, you-name-it. It seems incredible to think of such vast numbers of people "struggling" across uncharted lands full of hardships and dangers, Indian attacks, and sudden death around every corner.

Why did they do it? Why would so many people risk life and limb, property and prosperity — and take their children along, too? Is that what you wonder? Is that how you feel about this great American western migration on the Platte River trail? If so, you're wrong. It was never a "slaughter of the innocents." Instead, it was the thing to do. It was the "in" thing in the mid-1800's. Yes, believe it or not, migrating west was a great adventure for Americans of all ages with their energy and optomism and pot-of-gold-at-the-end-of-the-rainbow dreams.

Nor did they travel alone. Most emigrants teamed up with other travelers. Sometimes they formed a true wagon train and hired a wagon-master with scouts to lead the way — as portrayed so often on television or movies. Others traveled in loose-knit groups that camped together at night. Many cooked over the same fire. Some shared their food — often their game, if one of the party had been lucky in hunting.

They sang songs together, told stories around the campfire together, tended the sick together, made plans together, and argued over which way to go in the morning together, as well.

By the time they reached Fort Kearny, their sore muscles had hardened, the weak and lame ones had dropped out or turned back, and the rest greeted each morning sunrise with a happy heart and spirit. What would the new day bring? Maybe a fascinating prairie-dog town with its yelps and barks and scurryings. Perhaps a military post with flags fluttering and handsome blue-uniformed troopers a-gallop. Always a stage station with extra supplies and stock at hand, and maybe a message from a friend on the trail up ahead.

They left their names inscribed on every rocky landmark along the trail. They filled their letters and diaries with descriptions of the wonders they were encountering. And they wrote books about their adventures when they finally arrived. Mark Twain's powers of description in ROUGHING IT, almost carry us with him on those wonderful stagecoach mornings: "It was now just dawn; and as we stretched out cramped legs full length on the mail-sacks, and gazed out through the windows across the wide wastes of greensward clad in cool, powdery mist, to where there was an expectant look in the eastern horizon, our perfect enjoyment took the form of a tranquil and contented ecstasy.

"After breakfast, at some station whose name I have forgotten, we three climbed up on the seat behind the driver, and let the conductor have our bed for a nap. And by and by, when the sun made me drowsy, I lay down on my face on top of the coach, grasping the slender iron railing, and slept for an hour or more. That will give one an appreciable idea of those matchless roads."

THE DANGERS

Were there no dangers or difficulties, then? Of course there were. Just as every form of travel has its problems, so did migrating west across the Platte River Trail. A wagon breakdown was not ordinarily a serious one. Everybody carried spare parts and know-how. If that was not enough, there was usually a stage station up the road ten miles or so. Nevertheless, Samuel Clemens was alarmed to hear his driver exclaim:

"The Thoroughbrace is Broke"

"By George, the thoroughbrace is broke!"
This startled me broad awake — as an undefined sense of calamity is always apt to do. I said to myself: "Now, a thoroughbrace is probably part of a horse; and doubtless a vital part, too, from the dismay in the driver's voice. Leg, maybe — and yet how could he break his leg waltzing along such a road as this? No, it can't be his leg. This is im-

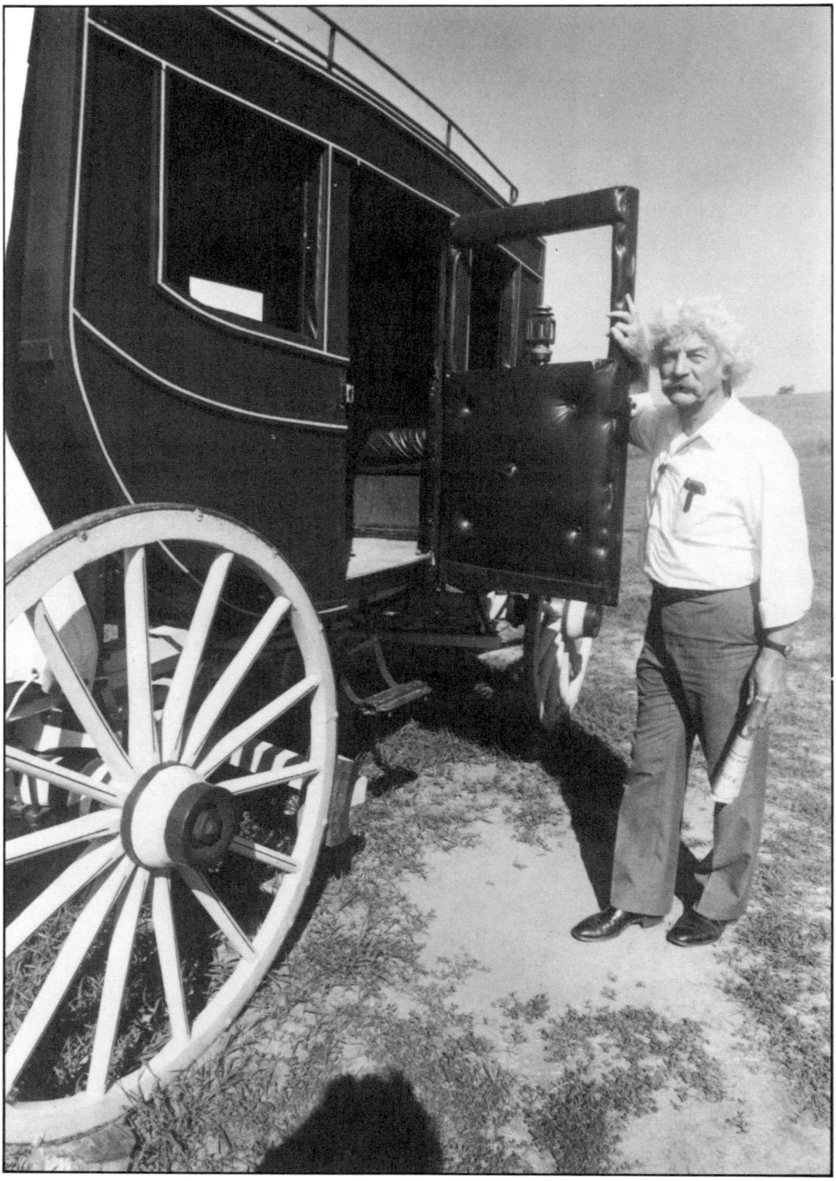

possible, unless he was reaching for the driver. Now, what can be the thoroughbrace of a horse, I wonder? Well, whatever comes, I shall not air my ignorance in this crowd, anyway."

Just then the conductor's face appeared at a lifted curtain, and his lantern glared in on us and our wall of mail matter. He said:

"Gents, you'll have to turn out a spell. Thoroughbrace is broke."

We climbed out into a chill drizzle, and felt ever so homeless and dreary. When I found that the thing they called a "thoroughbrace" was the massive combination of belts and springs which the coach rocks itself in, I said to the driver:

"I never saw a thoroughbrace used up like that, before, that I can remember. How did it happen?"

"Why, it happened by trying to make one coach carry three days' mail — that's how it happened," said he. "And right here is the very direction which is wrote on all the newspaper-bags which was to be put out for the Injuns for to keep 'em quiet. It's most uncommon luck, becuz it's so nation dark I should 'a' gone by unbeknowns if that air thoroughbrace hadn't broke. . . ."

The conductor said he would send back a guard from the next station to take charge of the abandoned mail-bags, and we drove on. (Twain, ROUGHING IT, 1913)

*****

Indians were always a possible danger in the 1850's and 1860's, but most western travelers did not actually encounter the fierce ones. There were more tales of scalpings and killings than actual occurrences. Mark Twain points this out in his own original way in ROUGHING IT when he describes one such incident:

"The Indian Mail Robbery and Massacre"

We crossed the sand-hills near the scene of the Indian mail robbery and massacre of 1856, wherein the driver and conductor perished, and also all of the passengers but one, it was supposed; but this must have been a mistake, for at different times afterward on the Pacific coast I was personally acquainted with a hundred and thirty-three or four people who were wounded during that massacre, and barely escaped with their lives. There was no doubt of the truth of it — I had it from their own lips.

*****

But there was one real dread that all emigrants feared, especially along the Platte River Trail in the 1850's: Asiatic cholera. It could strike at any time and cut down its victims swiftly — sometimes in a day. Graves of cholera victims dotted the trails, especially around the springs and watering holes.

JANSSEN AND BEATY AT COZAD AND GOTHENBURG

Modern interstate highway I-80 runs north of the Platte River from Kearney to beyond Gothenburg, Nebraska. So does U.S.30. The authors opted to follow the latter to two old stage stations open to the public. Willow Island Station in the town park at Cozad was the first of them. The small chinked log cabin with a shingled roof was said to be part of the original Willow Island Station, moved to the park for protection and public access. The town of Cozad also enjoyed some fame by being located squarely on the 100th Meridian. The next station on the trail, Midway, was also still standing, but on private property not open to the public.

In the town park at Gothenburg, ten miles west on the same road, stood still another chinked log building with its door open. Inside was a pioneer museum and gift shop. This building, probably part of the famous Gilman's Ranch Station, was originally located seven miles west of town. The building was supposedly part of a two-story cedar log structure with the station above and stables below. Only the upper portion was relocated to Gothenburg. Because of its two-story construction, Gilman's Station was more easily defended than some of the other stage stops along the Platte River Trail, and thus survived the Indian troubles of the mid-1860's, according to some accounts.

This building, like Willow Island Station, was originally located south of the Platte River on the California-Oregon Trail. In the early days the Gilman Ranch was operated by two brothers who made their money not only by servicing the Pony Express and stagecoaches, but mainly by trading with travelers. They would trade one of their well

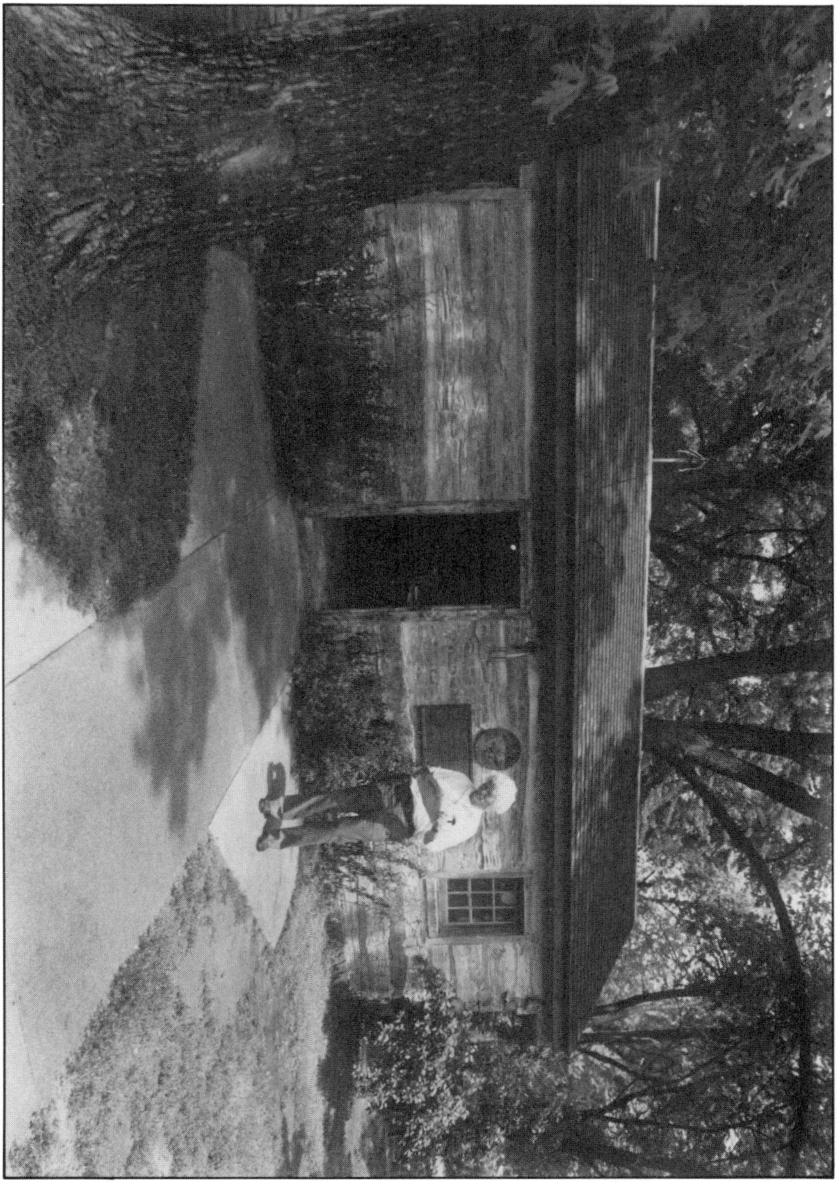

animals for any two footsore animals that an emigrant had to leave behind, and consider it an even trade! Thus they maintained a full stock of trade goods and an even larger stock of horses, mules, and oxen on-the-mend.

Janssen met by chance a man who had once lived on the Gilman Ranch. It was true about the emigrants coming through: their wheel ruts could still be seen on the ranch property, he related.

JANSSEN AT GOTHENBURG

When the authors arrived at the log cabin Pony Express museum in the Gothenburg town park, the visitors greeted Dale Janssen with the same surprise and delight that he had experienced all along the trail. What was "Mark Twain" doing in Nebraska, they wanted to know? Most people were unaware that Samuel Clemens had ever traveled west by stagecoach. Yes, they had heard about his book ROUGHING IT, but they thought that it was mainly about his California mining adventures. How Mark Twain got out to California in the first place, was really not part of their knowledge.

But they wanted photos of Janssen, all the same. It was really *something* to meet such a natural Mark Twain look-alike in a pioneer museum! "Did anyone ever tell you, you look like Mark Twain?" was often the first shy opener. Then when it was apparent that many people had, the questioner became even more excited and bold. "Brian! Jennifer!" they would call to their kids, "come on over here and meet Mark Twain! Maybe he'll give you his autograph!"

Janssen was happy to comply, but also anxious to get back on the modern highway "trail" following Twain and transportation across the West.

ON TO NORTH PLATTE, NEBRASKA

Some thirty-five miles ahead at North Platte, the broad flat Platte River of the plains was split into two rivers: the North Platte which continued on into Wyoming, and the South Platte which dipped down into Colorado. Obviously, since these streams were flowing west to east, they were actually the north and south branches of the main river that came together to form the Platte. All the trails except the Mormon Trail continued along the south side of the river. Thus, most emigrants ended up following the South Platte River across Nebraska to the border of Colorado. Then they were forced to ford the South Platte in order to work their way up to the North Platte Valley which would carry them across the rest of Nebraska to the Sweetwater River of Wyoming, and on over the Rockies.

When Janssen and Beaty arrived at this confluence of rivers, they realized that the thriving city of North Platte, Nebraska had spread itself across both river forks. Bridges at either side of the city crossed the two branches. In fact, it was hard to tell which was which, without a sign. They were low flowing rivers divided by numerous sand bars. But they were not the mile-wide rivers described by the early trail trekkers. Dams and irrigation drain-off had cut them down to size.

Originally founded by the Union Pacific Railroad in 1866, North Platte was laid out as a construction camp for the new railroad. Its first newspaper *Pioneer on Wheels* was printed in a box car. In 1988 the railroad was only one of the many forms of transportation apparent in the city. Yet North Platte had not forgotten its railroad heritage. In fact, its major celebration in 1988 was a "Canteen Reunion" honoring the hosting of over six million servicemen at the Canteen in the Union Pacific Depot during World War II. A stage musical about train travelers during World War II, a USO-style show, and a parade with the President of the Union Pacific Railroad as the grand marshal were on tap. The city's Western Heritage Museum featured for the first time a historical display of its famed World War II Canteen.

Such doings excited Dale Janssen, another railroad devotee. His transportation consulting work had brought him in close contact with a number of western railroads, including the Union Pacific. But when Dale began talking with people in North Platte, he was greeted with quite a different opening than usual.

"Did anyone ever tell you, you look like Buffalo Bill?" was a question that often opened a conversation. Hmmm. Now, what did that mean, wondered Dale?

THE BUFFALO BILL CONNECTION

Then the authors began looking around them. They soon noted that William "Buffalo Bill" Cody's name and picture were quite evident in North Platte. There was a park, a number of businesses, and many portraits of Cody displayed in the city. Pictures of the mature Cody showed him with a prominent shock of white hair, something like Mark

Twain's. When seen together the two did not really resemble one another, but apart one could make a connection.

Then Beaty began to laugh. Yes, there really was a connection with Buffalo Bill. As a Mark Twain researcher she had run across several incidents of their meetings and non-meetings. They were both in London at the same time, for instance, when another case of mistaken identity occurred: Twain's daughter Clara tells of his walking alone in London when "a well-dressed, pleasant-faced woman rushed up to him and grabbed both his hands. 'I am so delighted to see you, face to face,' she exclaimed. 'I have always admired you so much.' 'Indeed!' said the proud author, elevating his chest a little. 'Yes.' continued the woman, 'everybody here in England admires you. How proud America must be of you!' 'And you recognized me' — began Mark. 'By your pictures, of course. As soon as I set eyes on you, I said to myself: That's Buffalo Bill — the great Buffalo Bill!' " (Zall, P.M., MARK TWAIN LAUGHING, 1985, p. 115).

But what was Buffalo Bill doing in North Platte, wondered the authors? Hadn't he lived in Cody, Wyoming? Yes, he had. But his principal home and ranch was located at North Platte — now a state historical site. "Wouldn't you like to visit Buffalo Bill's ranch?" was the offer.

Thus, the Platte, or rather North Platte did have a decided effect on the authors' journey west. It sent them northwest on a diversionary quest to explore the connection between Mark Twain and Buffalo Bill Cody.

*****

REFERENCES

Federal Writers' Project, NEBRASKA, A GUIDE TO THE CORNHUSKER STATE, Lincoln, Nebraska: University of Nebraska Press, 1979.
Franzwa, Gregory M., THE OREGON TRAIL REVISITED, Gerald, Missouri: The Patrice Press, 1972.
Haines, Aubrey L., HISTORIC SITES ALONG THE OREGON TRAIL, Gerald, Missouri: The Patrice Press, 1981.
Mattes, Merrill J., "Chimney Rock, Nebraska," *Nebraska History,* Vol. 26, No. 1, 1955.
Twain, Mark, ROUGHING IT, New York: Harper and Brothers, 1913.
Zall, Paul M., MARK TWAIN LAUGHING, Knoxville: University of Tennessee Press, 1985. Passage reprinted by permission of publisher.

*****

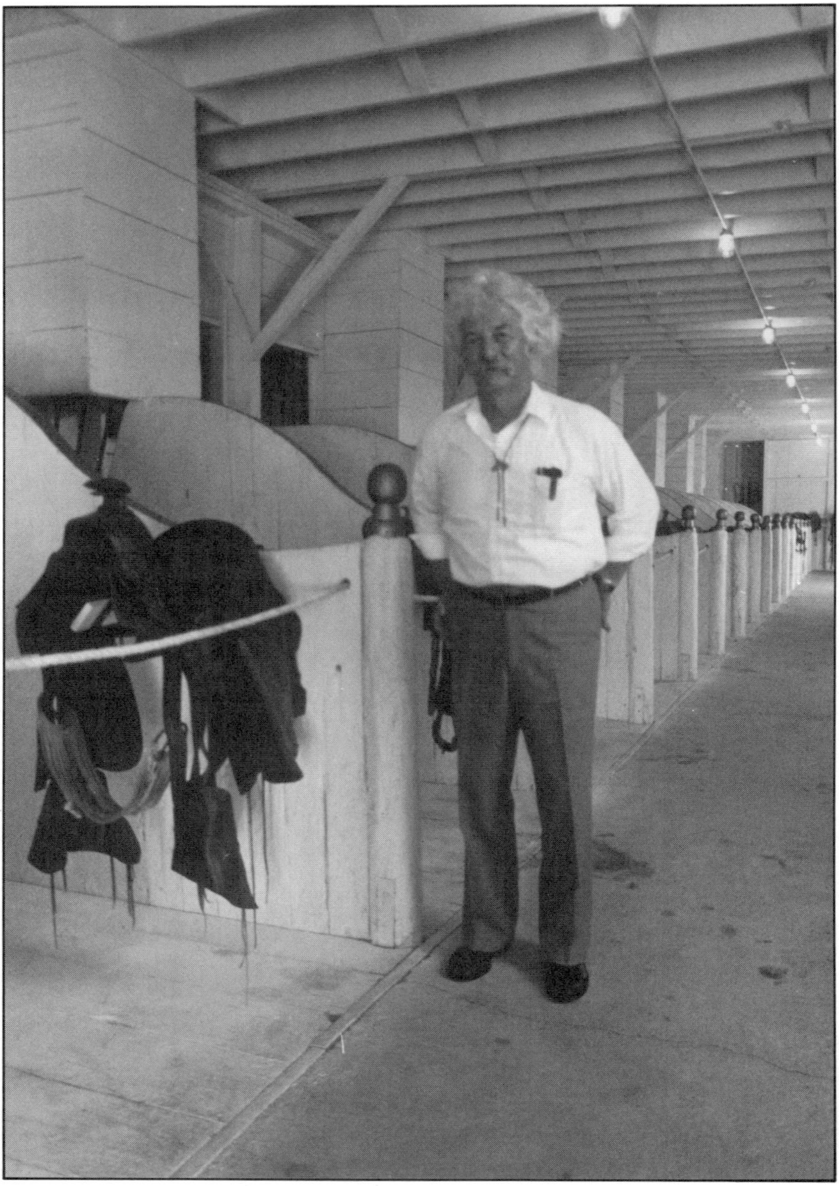

CHAPTER 6

THE BUFFALO BILL CONNECTION

SCOUT'S REST RANCH

But first the two authors drove out to Bill Cody's Scout's Rest Ranch near the Western Heritage Museum, to learn more about North Platte's most famous citizen, Buffalo Bill. The ranch occupied twenty-five acres of what was once a 4,000-acre spread where Cody raised cattle and horses from blooded stock, and rested between seasons of his Wild West Show. While the elegant three-story Victorian house was undoubtedly his pride and joy, it was the gigantic barn that was the first thing to catch the authors' eyes. It could stable up to 180 horses and their trappings. The row of white-washed stalls seemed to go on forever. Besides stabling horses, Cody used the building for rehearsing his Wild West Shows. Both buildings had been restored to appear much as they did when Cody had them built in 1886-7.

Cody had a house in town as well, called "Welcome Wigwam," where his wife spent much of her time while he was on the road, but it was the ranch house he enjoyed "resting" in so well during the off-season, that he called it "Scout's Rest Ranch" and painted the name on the barn roof in letters "big enough to be read from the Union Pacific a mile away," noted Don Russell (THE LIVES AND LEGENDS OF BUFFALO BILL, 1960, p. 422).

Once again Nebraska showed its pride and good sense by preserving the buildings and entire grounds as the Buffalo Bill State Historical Park. The house was a museum of period furniture and Cody memorabilia. The barn displayed original posters from the Wild West Shows as well as saddles and farm implements.

While Janssen was exploring the barn, visitors and staff alike were eyeing him knowingly. "Did anyone ever tell you that you look like . . . . . " It was starting again. And this time it was Buffalo Bill they had in mind. What Mark Twain looked like was not as well known in North Platte, it seemed.

Then one of the staff mentioned to Janssen that North Platte actually had its own "Buffalo Bill," a gentleman who looked exactly like Buffalo Bill with shoulder-length white hair, mustache and goatee. He lived on a ranch outside of town, and until quite recently had ridden in rodeo parades around the country as "Buffalo Bill." He had even appeared as Buffalo Bill in Europe. Wouldn't it be fascinating if the two look-alike men could meet?

BUFFALO STEW COOKOUT

Before they knew what was happening, Janssen and Beaty were accepting an invitation to a buffalo stew cookout at the ranch that evening; and yes, Charlie Evans, North Platte's "Buffalo Bill," would be there. The stew and cornbread were scrumptious, the guitar sing-along entertainment was outstanding, the good-guys-bad-guys melodrama was reminiscent of the old wild west shows; but the highlight of the evening for the authors was the meeting of Mr. and Mrs. Charlie Evans. It was true: here was another "spittin' image." Mr. Evans talked about his role as Buffalo Bill which he had played regularly until a few years ago when his white horse died. Now he lived on a ranch twelve miles out of town run by his son. And yes, he could appreciate Janssen and Beaty's trail quest that summer, for the Mormon Trail ran right through his ranch.

Mr. Evans was not aware of the Mark Twain-Buffalo Bill connection, but if the two men were contemporaries (and they were), they were certainly both famous and well-known enough to have met. He suggested, as did several others, that the authors take a detour up to Cody, Wyoming, to visit the Buffalo Bill home, museum, and the Irma Hotel that Buffalo Bill had built in his later years. And if we were following the Pony Express Trail . . . did we know that Buffalo Bill had been a Pony Express rider out of Julesburg, Colorado? Julesburg, Colorado . . . you mean the place where Samuel Clemens' stagecoach crossed the South Platte River, we wondered?

That clinched it. Suddenly we could see the parallels in the two lives. William Cody and Samuel Clemens, two young men of the West: each of them "originals"; each of them strong-willed individualists with a taste for adventure, and with a confidence and flair that would carry them beyond adventure to glory. But no one had mentioned before that the two of them had been at the same place at the same time on the western Overland Trail. Perhaps, no one knew . . .

OTHER PARALLELS

Some of the parallels in the two men's lives were startling, to say the least. Cody was born in 1846 in Le Claire, Iowa, near Davenport on the Mississippi River. Samuel Clemens had been born eleven years earlier in Florida, Missouri, inland from Hannibal on the Mississippi River. Cody's father died when he was eleven years old, just as did Samuel Clemens' father. As boys and men, both of them helped to support their mothers, their sisters and their brothers all of their lives. By then the Cody family had moved to Kansas where young Cody, even at eleven, had become a good rider and a crack shot. As he watched the emigrants pass through Kansas on the Oregon Trail (40,000 passed his mother's door), he itched to be part of this "westering" movement.

His first job at eleven was as a messenger riding between wagon trains on the road to Utah. Later he was a herder and then a "bullwhacker" on the wagon trains. At Fort Laramie he met Kit Carson and Jim Bridger. They became his heroes. He resolved to become a scout like them.

THE PONY EXPRESS

But first there was the Pony Express. In its short life of eighteen months from April of 1860 to November of 1861, the Pony Express caught the attention of the entire nation. Boys dreamed of being a rider, of galloping into glory carrying the mail across mountains and deserts, through Indian ambushes and difficult mountain passes. Travelers on the western trails hoped just to catch sight of such a rider. It was a thrill not to be forgotten.

Even Mark Twain caught the fever, or as he tells it in ROUGHING IT:

"A Consuming Desire to See a Pony-Rider"

> We had had a consuming desire, from the beginning, to see a pony-rider, but somehow or other all that passed us and all that met us managed to streak by in the night, and so we heard only a whiz and a hail, and the swift phantom of the desert was gone before we could get our heads out of the windows. But now we were expecting one along every moment, and would see him in broad daylight. Presently the driver exclaims:
> "HERE HE COMES!"
> Every neck is stretched further, and every eye strained wider. Away across the endless dead level of the prairie a black speck appears against the sky, and it is plain that it

moves. Well, I should think so! In a second or two it becomes a horse and rider, rising and falling, rising and falling — sweeping toward us nearer and nearer — growing more and more distinct, more and more sharply defined — nearer and still nearer, and the flutter of the hoofs comes faintly to the ear — another instant a whoop and a hurrah from our upper deck, a wave of the rider's hand, but no reply, and man and horse burst past our excited faces, and go swinging away like a belated fragment of a storm!

*****

BUFFALO BILL, A PONY RIDER

Buffalo Bill was fourteen and still known as Will Cody when he attempted to become a Pony Express rider. He went with a wagon train up the trail from Ft. Laramie to Horseshoe Station where the Division Superintendent Alf Slade was headquartered, looking for a job. Slade supervised the trail section from Julesburg, Colorado, through a corner of Nebraska and across Wyoming to South Pass Station. His headquarters at Horseshoe Station was halfway between the two outer stations with thirty-six other stations in between. He was appointed Division Superintendent because of his reputation for "cleaning up" a place with his fierce reputation and sharp shooting skills. Mark Twain was so impressed with Slade that he wrote two whole chapters about him in ROUGHING IT:

"This Desperado Slade"

And from the hour we had left Overland City (Julesburg) we had heard drivers and conductors talk about only three things — "Californy," the Nevada silver-mines, and this desperado Slade. And a deal of the talk was about Slade. We had gradually come to have a realizing sense of the fact that Slade was a man whose heart and hands and soul were steeped in the blood of offenders against his dignity; a man who awfully avenged all injuries, affronts, insults or slights, of whatever kind — on the spot if he could, years afterward if lack of earlier opportunity compelled it; a man whose hate tortured him day and night till vengeance appeased it — and not an ordinary vengeance either, but his enemy's absolute death — nothing less; a man whose face would

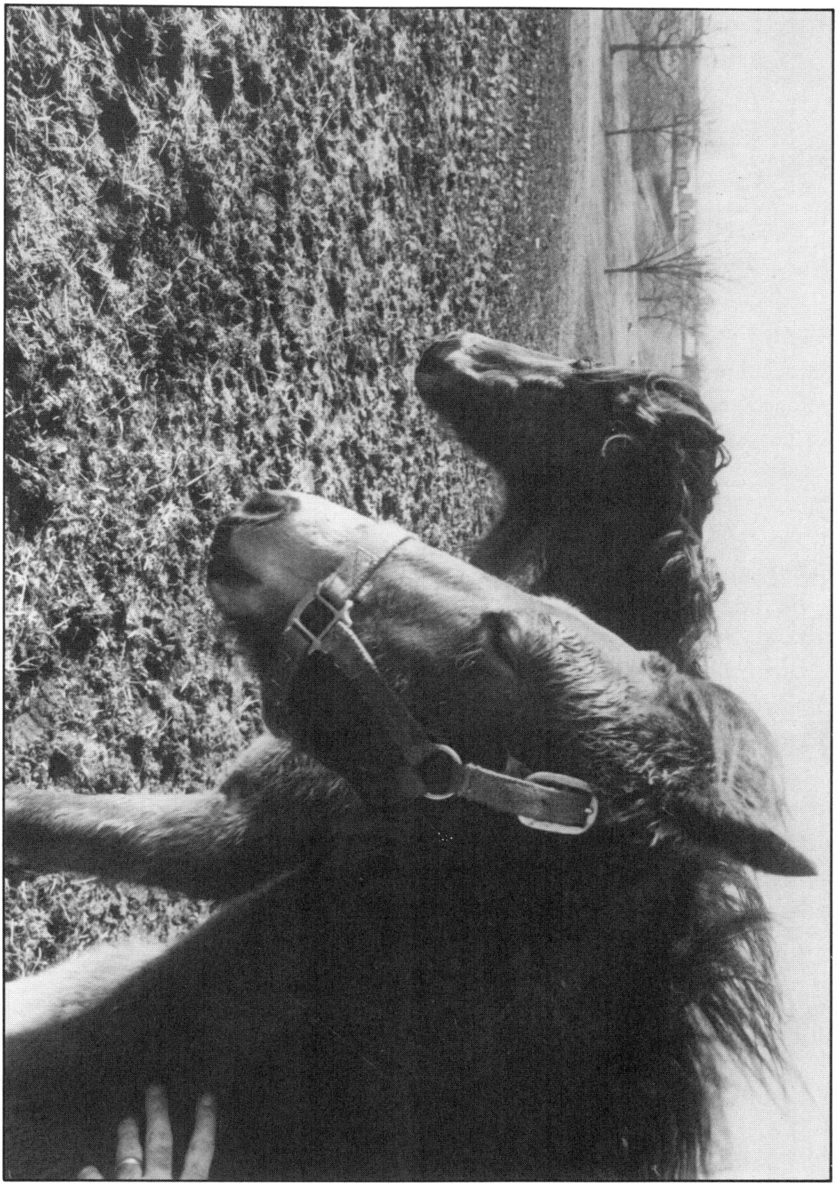

light up with a terrible joy when he surprised a foe and had him at a disadvantage. A high and efficient servant of the Overland, an outlaw among outlaws and yet their relentless scourge, Slade was at once the most bloody, the most dangerous, and the most valuable citizen that inhabited the savage fastness of the mountains.

*****

How Will Cody felt about Slade is not known. But how Slade felt about Will Cody was quite evident: he objected to him as a pony rider because he was so young. Nevertheless, he gave him a trial run between Red Buttes and Three Crossings Stations, a 76 mile run. Will must have passed the test, for he tells in his autobiography several anecdotes about the Red Buttes-to-Three-Crossings run. Once when he reached Three Crossings he found that the pony rider who was to relieve him had been killed the night before. Cody got a new horse and rode on for 85 more miles, and then rode back to Red Buttes, making a total of 322 miles in 21 hours, 40 minutes, using 21 horses. Although many stories about Cody's life were highly exaggerated or outright fiction, this particular ride seemed plausible according to researchers.

During 1861 the fifteen-year-old Cody worked mainly out of Horseshoe Station as a stock herder and an occasional Pony Express rider. Was he there when Samuel Clemens came through on the Overland Stage? It is certainly possible. The Clemens boys had breakfast at Horseshoe Station on Thursday, August 1. There were shots in the night and talk of hostile Indians. The next morning they sat down to breakfast at Horse Creek Station, or as Mark Twain put it in ROUGHING IT:

"We Sat Down to Breakfast"

In due time we rattled up to a stage-station, and sat down to breakfast with a half-savage, half civilized company of armed and bearded mountaineers, ranchmen and station employees. The most gentlemanly-appearing, quiet, and affable officer we had yet found along the road in the Overland Company's service was the person who sat at the head of the table, at my elbow. Never youth stared and shivered as I did when I heard them call him SLADE!

Here was romance, and I was sitting face to face with it! — looking upon it — touching it — hobnobbing with it, as it were! Here, right by my side, was the actual ogre who, in fights and brawls and various ways, *had taken the lives of twenty-six human beings*, or all men lied about him! I suppose I was the proudest stripling that ever traveled to see strange lands and wonderful people . . .

The coffee ran out. At least it was reduced to one tin cupful, and Slade was about to take it when he saw that my cup was empty. He politely offered to fill it, but although I wanted it, I politely declined. I was afraid he had not killed anybody that morning, and might be needing diversion. But still with firm politeness he insisted on filling my cup, and said I had traveled all night and better deserved it than he — and while he talked placidly poured the fluid, to the last drop. I thanked him and drank it, but it gave me no comfort, for I could not feel sure that he would not be sorry, presently, that he had given it away, and proceed to kill me to distract his thoughts from the loss. But nothing of the kind occurred. We left him with only twenty-six dead people to account for, and I felt a tranquil satisfaction in the thought that in so judiciously taking care of No. 1 at that breakfast-table I had pleasantly escaped being No. 27.

* * * * *

Was Bill Cody somewhere around at this station or another on Clemens' route? Quite probably. Since neither of the two of them was famous enough to be recognized or their names to be recorded at this point, we shall never really know, but only guess that Mark Twain and Buffalo Bill first passed by one another and perhaps even saw one another during the summer of 1861 on the old Overland Trail to California.

ON THE BUFFALO BILL TRAIL

Up toward the town of Cody, Wyoming the two authors now decided to travel, reading about Buffalo Bill on the way. They found that after his Pony Express experiences, Will Cody served in the Civil War as a scout in Tennessee, as a hospital orderly in St. Louis, and as a scout in the West for General Sherman. He met and married his wife Louisa in

St. Louis, but the western frontier lured him back, first as a stagecoach driver, then as an army scout, and finally as a buffalo hunter for the Union Pacific railroad crews, where he earned his nickname "Buffalo Bill." Dime novelist Ned Buntline met him and began writing the first of hundreds of dime novels featuring Buffalo Bill as the hero of the prairies.

He was invited to New York City, and eventually transformed himself from frontiersman to actor in melodramas such as "Scouts of the Plains." It was clear to him that by now scouts were a dying breed, but to the American public they were heroes. If Buntline could exploit Cody's heroics in dime novels, why couldn't Cody exploit himself? He began appearing in western dramas during the winter, but returned to the West as an army scout when summer Indian uprisings called him back. Eventually he carried the "West" back east with him in spectacular live shows with hundreds of horses, real cowboys and Indians, bucking broncos, buffalo stampedes, Indian attacks, stagecoach robberies, Pony Express rides, shootouts, trick roping, and sharpshooting.

An item in *The Chemung Historical Journal* of Elmira, New York, (Samuel Clemens' wife's home town) notes: "William E. Cody (Buffalo Bill) in 1878 as part of a show at the Elmira Opera House shot a potato off the head of a lady at 30 paces, then turned his back and using a mirror did it again. It was his sixth tour of the country. He came again in 1882." (Hilbert, p. 3776). Mark Twain and his family visited Elmira in March of 1878. They summered in Elmira during June, July, and August of 1882. Could Twain have seen the show? If not, he may have visited Cody's original Wild West Show in Hartford, Connecticut, (Twain's principal residence), when the show made its appearance there in 1883. If not there, he surely saw it in the New York City environs where it played for a whole season at a time.

At any rate, Mark Twain in his later years was captivated by Buffalo Bill's Wild West Shows. They seemed so extravagant that the general public could hardly believe they were true-to-life. Mark Twain knew better, for he had been there too. Without hesitation he wrote to Buffalo Bill after seeing a performance: "Down to its smallest details the Show is genuine. It brought back vividly the breezy wild life of the Plains and the Rocky Mountains. It is wholly free from sham and insincerity and the effects it produced upon me by its spectacles were identical with those wrought upon me a long time ago on the frontier. Your pony expressman was as tremendous an interest to me as he was twenty-three years ago when he used to come whizzing by from over the desert with his war news; and your bucking horses were even painfully real to me as I rode one of those outrages for nearly a quarter of a minute. It is often said on the other side of the water that none of the exhibitions which we send to England are purely and distinctly American. If you will take the Wild West Show over there you can remove that reproach." (Sell and Weybright, 1979, p. 151) Buffalo Bill did take his show abroad and spent many successful seasons performing in England and Europe.

ACROSS THE SANDHILLS OF NEBRASKA

Meanwhile, the two authors were heading north and west toward Cody, Wyoming through a fascinating land formation known as Nebraska's "sandhills." They drove due north from North Platte on U.S. 83 through the center of the sandhills: rounded humps of land covered with prairie grass or pocked with "blowouts" of various sizes. These were bare round holes blown out by the relentless sweep of the prairie wind over sandy soil that cattle had trampled loose. The hills themselves were actually sand dunes from 20 to 400 feet high, anchored by prairie grass: the largest tract of sand dunes in North America in fact, covering some 19,000 square miles, a quarter of the state of Nebraska.

If it weren't for the grass, the land would have resembled the Sahara Desert with endless ridges, mounds, hills, and peaks of sand blown into dunes in ancient times by winds that swept across the exposed sandy bed of an ancient inland sea. Early homesteaders avoided the sandhills as a no-man's-land where cattle were swallowed up in the endless hollows, valleys, and pockets — all exactly alike and easy to get lost in. The pioneers especially avoided the "choppies", clumps of little sandhills less than 30 feet in height. What they did not know was that the dry-appearing sandhill region was actually a sponge of water underneath that would eventually provide unlimited underground water for modern irrigation.

What appeared as endless miles of arid hilly grasslands, was in fact some of the richest grazing land in the United States. Today ranchers raise enough cattle there to make Nebraska the third largest beef producer, the authors discovered. Most of the cattle work was surprisingly still done by cowboys on horses in the remote pockets, although some ranchers assisted their herders with aircraft surveillance.

The northern and western sections of the sandhills were dotted with lakes, ponds, and marshes wherever the water table came to the surface. Over 1,300 lakes in this area made it a fishermen's and hunters' paradise, as well. At Valentine were two protected areas: the Valentine National Wildlife Refuge for waterfowl and the Fort Niobrara National Wildlife Refuge containing one of the state's three buffalo herds. Free-roaming antelope, elk, and deer were also visible from the Refuge roads by sharp-eyed visitors. And like ghosts from the past, longhorn cattle were occasionally spotted — remnants of herds driven up from Texas in the 1870's and '80's.

Janssen and Beaty followed Route 83 on through the waterfowl Refuge south of Valentine. Just east of the town on U.S. 20 was the Niobrara Refuge with its buffalo herd and roads through the hills that made it possible for a closeup look.

Once the entire area was black with buffalo. But even by Samuel Clemens' day the herds had retreated into the fastness of the sandhills to escape slaughter by men with guns. In ROUGHING IT Mark Twain tells of an incredible Nebraska buffalo hunt they and their imaginery companion Bemis participated in:

"When the Buffalo Climbed the Tree"

We were to be delayed five or six hours, and therefore we took horses, by invitation, and joined a party who were just starting on a buffalo-hunt. It was a noble sport galloping over the plain in the dewy freshness of the morning, but our part of the hunt ended in disaster and disgrace, for a wounded buffalo bull chased the passenger Bemis nearly two miles, and then he forsook his horse and took to a lone tree . . . finally he (Bemis) said:

"If I had had a horse worth a cent — but no, the minute he saw that buffalo bull wheel on him and give a bellow, he raised straight up in the air and stood on his heels. The saddle began to slip, and I took him round the neck and laid close to him, and began to pray. Then he came down and stood up on the other end awhile, and the bull actually stopped pawing sand and bellowing to contemplate the inhuman spectacle. Then the bull made a pass at him and uttered a bellow that sounded perfectly frightful, it was so close to me, and that seemed to literally prostrate my horse's reason, and make a raving distracted maniac of him, and I wish I may die if he didn't stand on his head for a quarter of a minute and shed tears. He was absolutely out of his mind — he was, as sure as truth itself, and he really didn't know what he was doing. Then the bull came charging at us, and my horse dropped down on all fours and took a fresh start — and then for the next ten minutes he would actually throw one handspring after another so fast that the bull began to get unsettled, too, and didn't know where to start in — and so he stood there sneezing and shoveling dust over his back, and bellowing every now and then, and thinking he had got a fifteen-hundred-dollar circus horse for breakfast, certain. Well, I was first out on his neck — the horse's, not the bull's — and then underneath, and next on his rump, and sometimes head up and sometimes heels — but I tell you it seemed solemn and awful to be ripping and tearing and carrying on so in the presence of death, as you might say. Pretty soon the bull made a snatch for us and brought away some of my horse's tail (I suppose, but do not know, being pretty busy at the time), but *something* made him hungry for solitude and suggested to him to get up and hunt for it. And then you ought to have seen that spider-legged old skeleton go! and you ought to have seen the bull cut out after him, too — head down, tongue out, tail up, bellowing like everything, and actually mowing down the weeds, and tearing up the earth, and boosting up the sand like a whirlwind! By George, it was a hot race! I and the saddle were back on the rump, and I had the bridle in my teeth and holding on to the pommel with both hands. First we left the dogs behind; then we passed a jackass-rabbit; then we overtook a coyote, and were gaining on an antelope when the rotten girths let go and threw me about thirty yards off to the left, and as the saddle went down over the horse's rump he gave it a lift with his heels that sent it more than four hundred yards up in the air, I wish I may die in a minute if he didn't. I fell at the foot of the only solitary tree there was in nine counties adjacent (as any creature could see with the naked eye), and the next second I had hold of the bark with four sets of nails and my teeth, and the next second after that I was astraddle of the main limb and blaspheming my luck in a way that made my breath smell of brimstone. I *had* the bull, now, if he did not think of *one* thing. But that one thing I dreaded. I dreaded it very seriously. There was a possibility that the bull might not think of it, but there were greater chances that he would. I made up my mind what I would do in case he did. It was a little over forty feet to the ground from where I sat. I cautiously unwound the lariat from the pommel of my saddle —"

"Your *saddle*? Did you take your saddle up in the tree with you?"

"Take it up in the tree with me? Why, how you talk! Of course I didn't. No man could do that. It *fell* in the tree when it came down."

"Oh — exactly."

"Certainly. I unwound the lariat, and fastened one end of it to the limb. It was the very best green rawhide, and capable of sustaining tons. I made a slip-noose in the other end, and then hung it down to see the length. It reached down twenty-two feet — half-way to the ground. I then loaded every barrel of the Allen revolver with a double charge. I felt satisfied. I said to myself, if he never thinks of that one thing that I dread, all right — but if he does, all right anyhow — I am fixed for him. But don't you know that the very thing a man dreads is the thing that always happens? Indeed it is so. I watched the bull, now, with anxiety — anxiety which no one can conceive of who has not been in such a situation and felt that at any moment death might come. Presently a thought came into the bull's eye. I knew it! said I — if my nerve fails now, I am lost. Sure enough, it was just as I had dreaded, he started in to climb the tree —"

"What, the bull?"

"Of course — who else?"

"But a bull can't climb a tree."

"He can't, can't he? Since you know so much about it, did you ever see a bull try?"

"No, I never dreamt of such a thing."

"Well, then, what is the use of your talking that way, then? Because you never saw a thing done, is that any reason why it can't be done?"

"Well, all right — go on. What did you do?"

"The bull started up and got along well for about ten feet, then slipped and slid back. I breathed easier. He tried it again — got up a little higher — slipped again. But he came at it once more, and this time he was careful. He got gradually higher and higher, and my spirits went down more and more. Up he came — an inch at a time — with his eyes hot, and his tongue hanging out. Higher and higher — hitched his foot over the stump of a limb, and looked up, as much as to say, 'You are my meat, friend.' Up again — higher and higher, and getting more excited the closer he got. He was within ten feet of me! I took a long breath — and then said I, 'It is now or never.' I had the coil of the lariat all ready; I paid it out slowly, till it hung right over his head; all of a sudden I let go of the slack and the slip-noose fell fairly round his neck! Quicker than lightning I out with the Allen and let him have it in the face. It was an awful roar, and must have scared the bull out of his senses. When the smoke cleared away, there he was, dangling in the air, twenty foot from the ground, and going out of one convulsion and into another faster than you could count! I didn't stop to count, anyhow — I shinned down the tree and shot for home."

"Bemis, is all that true, just as you have stated it?"

"I wish I may rot in my tracks and die the death of a dog if it isn't."

"Well, we can't refuse to believe it, and we don't. But if there were some proofs —"

"Proofs! Did I bring back my lariat?"

"No."

"Did I bring back my horse?"

"No."

"Did you ever see the bull again?"

"No."

"Well, then, what more do you want? I never saw anybody as particular as you are about a little thing like that."

I made up my mind that if this man was not a liar he only missed it by the skin of his teeth.

*****

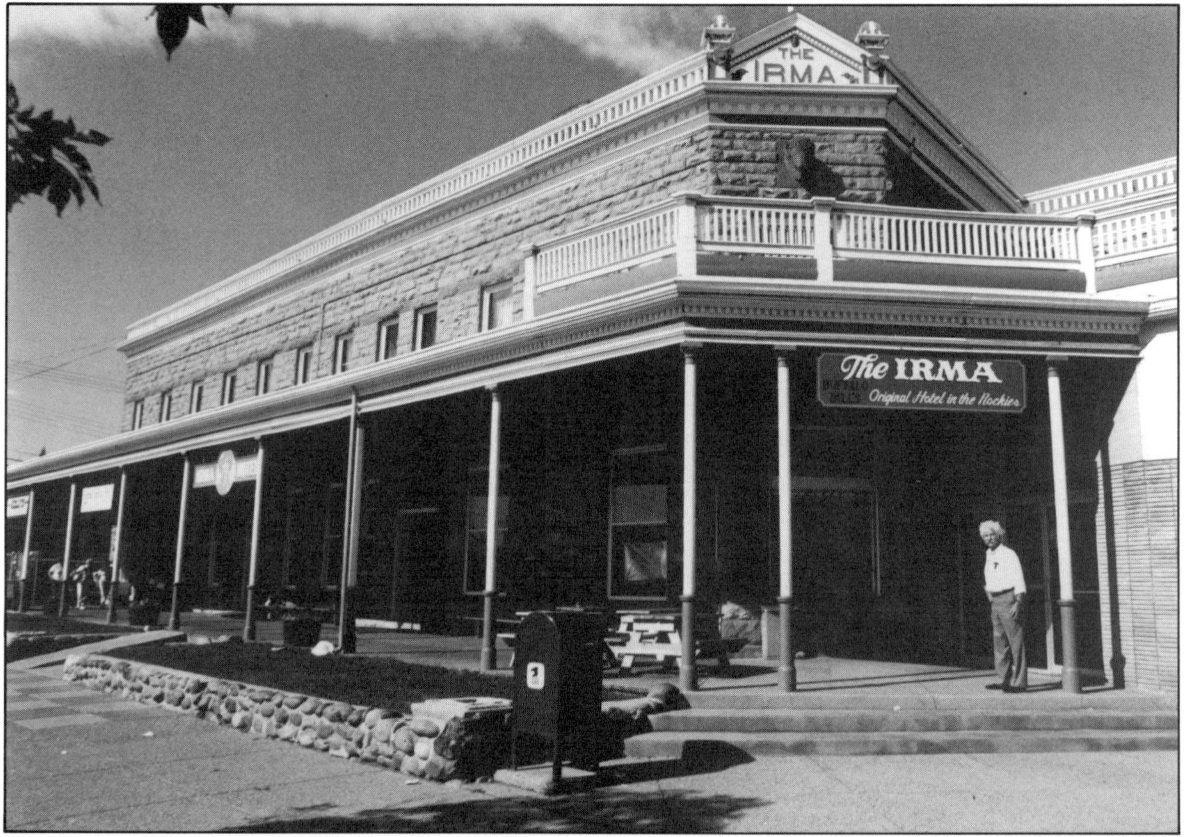
THE
IRMA
The IRMA
Original Hotel in the Rockies

What a tale! The authors remembered about it when they came as close as they cared to a small herd of buffalo in a fenced range outside of Thermopolis, Wyoming on their way up to Cody. The beasts looked placid enough. But all of them stopped grazing in unison to eye our stopped car and our camera. None of them snorted or pawed the earth. But we quickly took our pictures and went on our way. It was not our purpose to stay around until we might be forced to outdo Mark Twain with our own buffalo yarn! Little did we know that our own animal entanglement was yet to come!

AT CODY, WYOMING

Cody was the kind of western town that easterners picture a western town should be. Wide streets, low buildings (some of original sandstone), boot and saddle shops, pack trip outfitters, trading posts, fishing and hunting suppliers — all framed with spectacular mountains at the ends of the streets. A block party was on tap for the Cody Main Street Festival and rodeos were featured nightly during July and August.

Janssen and Beaty headed for The Irma ("Buffalo Bill's Hotel in the Rockies"). While the town of Cody was established by Bill Cody and his Shoshone Land Development partners in 1895-96, the first buildings were tents or frame. It was not until 1901 when Bill Cody's influence brought a railroad spur into Cody that the town took on a more substantial look. Cody built the Irma Hotel in 1902, naming it for his youngest daughter. A large two-story corner building of cut sandstone, the hotel today still features wonderful turn-of-the-century decor in its rooms. In fact the "Buffalo Bill Suite" contains Bill's original bed and furnishings that he designed for his two-room suite.

A large restaurant on the first floor housed the original cherrywood back bar running the length of the room, one of the most elaborately carved and ornamented back bars in the West, it is said. It was a gift to Cody from Queen Victoria in appreciation for his 1900 command performance in London, and was shipped over the mountains to Cody by horse-drawn freight wagons before the railroad was built. A modern ad reads: "For the past 80 years the Irma has been the gathering place for our local stockmen, woolgrowers and oilmen. Tens of thousands of dollars still change hands each year over a cup of coffee and a hand shake."

Modern tourists often know Cody, Wyoming as the Gateway to

Yellowstone National Park. It is, of course. But it is so much more. The entire town stands almost as a memorial to this man who promoted the West and its ideals through his Wild West Shows, his writings, and his investments in the land. A Buffalo Bill Historical Center now houses four "world-class" museums: Buffalo Bill Musuem, Whitney Gallery of Western Art, Plains Indian Museum, and the Winchester Museum, sometimes known collectively as the "Smithsonian of the West." Even Buffalo Bill's birthplace home has been moved to the area.

Where he died and is buried, however, is not in Cody, Wyoming, but outside his daughter's city of Denver, Colorado, atop Lookout Mountain.

The authors were even more impressed when they learned of other spinoffs from Buffalo Bill's fame and name. In his later years he was interested in the Boy Scout movement and helped one of its founders, Dan Beard by writing supportive articles. Beard, an artist, adopted for the Boy Scouts the stetson-like hat and scout neckerchief from the ones worn by Buffalo Bill. Dan Beard was also an artist for Mark Twain, and was best known for his illustrations in A CONNECTICUT YANKEE IN KING ARTHUR'S COURT. Beard enjoyed telling a story about Mark Twain's pride in being mistaken for Buffalo Bill by a Boy Scout on Fifth Avenue when he lived in New York.

More than that, Mark Twain was proud to be associated with the life and times of Buffalo Bill, for he also had crossed the plains when Indians were on the warpath and the Pony Express rider carried the mail. He also had experienced the life of the frontiersman and western miner. Mark Twain is so closely associated in the modern mind with the Mississippi River and steamboats, that people are often startled to hear about his western adventures. Not many of his readers realize that Mark Twain wrote a short story called "The Horse's Tale" about Buffalo Bill's horse, Pony Boy. The horse, in fact, narrates parts of this fictional account which begins:

"Buffalo Bill's Horse"

"I am Buffalo Bill's horse. I have spent my life under his saddle — with him in it, too, and he is good for two hundred pounds, without his clothes; and there is no telling how much he does weigh when he is out on the war-path and has his batteries belted on. He is over six feet, is young, hasn't an ounce of waste flesh, is straight, graceful, springy in his motions, quick as a cat, and has a handsome face, and black hair dangling down on his shoulders, and is beautiful to look at; and nobody is braver than he is, and nobody is stronger, except myself. Yes, a person that doubts that he is fine to see should see him in his beaded buckskins, on my back and his rifle peeping above his shoulder, chasing a hostile trail, with me going like the wind and his hair streaming out behind from the shelter of his broad slouch. Yes, he is a sight to look at then — and I'm part of it myself."

So there really was a Buffalo Bill connection, the authors realized as they read and talked to people about it. Samuel Clemens had not only known Buffalo Bill, but had also admired him for what he looked like, what he had done in the West, and what he stood for. And now this connection had carried the authors in yet another surprising direction. They realized that this was exactly the kind of thing Mark Twain himself would have done: that is, made digressions from his main theme — as he did over and over again in his writing. In fact it was becoming increasingly clear to Janssen and Beaty as they progressed, that what it really meant to "travel west Mark Twain style," had little to do with following a map.

*****

REFERENCES

Federal Writers' Project, NEBRASKA, A GUIDE TO THE CORNHUSKER STATE, Lincoln, Nebraska: University of Nebraska Press, 1979.
Hitchcock, Anthony and Jean Lindgreen, COUNTRY INNS, LODGES & HISTORIC HOTELS, MIDWEST & ROCKIES, New York: Burt Franklin & Company, 1987.
Hilbert, Alfred G. "Twin Tiers Trivia," *The Chemung Historical Journal*, Elmira, New York, June, 1988.
Kaplan, Justin (editor), THE SIGNET CLASSIC BOOK OF MARK TWAIN'S SHORT STORIES, New York: New American Library, 1985.
Madson, John, "Nebraska's Sand Hills: Land of Long Sunsets," *National Geographic Magazine*, Oct., 1978.
Russel, Don, THE LIVES AND LEGENDS OF BUFFALO BILL, Norman: University of Oklahoma Press, 1960.
Sell, Henry B. and Victor Weybright, BUFFALO BILL AND THE WILD WEST, Basin, Wyoming: Big Horn Books, 1979. Passage reprinted by permission of publisher.
Twain, Mark, ROUGHING IT, New York: Harper and Brothers, 1913.

*****

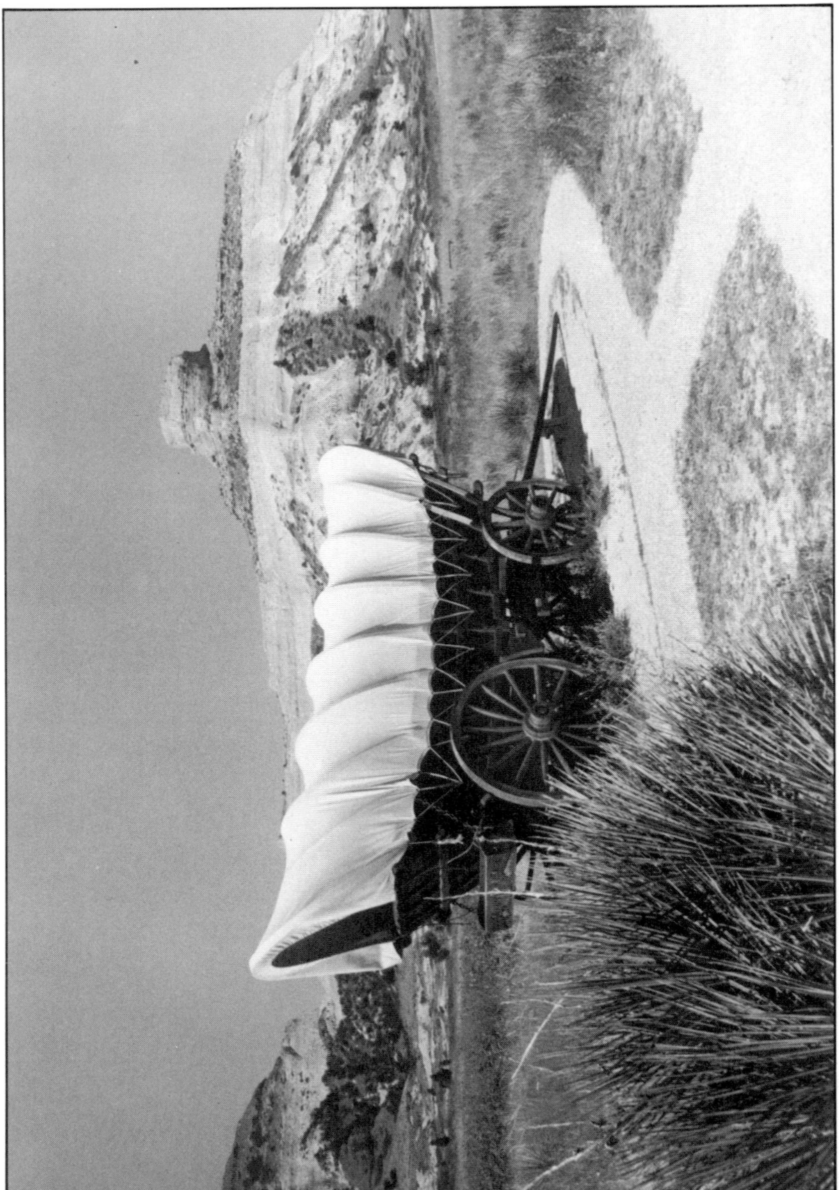

CHAPTER 7
LANDMARKS ON THE TRAIL

The emigrants had no maps to follow, nor any road signs. But they found their way across the plains, over the rivers, and through the mountains just as unerringly as though the route had been paved and fenced. Wheel ruts and stage stations marked the first part of the trail. The Platte River itself marked the next portion. But once they had crossed the South Platte River at Julesburg, Colorado, all trail travelers kept an eye peeled for the natural landmarks that would show them the remainder of the way through Nebraska and Wyoming.

They knew the markers by heart. They recited them over and over almost like a litany:

Courthouse Rock, Jail Rock, Chimney Rock, Scott's Bluff, Independence Rock by the Fourth of July; then Devil's Gate, Ice House Slough, and South Pass — and they were over the Rockies, hurrah!

COURTHOUSE ROCK AND JAIL ROCK

Courthouse Rock was the first of the carved butte landmarks visible on the California/Oregon Trail. It rose up as a massive sandstone monolith visible for days across the plains in the distance. Yes, it did resemble a courthouse, agreed the travelers at their first sighting. Something like the courthouse in St. Louis, someone remarked. And there standing next to it was another somewhat smaller, squared off rock that certainly looked like a jail. As the travelers approached, the Courthouse seemed to change size and shape.

They were fascinating sentinels of the trail, and who could resist hiking over to scratch his name at the base? It couldn't be more than a mile from the trail, many emigrants felt certain. But as they slogged along, the Courthouse did not seem to get any closer. Distances were deceiving in the clear air of the western plains, they learned to their chagrin. Courthouse Rock actually stood four miles from the closest point on the trail. Nevertheless thousands of emigrants hiked to the butte and cut their names in it, only to have them eventually erased by the winds and rains of seasons to follow.

Journals kept by the travelers remarked about the deceptive distance to Courthouse Rock. John Bidwell who guided the first emigrant wagon train west in 1841 wrote: "Its distance from us no one

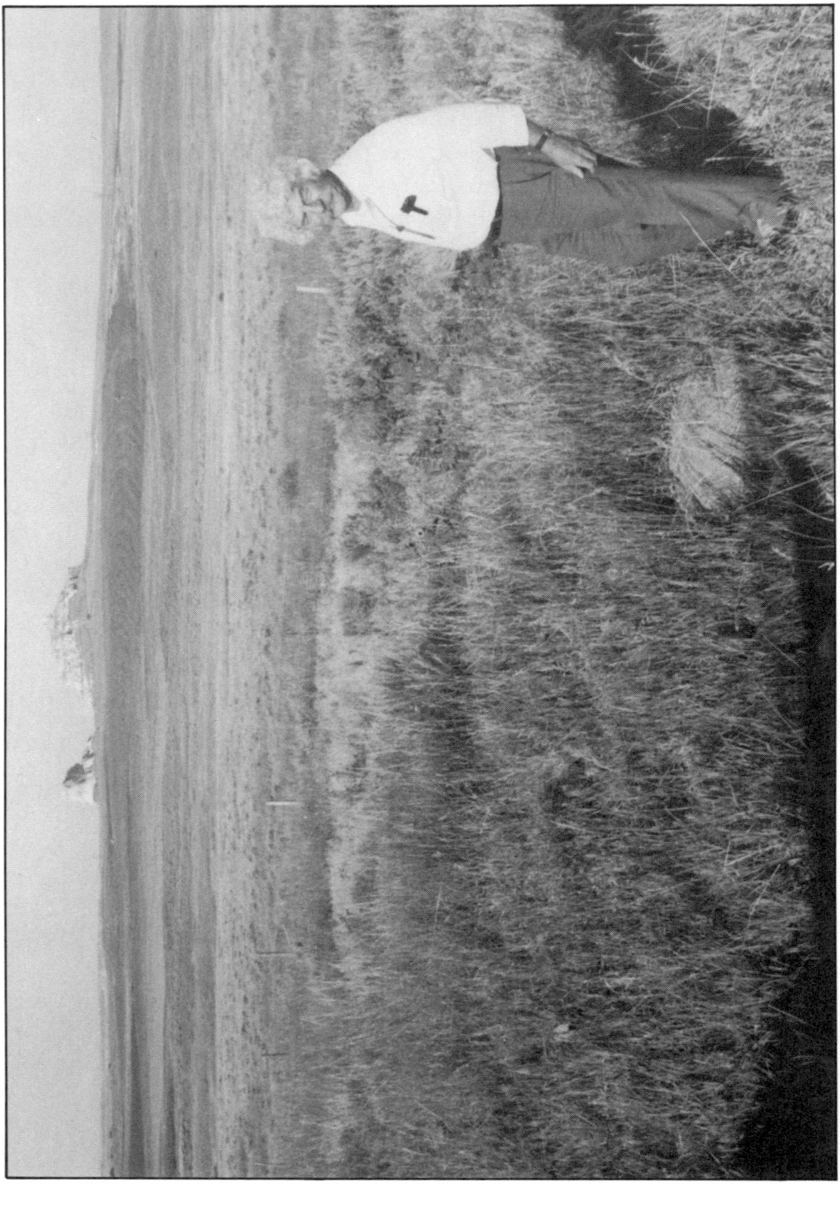

supposed more than 1½ miles, and yet it was at least 7 — this deception was owing to the pure atmosphere through which it was viewed, and the want of objects by which only, accurate ideas of distance can be acquired without measure." (Harris, 1962, p. 11)

Some brave or foolhardy travelers climbed to the top — a rough haul up the crumbling sandstone. Others had been there before them. Pawnee Indians had retreated to the top of the rock in times long past when they were pursued by the Sioux. Believing they had their enemies trapped, the proud Sioux warriors marched around the base of the rock singing a victory song. But in the night the Pawnees escaped through a crevice by letting down their lariats, so the story goes. Legend has it that visitors to the rock at night can sometimes hear the Sioux marching and singing.

On Wednesday, July 31, 1861 Samuel and Orion Clemens passed "Court House Rock" at sunrise according to Orion's letter to his wife giving an account of their journey. Courthouse Rock Pony Express Station served the Overland Stage as well, providing fresh horses or mules as needed. The Clemenses had exchanged their stagecoach in Julesburg for a "mud wagon" (a stripped-down stagecoach) for the crossing of the South Platte and the journey ahead through high plains and mountains. Mules had been substituted for horses, as well, for their pulling power and stamina. Orion described the landscape as being elevated plains covered with sage brush and cactus.

Janssen and Beaty experienced the excitement of viewing Courthouse Rock in the late afternoon driving north on U.S. 385 from Sidney, Nebraska to Bridgeport on the North Platte River. There it was in the far distance, no doubt about it: a solitary butte in the shape of a courthouse with a dome on top. Soon the second smaller butte came in sight, the Jail Rock. As they progressed north, they too noted that the Courthouse did seem to change in shape when viewed from a different perspective.

Next morning, the two travelers drove south from Bridgeport five miles on a paved road and then west for a short distance on a gravel road to the very base of the two rocks. They were huge and impressive. The Jail looked as enormous as the Courthouse from close up. A historical marker described the buttes as being 400 feet high, of four strata with Brule clay at the bottom, sandstone and limestone next, gray sandstone and volcanic ash next, and topped with a hard concretion. A warning to watch out for rattlesnakes in the rocks kept the travelers alert, but all they saw was a hen pheasant and her poults scurrying across the road. The landscape was different, though, from that seen by the Clemens boys. Irrigated fields of beans and alfalfa dotted the plains and the valley of the North Platte in the distance. The sweeping vistas of sagebrush prairies were still ahead in Wyoming.

Mark Twain doesn't really mention Courthouse Rock in his ROUGHING IT account. What he does say about coming up from the South Platte crossing is this:

"Horace Greeley's Stagecoach Ride"

Just after we left Julesburg, on the Platte, I was sitting with the driver, and he said:

"I can tell you a most laughable thing indeed, if you would like to listen to it. Horace Greeley went over this road once. When he was leaving Carson City he told the driver, Hank Monk, that he had an engagement to lecture at Placerville and was very anxious to go through quick. Hank Monk cracked his whip and started off at an awful pace. The coach bounced up and down in such a terrific way that it jolted the buttons all off of Horace's coat, and finally shot his head clean through the roof of the stage, and then he yelled at Hank Monk and begged him to go easier — said he warn't in as much of a hurry as he was a while ago. But Hank Monk said, 'Keep your seat, Horace, and I'll get you there on time' — and you bet you he did, too, what was left of him!"

* * * * *

CHIMNEY ROCK

Most distinctive of the butte landmarks along the trail was surely the next one, Chimney Rock, a needle of stone rising from a pyramid base, and now a National Historic Site. No traveler could ignore it. Those coming up from the South Platte Crossing at Julesburg like the Clemenses, had to turn west along the trail when they reached the North Platte River. Then they all kept their eyes peeled for Chimney Rock, not only a striking natural monument on the trail west, but also a marker telling them that the flat and easy Platte River road was coming to an end, and they would soon be on higher, rougher ground. Early emigrants had Chimney Rock in sight for at least two days. They filled their diaries with sketches of it.

Many travelers felt compelled to hike over to it, climb its conical base, and inscribe their names on the Chimney. So striking was the appearance of this landmark that emigrants on the north side of the Platte River sometimes swam the river just to climb up "this great natural curiosity." (Mattes, 1955, p. 8) As with Courthouse Rock the distance was so deceptive that what seemed like a mile or so often turned out to be five or even ten miles, depending on where they left the trail. Actually it was two miles south of the main trail at its closest point. Travelers also misjudged its height, describing it as anywhere from 50 feet to 700 feet tall. Actually it was something over 300 feet in height.

Chimney Rock looked extremely fragile as though it was ready to split apart. Stories about it said that it was once much higher and now through erosion was quite a bit shorter. Actually comparisons showed that it had not changed substantially in the last one hundred years. Only the thousands of emigrant names that once crammed its walls were no longer visible.

The Clemens brothers passed by Chimney Rock on the morning of July 31, 1861. Orion called this land the "barren region" with sage brush and cactus covering the plains. The Pony Express and stage station stood somewhere near its base adjacent to a fine spring where emigrants camped.

Janssen and Beaty stopped at a mobile museum just off U.S. 92, to view Chimney Rock one and a half miles south. Modern covered wagon rides took visitors even closer, down a gravel road to within a half mile of the site. Hikers could also travel by foot over rough terrain to the foot of the butte.

It was exciting to view this renowned landmark of the trail just as the California-bound emigrants had. No matter what the road ahead, those who viewed Chimney Rock were elated that they had finally reached this famed monument.

SCOTTS BLUFF

Next landmark was one of the largest on the trail, Scotts Bluff: a magnificent promontory towering 800 feet above the valley floor twenty-three miles west of Chimney Rock. The Indians called it "me-a-pa-te" or "hill that is hard to go around." It seemed to block the trail in fact, until the emigrant road was improved through Mitchell Pass just south of the bluff.

Its name came from Hiram Scott, a huge 6'4" frontiersman who was left to die by members of a trapping expedition he was leading in 1829. The next spring his remains were found 60 miles further along at the base of the bluff whose top was where he someday wanted to be buried. Thus the name "Scotts Bluff" was adopted by the travelers passing that way.

Emigrants called Scotts Bluff the "Gibralter of the Plains." They were impressed by its size and grandeur, and relieved to realize that one-third of the trail to California lay behind them. Today the bluff is part of Scotts Bluff National Monument, 3,000 acres of prairie and butte lands with a road up to the top of the bluff and a visitors center museum at its base. Displays and brochures describe how the ancient "high plains" of the area were once several hundred feet higher than the Great Plains of today; that four or five million years ago the high plains began to erode away, leaving behind as tall buttes certain isolated patches capped with concretions of rock which prevented erosion. Thus Scotts Bluff like the other rock landmarks along the trail is really a petrified cross section of what is left of the high plains.

Original prairie grasses cover the present plains at the base of the bluffs today: clumps of little bluestem, western wheatgrass, and needle-and-thread; or sod like blue grama and buffalo grass. It was sod with its dense root clusters that the pioneers cut into squares to build their "soddie" houses. But it was the grama and buffalo grass itself that attracted the huge herds of buffalo, and with them the Indians, to the region. The prairie grass also made it possible for the emigrants to travel west like they did, since there was natural fodder for their animals during the summer all the way from the Missouri River to the deserts of Utah and Nevada.

Mark Twain was more impressed with the white alkali water in the road than he was with either the bluff or the grass. He tells about it in ROUGHING IT:

"Alkali Water"

We rattled through Scott's Bluffs Pass, by and by. It was along here somewhere that we first came across genuine and unmistakable alkali water in the road, and we cordially hailed it as a first-class curiosity, and a thing to be mentioned with eclat in letters to the ignorant at home. This water gave the road a soapy appearance, and in many places the ground looked as if it had been whitewashed. I think the strange alkali water excited us as much as any wonder we had come upon yet, and I know we felt very complacent and conceited, and better satisfied with life after we had added it to our list of things which *we* had seen and some other people had not.

* * * * *

Janssen and Beaty did not see alkali water. They were more impressed with further examples of pioneer "wheel ruts" in the pass. Finally they had arrived in real "wild west" country, and could almost imagine the Clemens' stagecoach rattling through the pass. Mark Twain's stage had evidently picked up a passenger from the Colorado gold mines (or did it?), for he tells in ROUGHING IT:

"Horace Greeley's Stagecoach Ride"

We picked up a Denver man at the crossroads, and he told us a good deal about the country and the Gregory Diggings. He seemed a very entertaining person and a man well posted in the affairs of Colorado. By and by he remarked:

"I can tell you a most laughable thing indeed, if you would like to listen to it. Horace Greeley went over this road once. When he was leaving Carson City he told the driver, Hank Monk, that he had an engagement to lecture at Placerville and was very anxious to go through quick. Hank Monk cracked his whip and started off at an awful pace. The coach bounced up and down in such a terrific way that it jolted the buttons all off of Horace's coat, and finally shot his head clean through the roof of the stage, and then he yelled at Hank Monk and begged him to go easier — said he warn't in as much of a hurry as he was a while ago. But Hank Monk said, 'Keep your seat, Horace, and I'll get you there on time!' — and you bet you he did, too, what was left of him!"

* * * * *

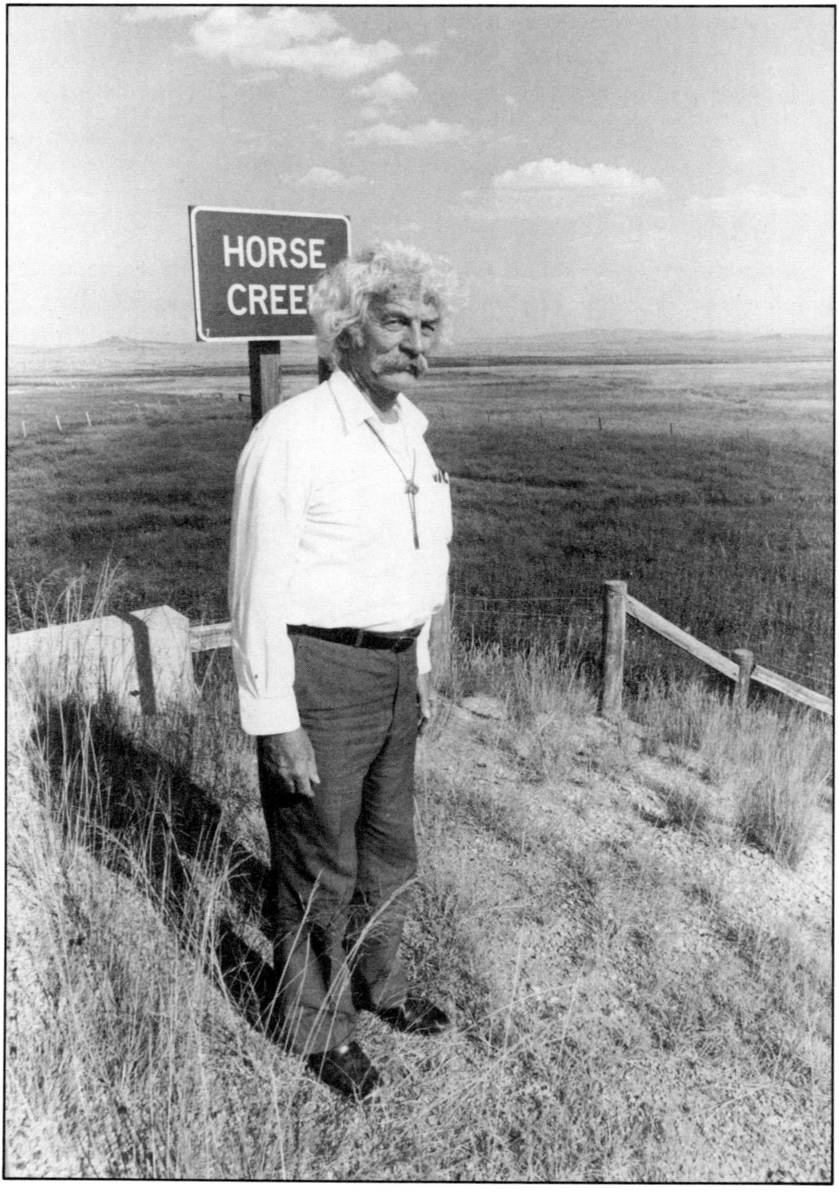
HORSE
CREEK

HORSE CREEK STATION

As the Clemens boys crossed into Wyoming in their own stagecoach, they realized they were at last in hostile Indian country. Talk of Indians and troopers on the move greeted them at the stage stops. Shots in the night were heard at one station. Then they had the excitement of sitting down to breakfast with the Division Superintendent, the desperado Slade, at the Horse Creek Station (as related in Chapter 6).

It was also at Horse Creek Station that the weary passengers had their first bath of the trip: in Horse Creek itself! Twain described it as a "limpid, sparkling stream" (until they bathed in it!), and that bathing of any kind was a luxury seldom indulged in on the Overland Stage Line. Their coach seldom halted any longer than four minutes, the time it took to change a team: "As our coach rattled up to each station six harnessed mules stepped gaily from the stable; and in the twinkling of an eye, almost, the old team was out and the new one in and we off and away again."

It was just past Horse Creek Station that they passed a Mormon wagon train, or as Mark Twain describes it in ROUGHING IT:

"Mormon Wagon Train"

Just beyond the breakfast-station we overtook a Mormon emigrant-train of thirty-three wagons; and tramping wearily along and driving their herd of loose cows, were dozens of coarse-clad and sad-looking men, women, and children, who had walked as they were walking now, day after day for eight lingering weeks, and in that time had compassed the distance our stage had come in *eight days and three hours* — seven hundred and ninety-eight miles! They were dusty and uncombed, hatless, bonnetless, and ragged, and they did look so tired!

* * * * *

Later Twain tells how they picked up a Mormon preacher at a stage stop:

A Mormon preacher got in with us at a way station — a gentle, soft-spoken, kindly man, and one whom any stranger would warm to at first sight. I can never forget the pathos that was in his voice as he told, in simple language, the story of his people's wanderings and unpitied sufferings. No pulpit eloquence was ever so moving and so beautiful as this outcast's picture of the first Mormon pilgrimage across the plains, struggling sorrowfully onward to the land of its banishment and marking its desolate way with graves and watering it with tears. His words so wrought upon us that it was a great relief to us all when the conversation drifted into a more cheerful channel and the natural features of the curious country we were in came under treatment. One matter after another was pleasantly discussed, and at length the stranger said:

"Horace Greeley's Stagecoach Ride"

"I can tell you a most laughable thing indeed, if you would like to listen to it. Horace Greeley went over this road once. When he was leaving Carson City he told the driver, Hank Monk, that he had an engagement to lecture in Placerville, and was very anxious to go through quick. Hank Monk cracked his whip and started off at an awful pace. The coach bounced up and down in such a terrific way that it jolted the buttons all off of Horace's coat, and finally shot his head clean through the roof of the stage, and then he yelled at Hank Monk and begged him to go easier — said he warn't in as much of a hurry as he was a while ago. But Hank Monk said, 'Keep your seat, Horace, and I'll get you there on time!' — and you bet you he did, too, what was left of him!"

*****

Janssen and Beaty also stopped at Horse Creek where it crossed Wyoming Route 220 southwest of Casper, but not to bathe. They were on the lookout for pronghorn antelope that they had been spotting near waterholes all day. Sure enough. A small herd grazed on the hillside in the distance, looking up nervously at the strangers' intrusion. The animals backed off cautiously and were soon out of camera range. Oh well, maybe a straggler or two would eventually be close enough to the road for a photo from the car window. Beaty was used to deer in the fields at the edge of the woods at twilight in Upstate New

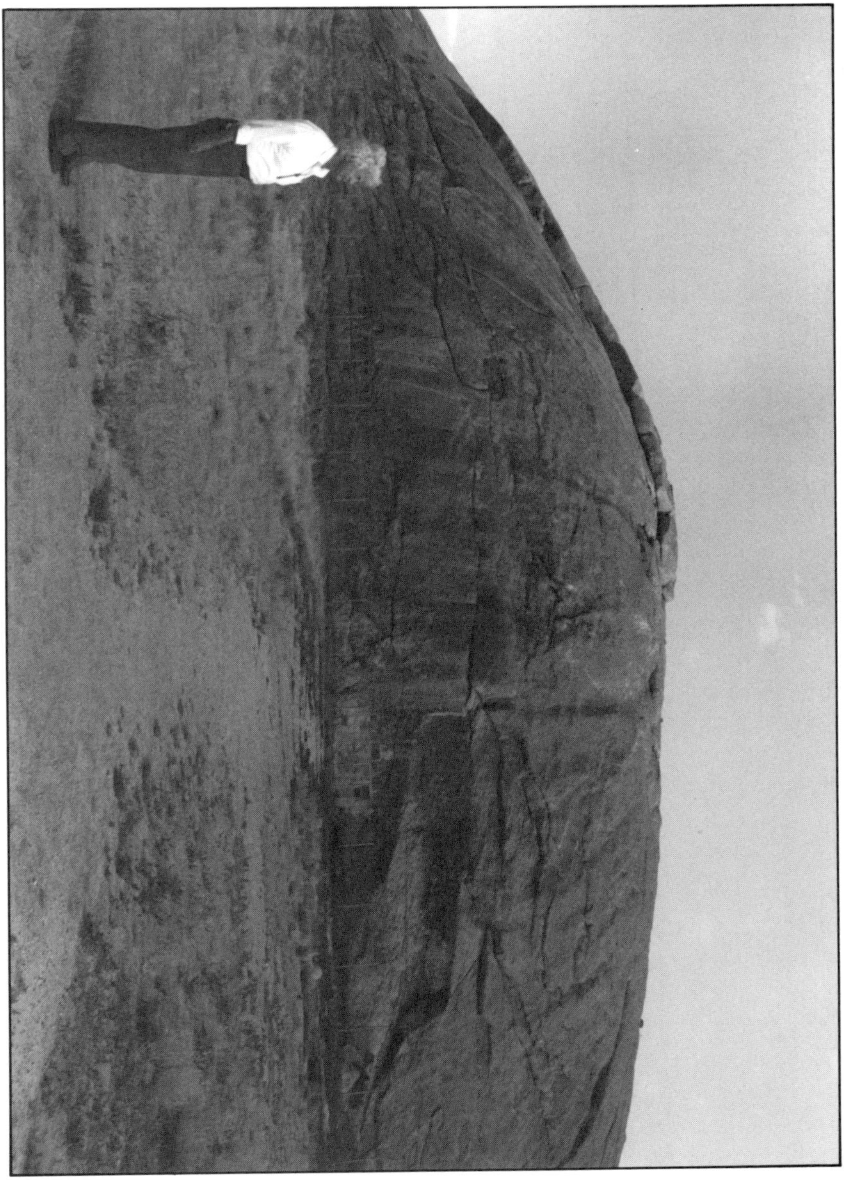

York. But seeing live antelope on the prairies — it was the real "wild west," like a dream come true, she felt!

INDEPENDENCE ROCK

Next natural landmark on the stagecoach trail west was Independence Rock. Now that the mountains had closed in on either side of Route 220, the authors realized that spotting a particular rock landmark might not be all that simple. For instance, there was a distinctive rock ahead standing separately on the left side of the road where the map indicated Independence Rock would be. Was that it? Would they be able to tell?

No. That was not it. It was too much like all of the other rock formations extending out from the mountains on either side of the road. Something told the authors that Independence Rock would be as distinctive for the modern car travelers as it had been for stage travelers on the Overland Trail in 1861.

There it was! A huge turtle-like hump of dark rock rose from the level prairie ahead about 50 miles southwest of Casper. A road sign confirmed it. Nearly 2,000 feet long, 850 feet wide, and from 167 to 193 feet high, this gray-brown granite monolith rose from the flat sagebrush prairie on the north bank of the Sweetwater River. Named by the Astorians from Oregon who passed it on their way east on the Fourth of July in 1812, it was eventually inscribed with over 50,000 names of emigrants going west in the 1840's, '50's, and '60's.

Its name also represented the goal of the western wagon travelers. They needed to reach Independence Rock by the Fourth of July in order to get through the Sierra Nevada Mountains and into California before snow blocked the passes. Imagine the sighs of relief from the emigrants who progressed down the Sweetwater Valley and finally caught a glimpse of Independence Rock in late June or early July! It was a grand confirmation! They finally knew they were really going to make it to destination!

The fleet Pony Express riders who rode from St. Joseph, Missouri to Sacramento, California in ten days, hailed Independence Rock for other reasons. It was near here that the trail left the North Platte River and entered the valley of the sparkling Sweetwater River. Raymond and Mary Settle claim that "the station keepers, stage drivers, and Pony Express riders affectionately spoke of it as 'her,' and the tinkling of its waters was music to the ear after having been associated with the gloomy, silent Platte." (Settle and Settle, SADDLES AND SPURS, 1955, pp. 134-5).

Travelers covered the great rock with their names — painted, scratched, etched, or inscribed with tar. Many names have weathered away, although many remain. Others have been preserved in bronze plaques honoring the Mormon emigrants; Narcissa Whitman, first white woman to cross Wyoming; Father De Smet, first Jesuit missionary in Wyoming; and commemorating Wyoming's first Masonic meeting held on top of the rock July 4, 1862, a year after Mark Twain passed it on the afternoon of Friday, August 2. Good water nearby made the rock a welcome campsite, as well.

DEVIL'S GATE

The next remarkable landmark on the trail was a 330-foot-deep cut in a solid granite wall through which the Sweetwater River gushed in a gorge at the bottom no more than 30 feet across. The walls of the chasm were of gray granite with a streak of black granite running from top to bottom. The trail ran around the cleft, but emigrants had to stop and hike over to it anyway for a look. One declared it to be: "one of the most notable features of its kind in the world." (WYOMING, 1941, p. 387) All who saw Devil's Gate were greatly impressed by its perpendicular walls of solid granite rising more than 300 feet. Some tried climbing the walls. A few were successful, but others fell.

Modern Highway 220 continued down the valley some way from Devil's Gate, although an overlook offered a distant view.

ICE HOUSE SLOUGH

Mark Twain had more to say about this natural curiosity: "In the night we sailed by a most notable curiosity, and one we had been hearing a good deal about for a day or two, and were suffering to see. This was what might be called a natural icehouse. It was August, now, and sweltering weather in the daytime, yet at one of the stations the men could scrape the soil on the hillside under the lee of a range of boulders, and at a depth of six inches cut out pure blocks of ice — hard, compactly frozen, and clear as crystal!"

SOUTH PASS

The discovery of the "South Pass" through the Rocky Mountains by the Astorians coming back from Oregon in 1812, made overland travel to California and Oregon possible. The Pass itself was hardly what travelers would call a mountain "pass." Instead it was a sloping plain between a break in the mountains. A gravel road off Wyoming Route 28 takes the modern visitor to South Pass City State Historic Site with its collection of frame and log buildings. Mark Twain's view in ROUGHING IT was not so different from a modern visitor's:

"South Pass City"

We hove in sight of South Pass City. The hotel-keeper, the postmaster, the blacksmith, the mayor, the constable, the city marshall, and the principal citizen and property-holder, all came out and greeted us cheerily, and we gave him good day. He gave us a little Indian news, and a little Rocky Mountain news, and we gave him some Plains information in return. He then retired to his lonely grandeur and we climbed on up among the bristling peaks and the ragged clouds. South Pass City consisted of four log cabins, one of which was unfinished, and the gentleman with all those offices and titles was the chiefest of the ten citizens of the place. Think of hotel-keeper, postmaster, blacksmith, mayor, constable, city marshal and principal citizen all condensed into one person and crammed into one skin. Bemis said he was "a perfect Allen's revolver of dignities." And he said that if he were to die as postmaster, or as blacksmith, or as postmaster and blacksmith both, the people might stand it; but if he were to die all over, it would be a frightful loss to the community.

*****

The Clemens brothers' stagecoach continued on over the summit, although as Mark Twain points out, 'it had been all summit to us and all equally level, for half an hour or more." They eventually came to Pacific Spring which sent some of its water east and some west for the first time. The travelers then met a wagon train, and Mark Twain recognized the horseman in charge as an old school friend from Hannibal. By midnight it began to rain so hard that the driver could not see the road. The pelting of the rain kept the horses moving, but the driver slowed them down as best he could until the rain slacked and he could determine exactly where they were.

When the rain finally stopped it was just as he feared: they were not on the road. The conductor took off with a lantern to look for it. As Mark Twain tells it: "the first dash he made was into a chasm about fourteen feet deep, his lantern following like a meteor. As soon as he touched bottom he sang out frantically: "Don't come here!" To which the driver, who was looking over the precipice where he had disappeared, replied, with an injured air: "Think I'm a dam' fool?"

"The conductor was more than an hour finding the road — a matter which showed us how far we had wandered and what chances we had been taking. He traced our wheel-tracks to the imminent verge of danger, in two places. I have always been glad that we were not killed that night. I do not have any particular reason, but I have always been glad." (Twain, ROUGHING IT, 1913)

JANSSEN AND BEATY ON THE ROAD

The authors, on the other hand, had no trouble following their Route 28, paved as it was, through rugged country with mountains in the distance and sloping sagebrush prairies on either side. As the sun dipped below the mountains it was a relief to know that such a thing as a rain storm could not throw them off course. With night coming on, they, like the Clemenses were far from any outpost of civilization. The afterglow of the sunset kept the sky light enough to show them what a wild, desolate place that old emigrant trail could be at night. Not a living thing in sight. Wait a minute! There was something up ahead. More than one "something," it seemed. Antelopes! A small family group of the animals was grazing alongside the road. Janssen slowed down. They didn't even move as the car passed by! At last Beaty had her wish fulfilled to see antelopes close up!

But look up ahead! There were more of them! By now the sky was definitely darker and headlights had to be turned on. The beams picked up the red eyes of the animals. Janssen slowed down even further. There were more of them up ahead, and on the other side too! Something about the highway at night attracted them. There was grass along the roadside. Perhaps the darkness erased their fears of approaching close to the road to graze. There surely were fewer cars on the road at night. None but the authors', to be exact.

By now it was pitch dark. And there up ahead was another car, high beams blazing. Just as it came abreast of the authors' car, an antelope from the right side of the road sprang out. Whump! We bumped it. It was necessary to keep going and we did. Slowly and carefully we progressed down the road in a gradual decline from the higher country of South Pass, eyes peeled for antelopes along the roadside — although what we could do about them other than to go slow, we didn't know. Was it better to see them first, and then hope they would stay put? Or not see them, and what we didn't know wouldn't hurt us? Whatever we did or didn't do, it was nerve-wracking to say the least! Who was it that wanted to see an antelope up close, in the first place? Did Mark Twain's stagecoach have trouble with antelopes at night?

Another car approached in the far distance, drew abreast, (we held our breath), and passed us by without incident. There were more antelopes. They raised their heads and look at us with red eyes as we passed. Maybe it was going to be all right. Maybe our one encounter was it. Whoops! There was a jackrabbit! And what was that? A badger! He stayed put and didn't move. Another jackrabbit! This one bounded across the road safely.

We got out the map and strained in the dimness of the glove compartment light to measure how far it was to the next town. 68 to Eden! Was that miles or a route number? Now what? Oh, a deer — a mule deer! Yes, this was beginning to seem like the Garden of Eden, all right! Now another car approached. Just as it drew up, we could see the silhouette of antelopes on the left side. Janssen slowed down. Whump! We bumped another one on the left side!

Would this night never end? But that was it. Two. We, like the passengers on that stagecoach so many years ago will always remember our "wheel-tracks on the imminent verge of danger, in two places" on our nighttime trip through the South Pass in Wyoming.

BREAKFAST AT FORT BRIDGER

The next morning the two authors aimed their car toward the town of Fort Bridger and the Fort Bridger National Historic Site, Wyoming's oldest permanent settlement. They enjoyed a fine Sunday breakfast of sausage, homemade biscuits, and excellent coffee at a restaurant across from the fort. Then they turned to ROUGHING IT and found that Mark Twain had also enjoyed a memorable breakfast at the next stage station after his own wild night ride through South Pass: "At the Green River Station we had breakfast — hot biscuits, fresh antelope steaks (!), and coffee — the only decent meal we tasted between the United States and Great Salt Lake City, and the only one we were ever really thankful for. Think of the monotonous execrableness of the thirty that went before it, to leave this one simple breakfast looming up in my memory like a shot-tower after all these years have gone by!" (He was writing ROUGHING IT ten years after the adventure had occurred.)

Mark Twain had other remarks to make about Fort Bridger:

"A Cavalry Sergeant"

At Fort Bridger . . . we took on board a cavalry sergeant, a very proper and soldierly person indeed. From no other man during the whole journey did we gather such a store of concise and well-arranged military information. It was surprising to find in the desolate wilds of our country a man so thoroughly acquainted with everything useful to know in his line of life, and yet of such inferior rank and unpretentious bearing. For as much as three hours we listened to him with unabated interest. Finally he got upon the subject of transcontinental travel, and presently said:

"Horace Greeley's Stagecoach Ride"

"I can tell you a very laughable thing indeed, if you would like to listen to it. Horace Greeley went over this road once. When he was leaving Carson City he told the driver, Hank Monk, that he had an engagement to lecture at Placerville and was very anxious to go through quick. Hank Monk cracked his whip and started off at an awful pace. The coach bounced up and down in such a terrific way that it jolted the buttons all off of Horace's coat, and finally shot his head clean through the roof of the stage, and then he yelled at Hank Monk and begged him to go easier — said he warn't in as much of a hurry as he was a while ago. But Hank Monk said, 'Keep your seat, Horace, and I'll get you there on time!' — and you bet you he did, too, what was left of him!"

*****

REFERENCES

Division of Publications, National Park Service, THE OVERLAND MIGRATIONS, Washington, D.C.: U.S. Department of the Interior, 1980.

Federal Writers' Project, WYOMING, A GUIDE TO ITS HISTORY, HIGHWAYS, AND PEOPLE, Lincoln: University of Nebraska Press, 1941.

Harris, Earl R. "Courthouse and Jail Rocks," *Nebraska History*, Vol. 43, No. 1, March, 1962.

Hill, William E. THE CALIFORNIA TRAIL YESTERDAY AND TODAY, Boulder, Colorado: Pruet Publishing Company, 1986.

Mattes, Merrill J. "Chimney Rock, Nebraska," *Nebraska History*, Vol. 26, No. 1, 1955.

Settle, Raymond W. and Mary Lund Settle, SADDLES & SPURS, THE PONY EXPRESS SAGA, Lincoln: University of Nebraska Press, 1955.

Twain, Mark, ROUGHING IT, Berkeley: University of California Press, 1972.

Twain, Mark, ROUGHING IT, New York: Harper and Brothers, Publishers, 1913.

*****

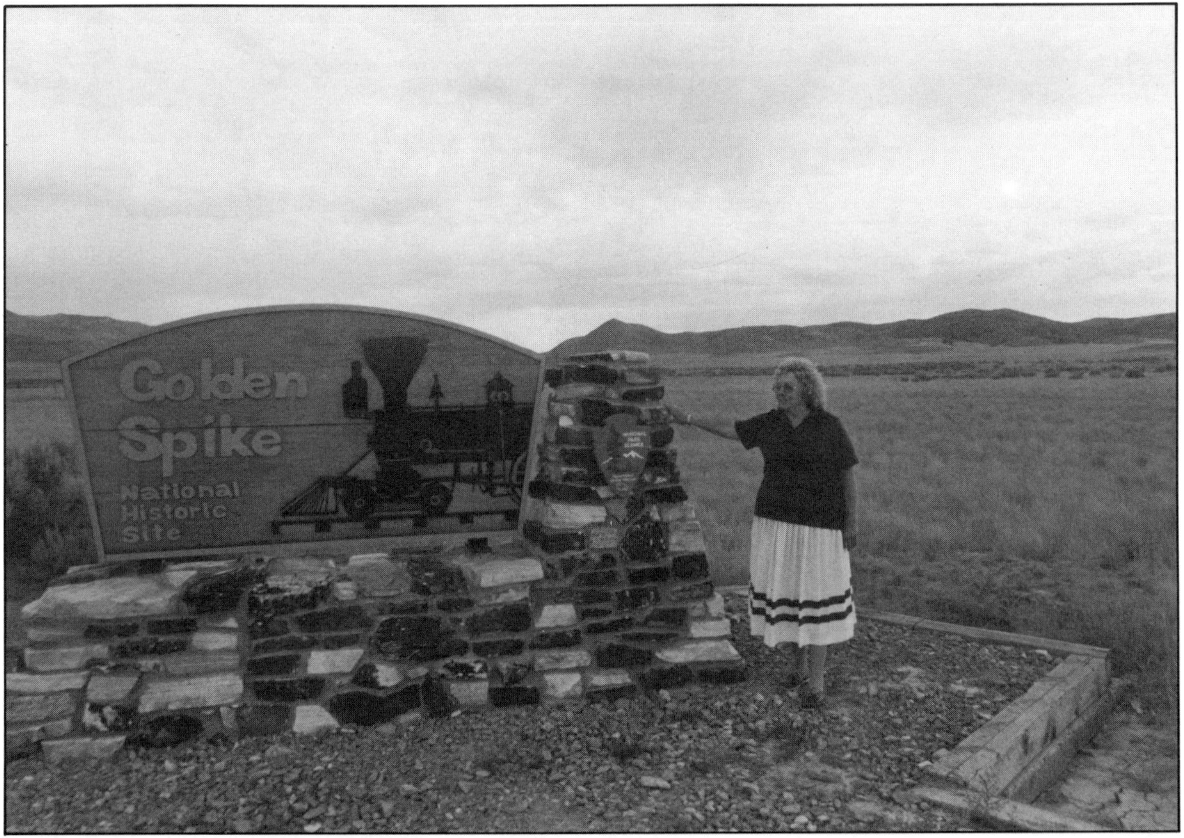
Golden
Spike
National
Historic
Site

CHAPTER 8
A GOLDEN SPIKE IN UTAH

ECHO CANYON, UTAH

Down, down through spectacular Echo Canyon in Utah the authors' trail carried them, now on highway I-80. Brilliant red walls of eroded rock rose 300 to 400 feet on either side of the road. Mark Twain appreciated his swift passage through the canyon as he related in ROUGHING IT: "Echo Canyon is twenty miles long. It was like a long, smooth, narrow street, with a gradual descending grade, and shut in by enormous perpendicular walls of coarse conglomerate, four hundred feet high in many places, and turreted like medieval castles. This was the most faultless piece of road in the mountains, and the driver said he would 'let his team out.' He did, and if the Pacific express-trains whiz through there now any faster than we did then in the stagecoach, I envy the passengers the exhilaration of it. We fairly seemed to pick up our wheels and fly — and the mail matter was lifted up free from everything and held in solution! I am not given to exaggeration, and when I say a thing I mean it."

Janssen and Beaty, however, were pleased to find a roadside rest along the Interstate Highway where they could enjoy a more leisurely view of the magnificent scenery as they ate their lunch. Car and truck traffic was heavy, but Mark Twain was right, there were trains running through the canyon, although principally hauling freight these days.

SUNSETS AND RAINBOWS

The road continued down just as it did in Mark Twain's day, but eventually went up to the summit of Big Mountain where the traveler had his first view of the Great Salt Lake. Twain related: "At four in the afternoon we arrived on the summit of Big Mountain, fifteen miles from Salt Lake City, when all the world was glorified with the setting sun, and the most stupendous panorama of mountain peaks yet encountered burst on our sight. We looked out upon this sublime spectacle from under the arch of a brilliant rainbow! Even the Overland stage driver stopped his horses and gazed!" (Twain, ROUGHING IT, 1913)

Samuel Clemens had a special place in his heart for sunsets.

Wherever he went he commented upon them. In his book LIFE ON THE MISSISSIPPI he wrote about the sunsets in Muscatine, Iowa on the Upper Mississippi where he had worked for a few months in his brother's newspaper office: "I remember Muscatine — still more pleasantly — for its summer sunsets. I have never seen any, on either side of the ocean, that equaled them . . . All the Upper Mississippi region has these extraordinary sunsets as a familiar spectacle. It is the true Sunset Land; I am sure no other country can show so good a right to the name. The sunrises are also said to be exceedingly fine. I do not know."

Rainbows meant something special to Samuel Clemens, as well. Maybe he thought of them as God's promise to Noah, one of his particular Biblical heroes. Rare lunar rainbows made at night by moonlight, he considered marker events in his life, and he mentions at least three of them. They seemed to indicate to him good fortune around the bend. Imagine, then, his seeing a wonderful sunset from under the arch of a rainbow!

THE GREAT SALT LAKE DESERT

Once down on the level Utah desert, the authors route and Samuel Clemens' trail parted company. The old stage trail went due south of Salt Lake City for some miles before turning west near historic Camp Floyd, crossing the desert, and proceeding through what is today the Goshute Indian Reservation. Unpaved roads across the desert and over the mountains into Nevada along this route made modern car travel difficult. The authors chose to follow I-80 instead, across the middle portion of the Great Salt Lake Desert, picking up the stagecoach trail once into Nevada.

Skirting the south edge of the Great Salt Lake, the authors followed an arrow straight highway for 77 miles between Rowley Junction and the Bonneville Salt Flats near Wendover. The mountains fell away revealing a flat arid desert with sparser and sparser vegetation. Glaring sun baked both highway and travelers. Then to the right was a glistening silvery lake with two islands in its midst. Why didn't it show up on the map? And why didn't they come any closer to the lake no matter how far they drove?

Finally it dawned on Beaty (who had lived in Arizona 25 years earlier), that they were witnessing a mirage! That settled, the two travelers watched either side of the road with interest for another recurrence of this fascinating desert phenomenon. Conditions seemed to be right that afternoon, for again a lake appeared to the right — this time a beautiful translucent green. It was hard to believe that there was nothing there but bare earth — scorched earth and shimmering heat waves that could bend and refract light. This time the "lake" seemed to shimmer just above the desert for miles ahead before it disappeared.

But in the distance was something more ominous: dark-looking cumulus clouds towering into the sky and stirring up something below them with a foggy, dusty appearance. Oh-oh, a dust storm! Beaty's memories of Arizona returned in full force. She remembered what the blast of dust-ladened wind could do to the paint on a car. And this cloud of dust in the distance had a decidedly white appearance. The map showed the Bonneville Salt Flats ahead. Now white sand on either side of the road confirmed its approach. What would a dust storm of alkali sand do to a car?

Janssen was more relaxed in his assessment of the situation. It was obviously a rain storm. Look at the clouds in the sky. Beaty explained that dust storms were like rain storms without any rain. It might even lightning and thunder, but that no rain would fall — only blowing dust that would blot out everything else and make breathing difficult for those caught outside. Janssen suggested they pull off at the Bonneville Salt Flats rest area, which they did.

The wind picked up in volume although the storm was some miles distant. A few tourists were out romping on the salt flats where speed records for the fastest cars on earth had been broken; or they were washing off their bare feet in the spigot provided at the edge of the desert before reentering their cars. Others were gathering up picnic supplies and heading for the shelter of vans or cars. A native American family in the back of a pickup truck was ducking under canvas to ward off the wind. (Could they be Goshute Indians?)

Then without further ado, a splat of rain struck the authors' windshield, and another, and another. It was no fullfledged rain storm, Beaty pointed out in defense as they pulled back onto the highway; and it looked more like the white "dust storm" had veered off to the south. Oh well, let's see what Mark Twain had to say about this desert in ROUGHING IT.

MARK TWAIN ON THE GREAT SALT LAKE DESERT

"And now we entered upon one of that species of deserts whose concentrated hideousness shames the diffused and diluted horrors of Sahara — an "alkali" desert. For sixty-eight miles there was but one break in it. I do not remember that this was really a break; indeed, it seems to me that it was nothing but a watering-depot *in the midst* of the stretch of sixty-eight miles. If my memory serves me, there was no well or spring at this place, but the water was hauled there by mule and ox teams from the further side of the desert. There was a stage station there. It was forty-five miles from the beginning of the desert, and twenty-three from the end of it.

"We plowed and dragged and groped along, the whole livelong night, and at the end of this uncomfortable twelve hours we finished the forty-five miles of the desert and got to the stage-station where the imported water was. The sun was just rising. It was easy enough to cross a desert in the night while we were asleep; and it was pleasant to reflect in the morning, that we in actual person *had* encountered an absolute desert and could always speak knowingly of deserts in presence of the ignorant thenceforward . . . but now we were to cross a desert in *daylight*. This was fine — novel — romantic — dramatically adventurous — this, indeed, was worth living for, worth traveling for! We would write home all about it."

"A Vast Waveless Ocean"

This enthusiasm, this stern thirst for adventure, wilted under the sultry August sun and did not last above one hour. One poor little hour — and then we were ashamed that we had 'gushed' so. The poetry was all in the anticipation — there is none in the reality. Imagine a vast, waveless ocean stricken dead and turned to ashes; imagine this solemn waste tufted with ash-dusted sage-bushes; imagine the lifeless silence and solitude that belong to such a place; imagine a coach, creeping like a bug through the midst of this shoreless level, and sending up tumbled volumes of dust as if it were a bug that went by steam; imagine this aching monotony of toiling and plowing kept up hour after hour, and the shore still as far away as ever, apparently; imagine team, driver, coach, and passengers so deeply coated with ashes that they are all one colorless color; imagine ash-drifts roosting above mustaches and eyebrows like snow accumulations on boughs and bushes. This is the reality of it.

The sun beats down with dead, blistering, relentless malignity; the perspiration is welling from every pore in man and beast, but scarcely a sign of it finds its way to the surface — it is absorbed before it gets there; there is not the faintest breath of air stirring; there is not a merciful shred of cloud in all the brilliant firmament . . .

The mules, under violent swearing, coaxing, and whip-cracking, would make at stated intervals a 'spurt,' and drag the coach a hundred or maybe two hundred yards, stirring up a billowy cloud of dust that rolled back, enveloping the vehicle to the wheel-tops or higher, and making it seem afloat in a fog. Then a rest followed, with the usual sneezing and bit-champing. Then another 'spurt' of a hundred yards and another rest at the end of it. All day long we kept this up, without water for the mules and without ever changing the team . . . And it was so hot! and so close! and our water canteens went dry in the middle of the day and we got so thirsty! . . .The alkali dust cut through the delicate membranes and made our noses bleed and *kept* them bleeding — and truly and seriously the romance all faded far away and disappeared, and left the desert trip nothing but a harsh reality — a thirsty, sweltering, longing hateful reality!

* * * * *

WINDS OF CHANGE

Now, that's a description of a desert, Beaty decided! She looked to see if any of the alkali dust had accumulated on Janssen's mustache. No. Nothing but raindrops.

Was this it, then? Was this all of Utah that would affect the authors' trip west? Hardly. Before the wind had blown itself out, revised travel plans were afoot. Mark Twain's chance remark about trains in Echo Canyon at the beginning of his own trek across Utah proved significant for the authors, as well.

They realized that there were no trains in Utah when Samuel and Orion Clemens crossed the Territory by stage in 1861. Yet a mere eight years later on May 10, 1869 the biggest railroad event of all time occurred in Utah: the pounding in of a Golden Spike which joined

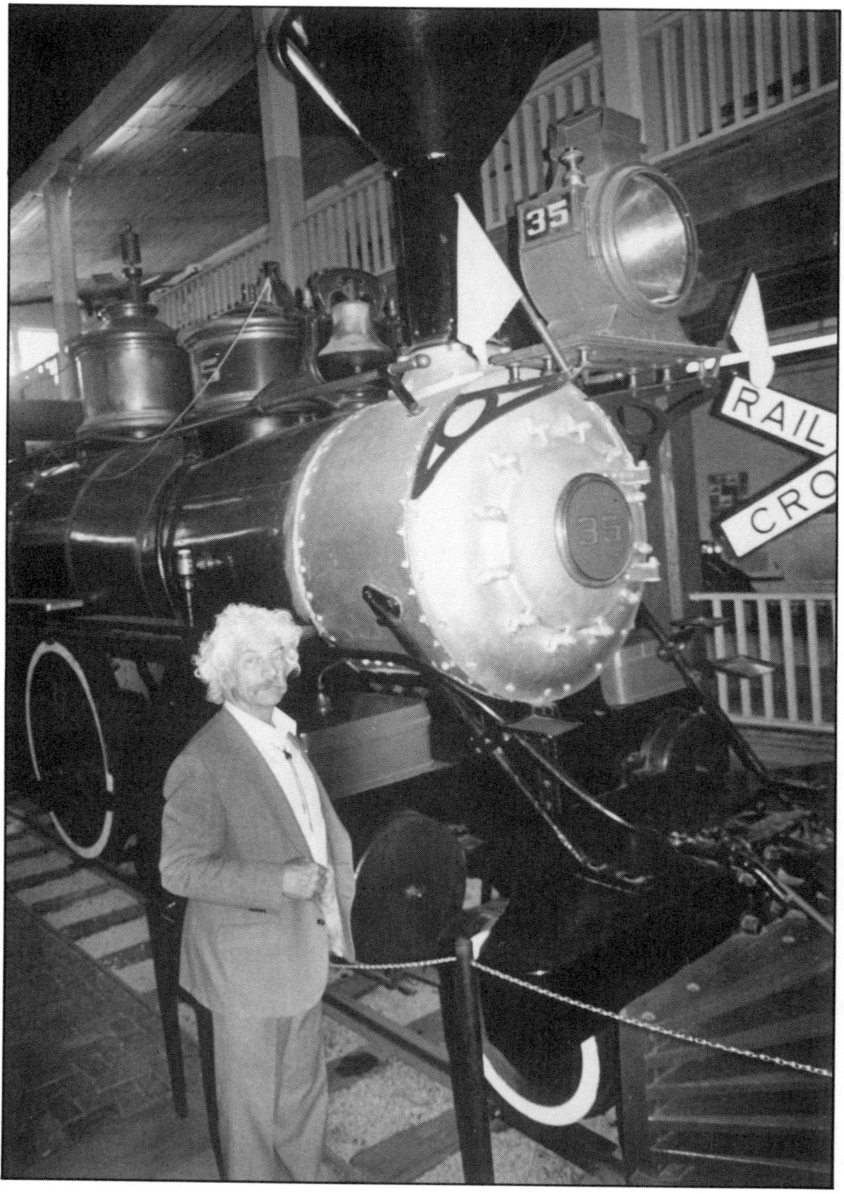
35
RAIL
CRO
35

together the Central Pacific Railroad and the Union Pacific Railroad at Promontory, Utah to form the first transcontinental railroad across the United States. East met West via rail on that day in 1869, and the United States was never afterwards the same.

When Dale Janssen discovered that this singular event had occurred in Utah, he was determined to leave no stone unturned in his effort to visit the spot. After all Janssen, a "transportation man" of long standing, was also researching the history of transportation across the United States in the 1860's. It was time to "rein in the horses" and veer north a bit, if Promontory, Utah was to become a part of that research. It would mean a bit of back-tracking just as the trip to Cody, Wyoming had, but a visit to the historic railroad site would be worth every minute of it, the authors concluded.

MARK TWAIN AND RAILROADS

How was Mark Twain tied to railroads? Not very strongly, was his own thought about it. Janssen says it best, perhaps, when he mentions in his Mark Twain appearances that: "As a riverboat pilot I'm concerned about these railroads, because they're building bridges for them across the Mississippi River; and you should also be concerned about these railroads because they may be the ruination of the country. They're in competition with the riverboats!" (Janssen and Beaty, MARK TWAIN WALKING AMERICA AGAIN, 1987, p. 106)

Mark Twain's father, John Marshall Clemens, knew better. He was interested in railroads from the start. When his ideas for a railroad or a canal up to his original location in Florida, Missouri came to nothing, he moved his family to Hannibal, Missouri on the Mississippi River. Among his several visionary ventures was his idea for a railroad from Hannibal across the state to St. Joseph on the western frontier. He hosted a public meeting in his Hannibal law office in the old Union Hotel in 1846 at which time the proposed route of the new line was laid out.

Although he did not live to see it begun, the Hannibal and St. Joseph Railroad was the first railroad to be completed in the State of Missouri (1857), connecting East with West via the Pony Express and Overland Stage to California which began at St. Joseph. One could almost say that John Marshall Clemens was, in fact, instrumental in bringing about the first transcontinental transportation system across the United States!

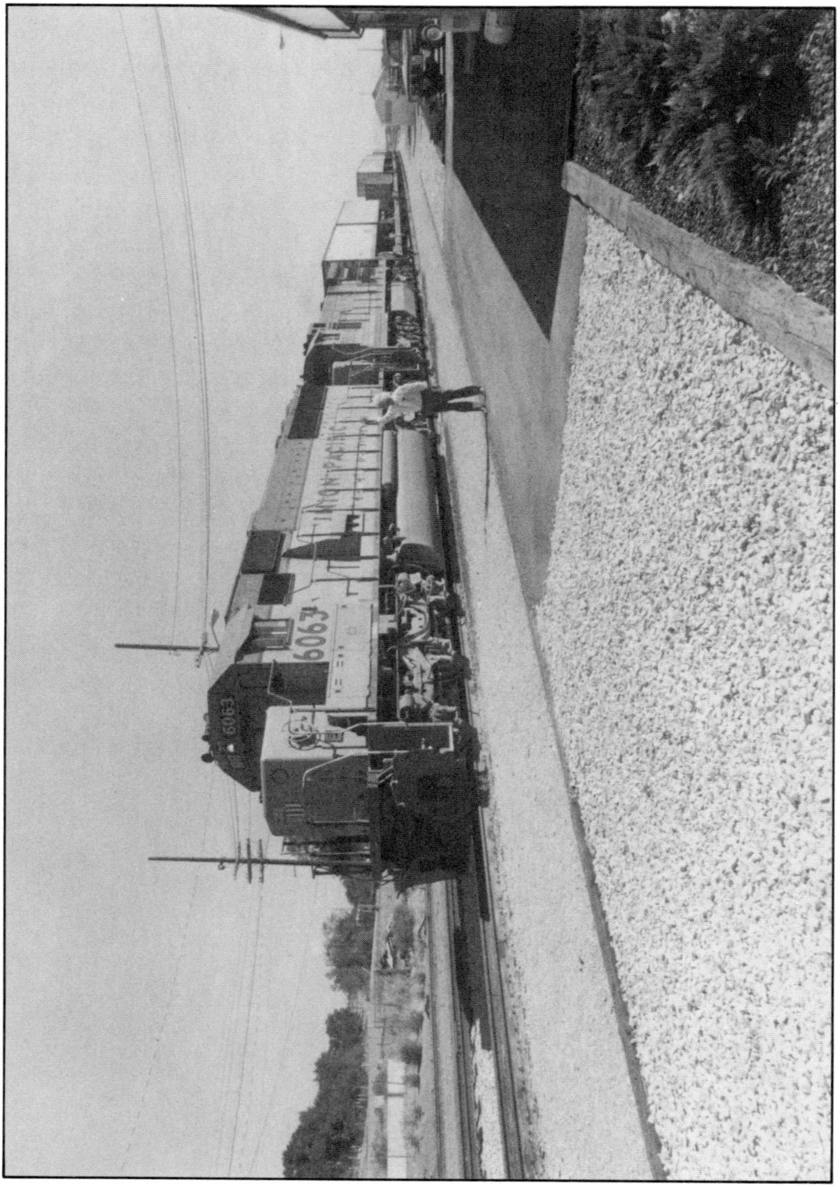
6063

When Mark Twain was later invited to attend an 1886 celebration of the railroad's foundation, he wrote from his Hartford, Connecticut home: "I have to thank you very much for your letter's astonishing information. I never knew before that my father was a pioneer railroad man; I knew he was interested in Salt River navigation, but this railroad matter is entirely new to me." (Wector, SAM CLEMENS OF HANNIBAL, 1961, p. 110.)

JANSSEN AND RAILROADS

Dale Janssen was more than familiar with railroads in Missouri and the Midwest. Early in his own career he had helped to establish the Transportation Section of the Missouri Farmers Association (MFA) which was concerned with transporting fertilizer and agricultural products by rail, barge, and truck lines as shown in the booklet *MFA: from a Vision to Reality in Missouri Agriculture* and Janssen's booklet *MFA Transportation Section: Its Accomplishments and Future*, that describe, among other things, his involvement with the great rail systems then in use. Later in his career as a transportation law practitioner, he was instrumental in preserving needed rail service by the Burlington Northern Railroad to a number of communities in western Iowa once served by the Milwaukee Railroad.

No wonder, then, that Janssen continued to emphasize railroads in his Mark Twain appearances. Audiences were delighted when he drew from Mark Twain's humor to tell the story:

"The Train with the Cowcatcher"

I remember this very slow passenger train that I was on, and I noticed that the conductor kept looking at his gold watch. Most railroad men have gold watches, and he seemed to be realizing it was a very slow train. It was so slow that one of the passengers said, "Mister conductor, you have on the front of your train a 'cowcatcher' that causes the cows to move out of the way so the train can speed across the prairies faster. This train is so slow you should take that cowcatcher off the front of the train and put it back of the caboose, so that the cows can walk up and ride along with us people!" (Janssen and Beaty, STORYTELLING MARK TWAIN STYLE, 1988, p. 132.)

*****

TO PROMONTORY

Now Janssen and Beaty were heading north on U.S.15 through Salt Lake City, past Ogden and Brigham City, turning left onto Route 13 and eventually out to Promontory, Utah, the Golden Spike National Historic Site.

The story of the building of the transcontinental railroad was as full of adventure, intrigue, and excitement as any epic ever written, the authors soon discovered. While the Pony Express riders had caught the nation's fancy with their day-and-night dashes over impossible and dangerous terrain, the thought of building an entire railroad 1800 miles from the Missouri River to the Pacific Coast over prairies, deserts, canyons, and impassable mountains was mind-boggling, indeed.

But Congress realized that it had to be done. Trade with the Orient was increasing. The settlement of Oregon in 1846 and the discovery of gold in California and later of silver in Nevada had created a tremendous surge of emigrants across the continent. The lumbering wagon trains on the overland route were too slow. The sailing vessels rounding Cape Horn or crossing to the Panama or Nicaraugua Isthmus were too time-consuming. Then came the Civil War and the added necessity of keeping California in the Union. The answer was a transcontinental railroad. President Lincoln signed the first Railroad Act in 1862.

Two railroads were chosen to build the line: the Central Pacific Railroad from Sacramento, California near the Pacific Coast and the Union Pacific Railroad from Omaha, Nebraska on the Missouri River. They were to meet and join lines at Ogden, Utah. The Mormon leader Brigham Young hoped they would come through Salt Lake City at the south end of the Great Salt Lake. Instead, they chose to build their lines north of the lake to avoid the treacherous salt flats at the southern end. "The great railroad race" was on, to see which company would reach Ogden first.

But Union Pacific surveying parties with their engineers, rodmen, flagmen, chainmen, axmen, teamsters, and herders soon leapfrogged ahead and staked out their line beyond Ogden. Graders, track layers, gaugers, spikers, and bolters hurried to catch up. Meanwhile, Central Pacific crews were scrambling across the Utah desert. When the two crews met, neither of them stopped. Since the companies were paid for the number of miles of line they laid, both railroads continued constructing their roadbeds parallel to one another but in opposite directions. Iron rang out against iron in the clear desert air: three strokes of a sledge hammer to a spike, ten spikes to a rail, four hundred rails to a mile. On April 10, 1869 Congress finally called a halt to the great railroad race by declaring that Promontory Summit, and not Ogden, was the place where the two lines would meet.

JANSSEN AND BEATY AT PROMONTORY

The authors arrived at Promontory late in the afternoon. It was a wild, desolate, off-the-beaten path place. Some would call it barren. Others see beauty and grandeur in sagebrush flats and sculpted mountains. Dark thunderheads arose in the west and distant glimpses of the Great Salt Lake appeared now and again from the road. The "promontory" was actually a large peninsula of land and mountains jutting into the Great Salt Lake at its northern end, nearly dividing the lake in two. The site of the joining of the railroads, though, was at the northern land end of the peninsula. A Visitors Center, a Locomotive Engine House, piles of neatly stacked railroad ties, several wagons, the railroad line itself, and of course the Monument clustered together at a central point. Miles of gravel roads provided self-guided auto tours east and west of the Center along the railroad right-of-way.

It was here that the great drama of April and May, 1869 was enacted. The visitor can still share in that excitement by driving eight miles west and then retracing the railroad route by actually driving on one of the roadbeds built by the two railroads. The Central Pacific graders were climbing up a gentle slope with their roadbed from the lowlands along the northern edge of the Great Salt Lake. The Union Pacific workers from the east had a more difficult task on the steeper eastern slopes. They eventually met and passed the Central Pacific roadbed going down in the opposite direction. The authors noted parallel grades, one usually higher than the other.

Cuts through the mountains were chipped away with picks and shovels or blasted with black powder. The rock and debris hauled out was used to fill in low places. Both companies did blasting, sometimes without warning the other. Armies of workers scurried back and forth day and night to push their own line forward. Second Lieutenant Charles Currier, U.S. Infantry, recorded his observations of the work:

> I can count five hundred men and one hundred fifty carts drawn by patient mules hauling dirt to grade the permanent

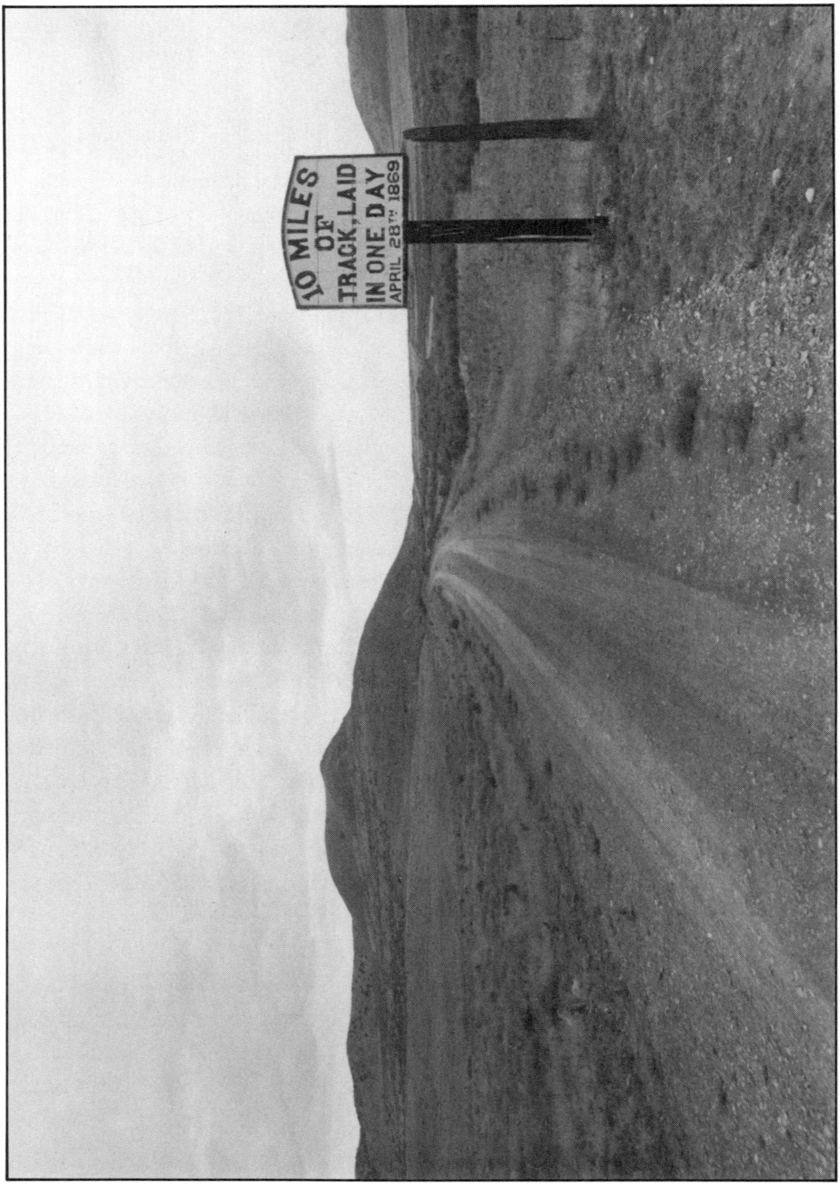
10 MILES
OF
TRACK, LAID
IN ONE DAY
APRIL 28TH 1869

track . . . there are plows, scrapers & etc. The mules are well trained; they climb up and down the bank, stop at the right place and wait till their load is dumped, then take their place in the line and go back to get another. They look like ants. The place is black with laborers; they stand as near together as they can shovel. It's a funny sight to see five hundred shovels going into the air at one time. (*The Promontory Trail*, 1988)

* * * * *

But the Union Pacific line was behind because they started work in the Promontory Mountains much later than the Central Pacific. To bridge one of the largest ravines, they resorted to the shortcut of building a wooden trestle rather than filling in the roadbed. Their rickety trestle, known as the "Big Trestle" ran parallel to the Central Pacific's "Big Fill," but was never considered very safe. The site of both crossings was still visible from a three-quarter mile walk from the road.

A natural phenomenon that the authors also stopped to examine along the road was a limestone formation known as "Chinamen's Arch" which eventually became a memorial to the thousands of Chinese employed by the Central Pacific to build its railroad. The lack of laborers in California induced the company to hire coolies directly from China. By 1868 over 11,000 were employed. A large Chinese camp remained at this spot for years after the lines were joined.

The Union Pacific, on the other hand, hired Civil War veterans, mostly Irish, as its laborers. But in Utah many Mormons joined both camps to give them the extra push needed to win "the great railroad race." Whoever won would be the carrier for the large Mormon trading centers of Salt Lake City and Ogden. While the Union Pacific reached Ogden first, the Central Pacific reached Promontory first; but by then the race had been called off by Congress, and only the actual joining of the lines counted.

TEN MILES OF TRACK

The Central Pacific, though, had another race in mind: a race they were determined to win. Early on, their Union Pacific rival had laid eight and one-half miles of track in one day. This feat, the U.P. boasted, would never be equaled. The Central Pacific believed that it could, but cleverly waited until the distance between the two lines was so short that the Union Pacific would not have room to retaliate. On April 28, 1869 the Central Pacific work gangs started at 7:15 A.M. with eight Irish track layers and an army of Chinese coolies. There were pioneers who set the ties, others who distributed spikes and bolts, spike-starters, track-straighteners, spike-drivers, bolt screwers, tampers with shovels and crowbars, mule teams hauling tools and water-wagons, and Chinamen with bamboo poles and buckets of water and tea.

The teams worked like well-oiled machines. Every man knew his job and worked in concert with every other man. Railroad flat cars piled high with iron rails rolled over the freshly laid track to the end of the line to keep the track-layers supplied. Wagons loaded with rough wooden ties rumbled ahead with teamsters in charge, followed by gangs of tie-setters. The San Francisco *Evening Bulletin* described the scene:

> The scene is a most animated one. From the first pioneer to the last tamper, perhaps two miles, there is a thin line of 1,000 men advancing a mile an hour; the iron cars, with their living and iron freight, running up and down; mounted men galloping backward and forward. Far in the rear are trains with material, with four or five locomotives, and their water-tanks and cars . . . Keeping pace with the track-layers was a telegraph construction party, hauling out, and hanging and insulating the wire . . . (*The Promontory Trail*, 1988)

* * * * *

Workers from the Union Pacific camp gathered around to watch. By noon the Central Pacific had laid six miles of track. When it was apparent they would break the record, they stopped for lunch at a spot named "Camp Victory." When they eventually stopped at seven P.M., ten miles, fifty-six feet of track had been laid: a record that has never been broken from that day to this.

The authors marveled at the "10 Miles" sign, knowing what it represented, as they looked down the roadbed to the distant hills. The tracks had long since been torn up when rails from the abandoned line were donated as scrap iron to the war effort during World War II. Today the railroad roadbed is a gravel auto road on the self-guided tour.

THE GOLDEN SPIKE

In some ways the pounding in of the Golden Spike, the last spike, was anticlimactic. It was decided that May 8 would be the big day. But the Union Pacific people informed the Central Pacific officials that they would not be ready until May 10. Their officials had not yet arrived, after being held up in Wyoming by railroad workers who demanded their pay and then by a rail washout in Echo Canyon, Utah after two days of torrential rains.

Finally on May 10 all the officials of both lines were gathered. Newspaper reporters were on hand. An army band played. The Central Pacific locomotive "Jupiter" rolled up to the last link of track. From the opposite direction the Union Pacific's Engine No. 119 steamed up. A telegraph man had wired one of the spikes and a sledge hammer to the telegraph armature so that it would automatically send the message of the pounding in of the last spike to an awaiting nation.

But delays and torrential rains had kept the crowd to five or six hundred, not the 30,000 that had been predicted. And those that were there swarmed over and around the two locomotives so thickly that even some of the dignitaries found no room. Then the officials of the two railroads could not agree on how the ceremony should be conducted. But finally it occurred anyway, much in the manner of the building of the railroad. President Leland Stanford of the Union Pacific swung the sledge at the wired spike — and missed, to the delight of the crowd! Then Dr. Thomas Durant, Vice-president of the Union Pacific swung the sledge — and he missed too; more cheers! The military officers present and their wives gave the spike a ceremonial tap with their sword hilts. And the telegraph operator sent the message to an awaiting nation anyway.

The ceremonial spikes (two were of gold) were removed, and ordinary iron spikes were driven in to join the two railroads and the continent of the United States at last. The crowd cheered and broke out the champagne. A bottle was broken over the last tie as a christening, and photographs were taken of the locomotives and the men.

Looking at the famous photograph of the pounding in of the Golden Spike, Janssen and Beaty saw what hundreds of other Americans must have since recognized. There was no spike in the picture. The railroad tracks were obscured. Only the stacks on the locomotives were visible.

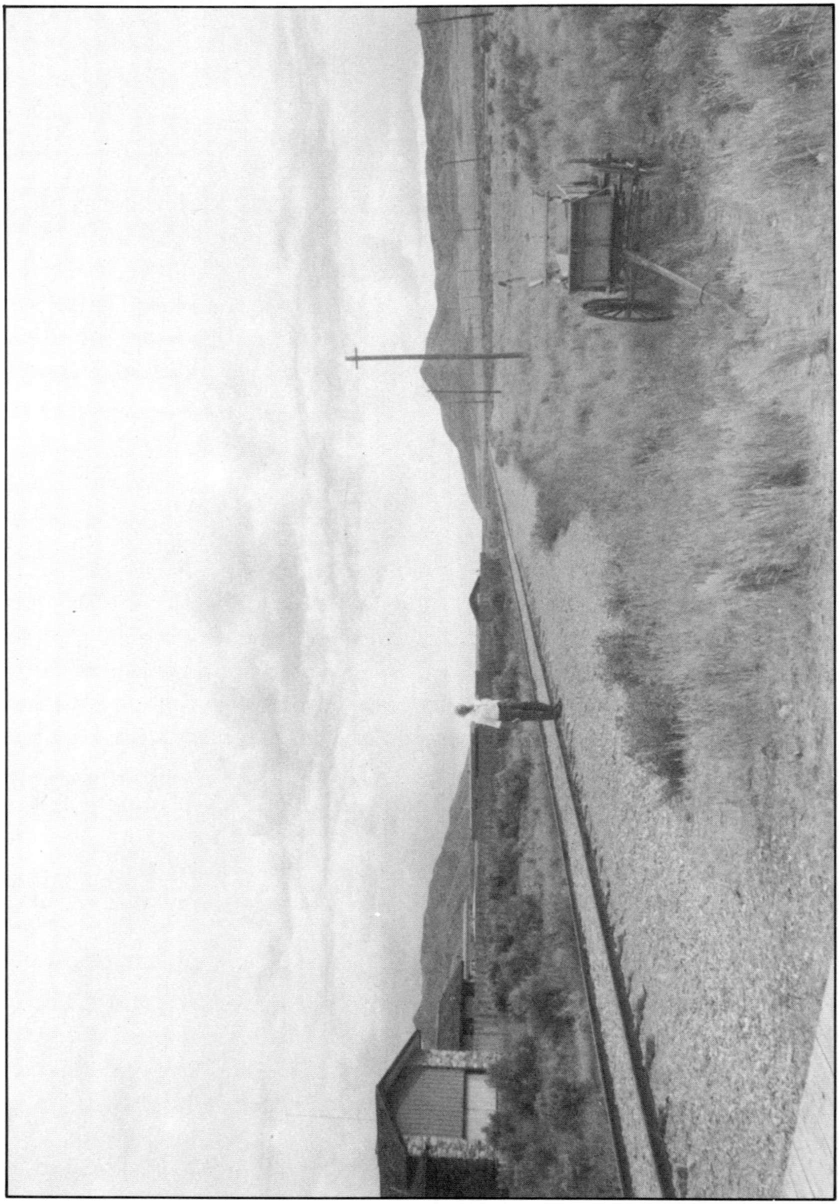

What the picture showed, instead, were men — the men that built the railroad, that gave their hearts and muscles and energy to make a dream come true. It was the Nineteenth Century version of our own Moon Landing. It made us proud to be Americans.

ANOTHER RAINBOW

Driving back to Ogden from Promontory, the authors mulled over what they had experienced: watching a video of the ceremony in the Visitors Center, driving the self-guided auto tour over the original roadbeds of the railroads, and visiting the ceremonial spot itself. What would Mark Twain have thought of it all, we wondered? He was in the forefront of new inventions and original applications of them. No matter how he complained about the telephone, he was one of the first home owners in Hartford to have one installed. No matter how he ridiculed the early typewriter, he was one of the first authors to compose a manuscript on one.

Before we could discuss the issue further, a brilliant rainbow appeared in the east over the mountains and ending on the desert. Then, before we could even gasp, another rainbow appeared — a double rainbow! And as the rainbows finally faded from sight, a sunset began — a red, red sunset, the sailor's delight. We knew what Mark Twain would have thought about all of those!

*****

REFERENCES

Alsberg, Henry G. THE AMERICAN GUIDE, New York: Hastings House, 1949.

Brown, Dee, LONESOME WHISTLE, THE STORY OF THE FIRST TRANSCONTINENTAL RAILROAD, New York: Holt, Rinehart, and Winston, 1980.

Janssen, Dale H., (compiler), *MFA: From a Vision to Reality in Missouri Agriculture,* March 21, 1949.

Janssen, Dale H., *MFA Transportation Section: Its Accomplishments and Future,* Jan. 28, 1955.

Janssen, Dale H. and Janice J. Beaty, MARK TWAIN WALKING AMERICA AGAIN, Columbia, Missouri: Janssen Education Enterprise, Inc., 1987.

Janssen, Dale H. and Janice J. Beaty, STORYTELLING MARK TWAIN STYLE, Columbia, Missouri: Janssen Education Enterprise, Inc., 1988.

Mark Twain Pilot House, "The First Railroad Built in 1857," Thursday, June 23, 1988, p. 2.

Paine, Albert Bigelow, MARK TWAIN, A BIOGRAPHY, New York: Harper & Row, 1912.

The Promontory Trail, Southwest Parks and Monuments Association, 1988.

Twain, Mark, LIFE ON THE MISSISSIPPI, New York: Harper & Row, 1917.

Twain, Mark, ROUGHING IT, New York: Harper & Row, 1913.

Utley, Robert M. and Francis A. Ketterson, Jr., *Golden Spike,* Washington, D.C.: Div. of Publications, National Park Service, U.S. Dept. of the Interior, 1969.

Wector, Dixon, SAM CLEMENS OF HANNIBAL, Boston: Houghton Mifflin Co., 1961.

*****

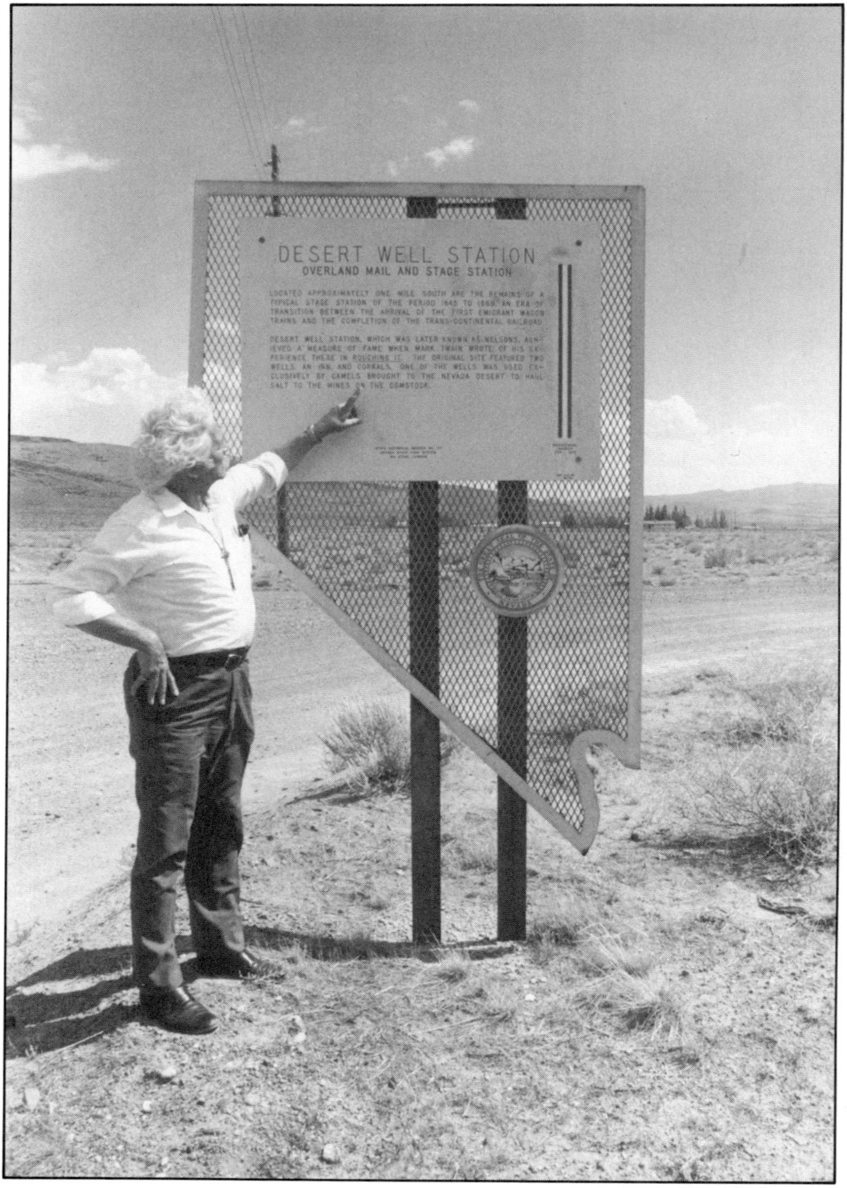
DESERT WELL STATION
OVERLAND MAIL AND STAGE STATION

CHAPTER 9
CARSON CITY, NEVADA

ACROSS NEVADA

More backtracking brought the authors once more over I-80 and across the Great Salt Lake Desert. This time they crossed the border into Nevada at Wendover and continued a few miles before turning south onto Alternate 93. This would take them south to Ely and Route 50 west. Once again they would be following the old stagecoach road to Carson City. Long desert vistas spread out before them with distant mountain ranges crossing their route in a north-south direction.

Up and over the first of the ranges, they cruised, to beautiful little Eureka tucked in the mountains at 7,000 feet. Very western and very 19th Century in appearance. Dozens of historic buildings remained. Once it was Nevada's second largest city with 10,000 people after silver had been discovered. Typical of western mining towns, Eureka boasted 125 saloons, 25 gambling houses, and 15 tent shows in 1878. The Clemens brothers had long since left the state by then.

Then down across the desert again in a straight line to the next range of mountains in the distance went the road. *Life Magazine* had once dubbed Highway 50 as "the loneliest road in America." People living there had taken up the motto, but with pride, as they pointed out its splendors to the many visitors. Each town along the way seemed packed with motels that filled up quickly in the evening. Casinos made their appearance as well, reflecting the wide-open nature of the state in yet another way.

True. The road had a natural beauty all its own. It stretched away in sweeping desert vistas on either side, and dissolved into barren mountain ramparts far ahead. Austin was the next town clinging to the mountains as the road looped down in switchbacks, doubling back upon itself. Austin's unmistakable appearance as a mining town was a reminder that silver had been discovered in 1862 only a year after the Clemens boys had come through, by a Pony Express rider who kicked over a rock and exposed a rich vein. Austin's other claim to fame was its nine camels brought in to haul salt for the quartz mills, and later turned loose. Prospectors claimed they saw wild camels here and there in the desert as late as 1901.

The next expanse of desert had an added feature: a gigantic Sand

Mountain that rose up 600 feet and stretched out two miles long and a mile wide. It was an ancient dune formed by sand-laden winds sweeping across the beaches of a prehistoric sea that once covered Nevada. U.S.50 continued on past vast salt deposits called Twelve Mile Flat and the site of Sand Springs stage station. The adobe remains of old Fort Churchill were off the highway on a side road near Lake Lahontan, a real lake in the desert, not a mirage.

Mark Twain described his nineteenth and next-to-the-last day of his stagecoach adventure as the day they crossed the Great American Desert, "forty memorable miles of bottomless sand, into which the coach wheels sank from six inches to a foot." They got out and walked. "From one extremity of this desert to the other, the road was white with the bones of oxen and horses," he related in ROUGHING IT. "It would hardly be an exaggeration to say that we could have walked the forty miles and set our feet on a bone at every step!"

THE "PASSENGER" AT RAGTOWN

At the western edge of the desert was Ragtown, once an emigrant trading post, now marked by a historical monument. Mark Twain told about one last "passenger" they picked up: "Ten miles out of Ragtown we found a poor wanderer who had lain down to die. He had walked as long as he could, but his limbs had failed him at last. Hunger and fatigue had conquered him. It would have been inhuman to leave him there. We paid his fare to Carson and lifted him into the coach. It was some little time before he showed any very decided signs of life; but by dint of chafing him and pouring brandy between his lips we finally brought him to a languid consciousness. Then we fed him a little, and by and by he seemed to comprehend the situation and a grateful light softened his eye. We made his mail-sack bed as comfortable as possible, and constructed a pillow for him with our coats. He seemed very thankful. Then he looked up in our faces, and said in a feeble voice that had a tremble of honest emotion in it:

'Gentlemen, I know not who you are, but you have saved my life; and although I can never be able to repay you for it, I feel that I can at least make one hour of your long journey lighter. I take it you are strangers to this great thoroughfare, but I am entirely familiar with it. In this connection I can tell you a most laughable thing indeed, if you would like to listen to it. Horace Greeley —'

"I said impressively:

"Suffering stranger, proceed at your peril. You see in me the melancholy wreck of a once stalwart and magnificent manhood. What has brought me to this? That thing which you are about to tell. Gradually, but surely, that tiresome old anecdote has sapped my strength, undermined my constitution, withered my life. Pity my helplessness. Spare me only just this once, and tell me about young George Washington and his little hatchet for a change."

JANSSEN'S HORACE GREELEY AND THE STAGECOACH STORY

Dale Janssen had also heard the anecdote many times. He knew about Mark Twain using it in his platform lectures. Janssen had tried it successfully during his own appearances as Mark Twain, using his own twist. It was, in fact, one of the audiences' favorite stories:

"Horace Greeley and the Stagecoach"

While in San Francisco and playing pool with some of my friends, they asked me what stories I was going to tell at my appearance that night, and I said I'd probably tell the story about this good friend of mine, Horace Greeley, and his ride on the stagecoach. They said, "Oh, Mr. Clemens, everybody's heard that story so many times. If you tell that tonight at your appearance no one will laugh, and you'll certainly not get any clapping." Well, I had a plan, and I said, "I'm going to tell that story, and I'll wager you each a five dollar gold piece that I'll tell that story and I'll bring the house down."

That evening at my appearance I said, "Folks, I'm glad to be here in San Francisco, and first I want to tell you a story about a good friend of mine, Horace Greeley. He was on his way to San Francisco for a very important engagement, and he didn't want to be late, and he said to the driver: 'Now, driver, I don't want to be late. I have a very important engagement to keep.' So the driver lashed out at the horses, and bounced Horace Greeley to the top of the stagecoach, and when he came down he said, 'Now, you can slow down just a little bit, driver. I'm not in that big of a hurry!' "

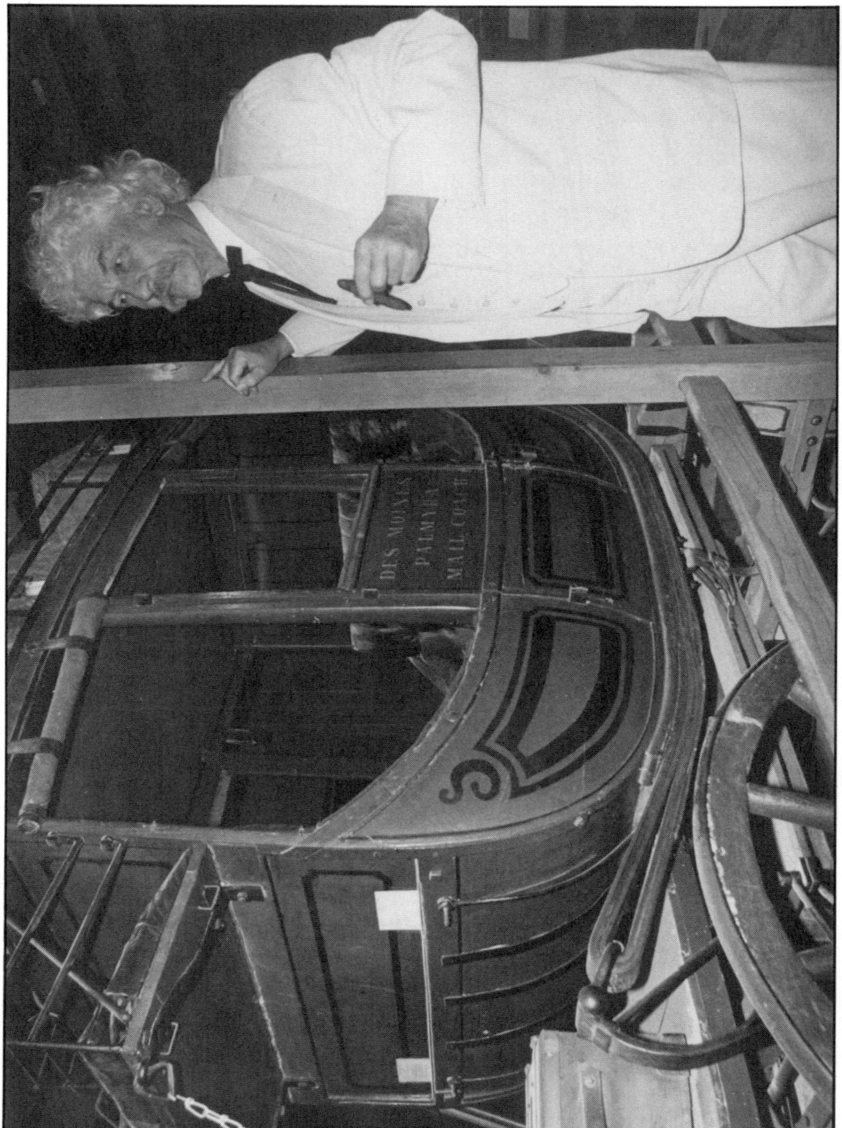

Well I noticed that not very many people were clapping, and there was no laughing. As I went ahead in my appearance, then, I paused and said to the audience: "While I'm here in San Francisco I want to tell you one of the funniest stories I ever heard, and this was about a friend of mine, Horace Greeley. He was on his way to San Francisco on this stagecoach, and he said to the driver, 'Hurry along there, driver, because I don't want to be late.' The driver lashed out at the horses, bounced Horace Greeley to the top of the stagecoach, and when he came back down on the seat he said to the driver: 'Now, you can slow down, driver. I'm not in that big of a hurry!' "

Now some of the folks in the audience thought I had forgot that I had already told that story. They started clapping and some started laughing.

Later on at the end of my appearance I said, "Folks, before I leave San Francisco I want to tell you one of the funniest stories I ever heard. It was about a good friend of mine, Horace Greeley. He was on the stagecoach on his way to San Francisco and he said to the driver: 'Now, hurry along there, driver, because I don't want to be late.' The driver lashed out at the horses, bounced Horace Greeley against the top of the stagecoach, and when he came back down in his seat, he said, 'Now, driver, you can slow down just a little bit, because I'm really not in that big of a hurry!' "

By this time the audience thought, Oh, that poor man. Now he's gone and told that story again, not remembering that he had already told it two times. Now the entire audience was laughing and clapping. The next morning I went around and collected my five dollar gold pieces! (Janssen and Beaty, STORYTELLING MARK TWAIN STYLE, 1988, p. 62).

*****

AT CARSON CITY

There was no gold to collect at the end of the Overland trip, either

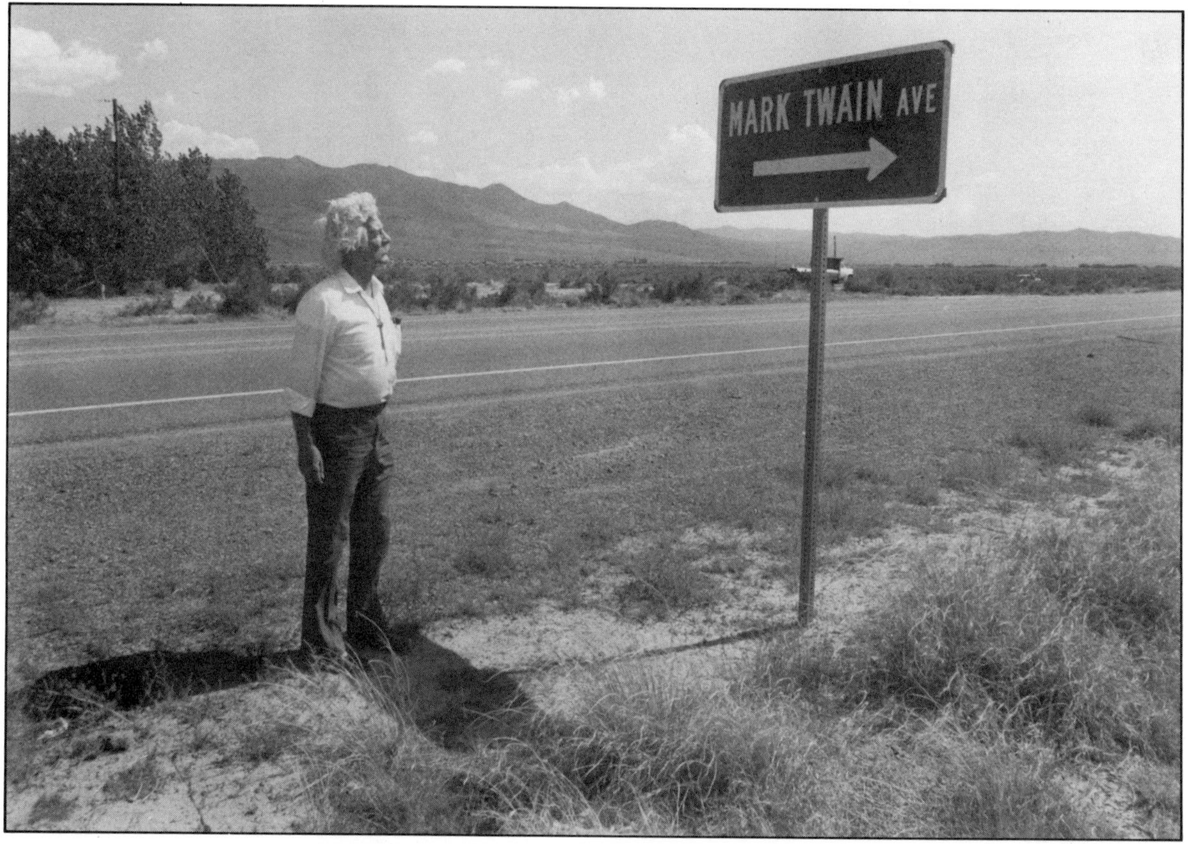
MARK TWAIN AVE

for Mark Twain or Dale Janssen — at least not yet. At noon on Wednesday, August 14, 1861 — 1,700 miles and 20 days out from St. Joseph, Missouri — the Clemens boys and their stagecoach finally arrived in Carson City, capital of the Nevada Territory, unofficially known as "Washoe."

At two P.M. on Monday, August 1, 1988, Janssen and Beaty emerged from the desert at the beginning of a developed area, when a street sign at the edge of the road caught their attention. "Mark Twain Avenue" it read. They quickly pulled over. The entire area was known as "Mark Twain Valley," they soon discovered. Straight down the highway eight or ten miles ahead lay Carson City.

THE "WASHOE ZEPHYR"

Mark Twain noted in ROUGHING IT that Carson City was a "wooden town" (to distinguish it from a tent town as many mining towns were), and that it consisted of four or five blocks of little white frame stores and houses, board sidewalks, a plaza, and two thousand souls.

That's all he saw when he first arrived, for (as he described later) "it was two o'clock now, and according to custom the daily 'Washoe Zephyr' set in; a soaring dust drift about the size of the United States set up edgewise came with it, and the capital of Nevada Territory disappeared from view. Still, there were sights to be seen which were not wholly uninteresting to newcomers; for the vast dust cloud was thickly freckled with things strange to the upper air — things living and dead, that flitted hither and thither; going and coming; appearing and disappearing among the rolling billows of dust — hats, chickens, and parasols sailing in the remote heavens; blankets, tin signs, sagebrush and shingles a shade lower; doormats and buffalo robes lower still; shovels and coal scuttles on the next grade; glass doors, coats and little children on the next; disrupted lumberyards, light buggies and wheelbarrows on the next; and down only thirty or forty feet above ground was a scurrying storm of emigrating roofs and vacant lots.

"It was something to see that much. I could have seen more, if I could have kept the dust out of my eyes." (ROUGHING IT, 1913).

Beaty peered into the radiant blue skies of a flawless Nevada afternoon for something similar. Nothing. Not a speck of dust. "Where are you when you're needed, 'Bonneville Zephyr'!" she sighed.

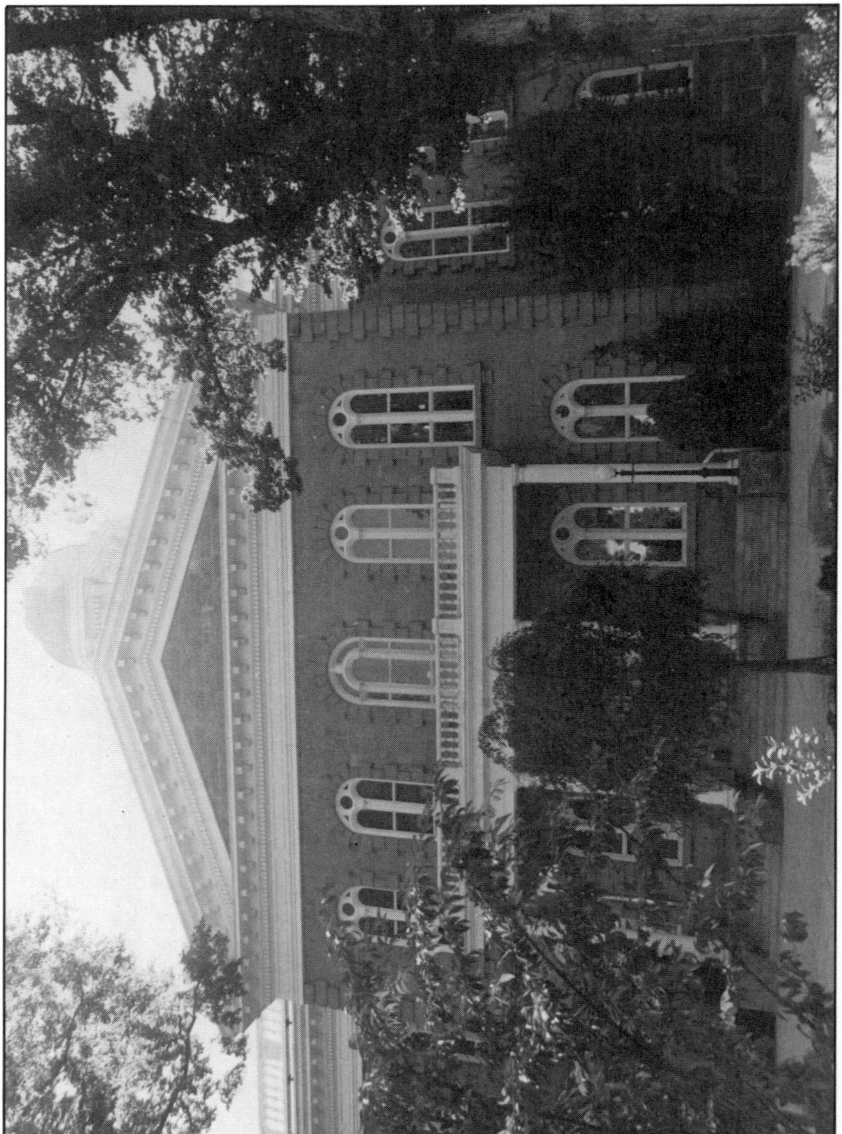

THE MODERN CITY

In a sense today's Carson City is as sleek and modern as any Nevada City with flashy casinos and traffic-filled downtown. But in another sense it still retains some of the flavor of another age as it was when Samuel and Orion Clemens were residents during the 1860's.

As Janssen and Beaty drove through town they noted that scattered throughout many square blocks of its downtown residential area were historic homes, businesses, and churches erected during that early era and preserved in tact to the present day. The old Ormsby House Hotel and Casino had been rebuilt into an imposing structure. But the State Capitol Building was the same handsome dressed-stone structure with cupola dome as early pictures showed it. The main difference was the trees: where once they were inconspicuous saplings, today they have grown to immense proportions, turning the capitol grounds into a shaded park.

THE 1861 TOWN

What impressed Samuel Clemens upon his arrival was a wide-open plaza: "a large, unfenced, level vacancy, with a liberty pole in it, and very useful as a place for public auctions, horse trades, and mass meetings, and likewise for teamsters to camp in. Two other sides of the plaza were faced by stores, offices, and stables. The rest of Carson City was pretty scattering." (ROUGHING IT, 1913).

Streets were wide and unpaved. Sidewalks were boards: "that were more or less loose and inclined to rattle when walked upon." There was not a tree to be seen — only sagebrush and greasewood up to the edge of town.

As the Clemens' stagecoach pulled up to the Ormsby House, it might be imagined that the weary travelers were thankful to have arrived and glad their exhausting overland journey was finished at last. They had been on the trail nearly non-stop for twenty days and 1,700 miles out of St. Joseph, Missouri.

Not Samuel Clemens. He was almost never happy for a journey to end. Travel was always for him the great adventure. Of the approaching end of their long journey, he exclaimed: "We were not glad, but sorry. It had been a fine pleasure trip; we had fed fat on wonders every day; and we were now well accustomed to stage life, and very fond of it; so the idea of coming to a standstill and settling down to a humdrum existence in a village was not agreeable, but on the contrary, depressing."

Samuel Clemens should have known that he would never come to a standstill, for his life was always one of exhilerating movement. Even when he was standing still physically, his brain was a ferment of energized activity. And as for "humdrum existence" — even in this raw frontier village there was sure to be excitement wherever Samuel Clemens was found.

A PLACE TO LIVE

At this moment of his arrival in Carson City, however, his first concern was finding a place to live. He and his brother the Secretary, finally took quarters on the first floor of Mrs. O'Flannigan's rooming house facing the plaza. Into their one room they stuffed a bed, a small table, two chairs, the government fireproof safe, and the unabridged dictionary. For luxuries, they added a carpet, a painted oilcloth window curtain, and a genuine queensware washing bowl. There might have even been room for a visitor if they squeezed, thought Sam.

However, he soon decided that there was not room for him, so he moved upstairs to a dorm room of "fourteen white-pine cot-bedsteads that stood in two long ranks in the one sole room of which the second floor consisted." The beds were occupied by a retinue of the new governor's men. During the day they were busy surveying for a railroad east across the desert from Carson City. In the evening they returned to the boarding house tired, dusty, and often with a few souvenirs from the desert: promising looking rocks they had picked up and always, as Mark Twain noted in ROUGHING IT: "a great store of prodigious hairy spiders — tarantulas." These they kept in covered tumblers arranged along the shelf of the dorm room.

One night during Twain's early days in Carson City a furious "zephyr" roared in at midnight and blew off the roof of an adjoining stable which in turn crashed through the side of the boarding house. The sleeping men jumped up so quickly out of a sound sleep that one of them hit the shelf with his head, knocking off the glasses containing the spiders. Instantly, in the pitch dark of the room he shouted:

"The Tarantulas is Loose!"

"Turn out, boys — the tarantulas is loose!"

No warning ever sounded so dreadful. Nobody tried, any longer, to leave the room, lest he might step on a tarantula.

Every man groped for a trunk or a bed, and jumped on it. Then followed the strangest silence — a silence of grisly suspense it was, too — waiting, expectancy, fear. It was as dark as pitch, and one had to imagine the spectacle of those fourteen scant-clad men roosting gingerly on trunks and beds, for not a thing could be seen. Then came occasional little interruptions of the silence, and one could recognize a man and tell his locality by his voice, or locate any other sound a sufferer made by his gropings or changes of position. The occasional voices were not given much to speaking — you simply heard a gentle ejaculation of "Ow!" followed by a solid thump, and you knew the gentleman had felt a hairy blanket or something touch his bare skin and had skipped from a bed to the floor. Another silence. Presently you would hear a gasping voice say:

"Su-su-something's crawling up the back of my neck!"

Every now and then you could hear a little subdued scramble and a sorrowful "O Lord!" and then you knew that somebody was getting away from something he took for a tarantula, and not losing any time about it, either. Directly a voice in the corner rang out wild and clear:

"I've got him! I've got him!" (Pause, and probably change of circumstances.) "No, he's got me! Oh, ain't they *never* going to fetch a lantern!"

The lantern came at that moment, in the hands of Mrs. O'Flannigan, whose anxiety to know the amount of damage done by the assaulting roof had not prevented her waiting a judicious interval, after getting out of bed and lighting up, to see if the wind was done, now, upstairs, or had a larger contract.

The landscape presented when the lantern flashed into the room was picturesque, and might have been funny to some people, but was not to us. Although we were perched so strangely upon boxes, trunks and beds, and so strangely attired, too, we were too earnestly distressed and too genuinely miserable to see any fun about it, and there was not the semblance of a smile anywhere visible. I know I am not capable of suffering more than I did during those few minutes of suspense in the dark, surrounded by those creeping bloody-minded tarantulas. I had skipped from bed to bed and from box to box in a cold agony, and every time I touched anything that was fuzzy I fancied I felt the fangs. I had rather go to war than live that episode over again. Nobody was hurt. The man who thought a tarantula had "got" him was mistaken — only a crack in a box had caught his finger. Not one of those escaped tarantulas was ever seen again. There were ten or twelve of them. We took candles and hunted the place high and low for them, but with no success. Did we go back to bed then? We did nothing of the kind. Money could not have persuaded us to do it. We sat up the rest of the night playing cribbage and keeping a sharp lookout for the enemy. (ROUGHING IT, 1913)

A HORSE TO RIDE

Sam found that he was not much needed by his brother Orion to be the secretary to the Secretary. Therefore, he had time on his hands. He explored Carson City, made a trip or two to the outlying area, and finally decided that what he really needed was a horse to ride:

"A Genuine Mexican Plug"

I resolved to have a horse to ride. I had never seen such wild, free, magnificent horsemanship outside of a circus as these picturesquely-clad Mexicans, Californians and Mexicanized-Americans displayed in Carson streets every day. How they rode! Leaning just gently forward out of the perpendicular, easy and nonchalant, with broad slouch-hat brim blown square up in front, and long riata swinging above the head, they swept through the town like the wind! The next minute they were only a sailing puff of dust on the far desert. If they trotted, they sat up gallantly and gracefully, and seemed part of the horse; did not go jiggering up and down after the silly Miss Nancy fashion of the riding schools. I had quickly learned to tell a horse from a cow, and was full of anxiety to learn more. I was resolved to buy a horse.

While the thought was rankling in my mind, the auctioneer came scurrying through the plaza on a black beast that had as many humps and corners on him as a dromedary, and was necessarily uncomely; but he was "going, going at twenty-two! — horse, saddle and bridle at twenty-two dollars, gentlemen!" and I could hardly resist.

A man whom I did not know (He turned out to be the auctioneer's brother) noticed the wistful look in my eye, and observed that that was a very remarkable horse to be going at such a price; and added that the saddle alone was worth the money . . .

"I know that horse — know him well. You are a stranger, I take it, and so you might think he was an American horse, maybe, but I assure you he is not. He is nothing of the kind; but — excuse my speaking in a low voice, other people being near — he is, without the shadow of a doubt, a Genuine Mexican Plug!"

I did not know what a genuine Mexican Plug was, but there was something about this man's way of saying it that made me swear inwardly that I would own a Genuine Mexican Plug or die.

He hooked his forefinger in the pocket of my army shirt, led me to one side, and breathed in my ear impressively these words:

"He can outbuck anything in America!"

"Going, going, going — at *twenty*-four dollars and a half, gen—"

"Twenty-seven!" I shouted in a frenzy.

"And sold!" said the auctioneer, and passed over the Genuine Mexican Plug to me.

I could scarcely contain my exultation. I paid the money, and put the animal in a neighboring livery stable to dine and rest himself.

In the afternoon I brought the creature into the plaza, and certain citizens held him by the head, and others by the tail, while I mounted him. As soon as they let go, he placed all his feet in a bunch together, lowered his back, and then suddenly arched it upward, and shot me straight into the air a matter of three or four feet! I came as straight down again, lit in the saddle, went instantly up again, came down almost on the high pommel, shot up again, and came down on the horse's neck — all in the space of three or four seconds. Then he rose and stood almost straight up on his hind feet,

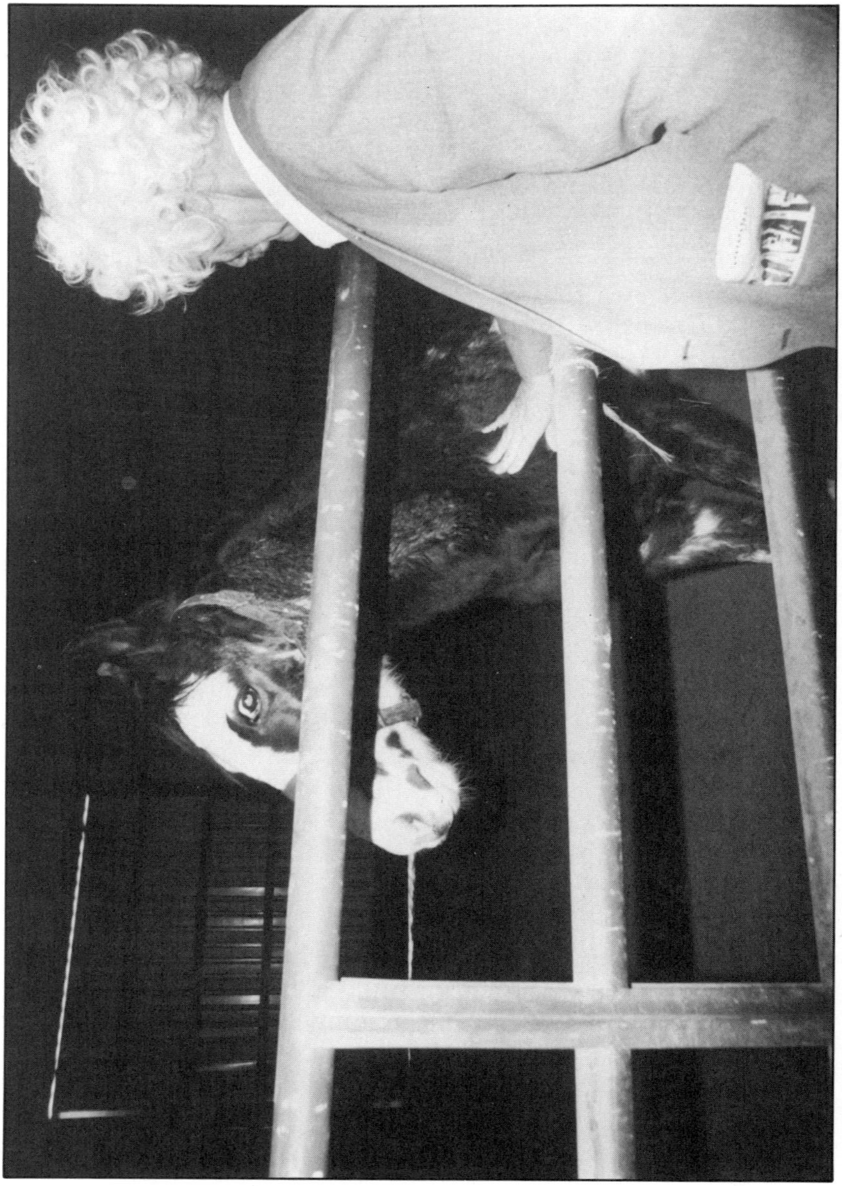

and I, clasping his lean neck desparately, slid back into the saddle, and held on. He came down, and immediately hoisted his heels into the air, delivering a vicious kick at the sky, and stood on his forefeet. And then down he came once more, and began the original exercise of shooting me straight up again. The third time I went up I heard a stranger say:

"Oh, *don't* he buck, though!"

While I was up, somebody struck the horse a sounding thwack with a leathern strap, and when I arrived again the Genuine Mexican Plug was not there . . .

One elderly-looking comforter said:

"Stranger, you've been taken in. Everybody in this camp knows that horse. Any child, any Injun, could have told you that he'd buck; he is the very worst devil to buck on the continent of America. You hear *me*. I'm Curry. *Old* Curry. Old *Abe* Curry. And moreover, he is a simon-pure, out-and-out, genuine d---d Mexican plug, and an uncommon mean one at that, too. Why, you turnip, if you had laid low and kept dark, there's chances to buy an *American* horse for mighty little more than you paid for that bloody foreign relic."

I gave no sign; but I made up my mind that if the auctioneer's brother's funeral took place while I was in the Territory I would postpone all other recreations and attend it. (ROUGHING IT, 1913)

* * * * *

JANSSEN'S HORSE STORY

Dale Janssen, on the other hand, was happy to arrive in Carson City — not because his long trip across the United States was finished (because it wasn't), but because at last he would see the actual location of the Mark Twain stories he enjoyed telling. Then he remembered that one of his favorites was the story of a real horse Twain had encountered while visiting the Hawaiian Islands in 1863. Janssen had adapted the story from ROUGHING IT and tells it as follows in his book STORYTELLING MARK TWAIN STYLE:

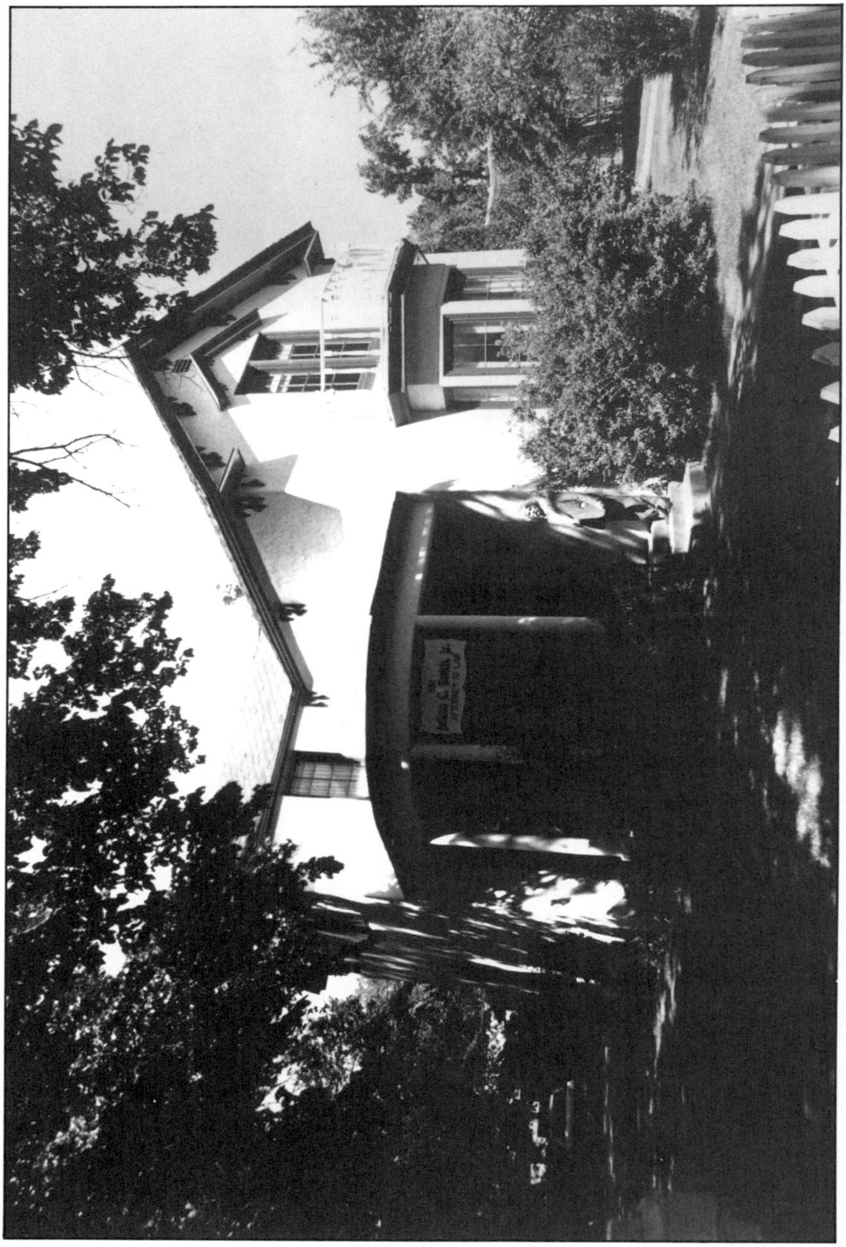

"A Horse in Honolulu"

While I was there in San Francisco, the newspaper sent me to the Sandwich Islands, and when I arrived at the Sandwich Islands I realized these were the Hawaiian Islands and I was to have this horse to ride. I was concerned about this horse because I could see that mischievous look in his eye. I had been thrown from one back in Carson City, Nevada. This one was a very good horse. A very slow horse. I was riding this horse along the water's edge, and right there was a pile of women's clothing. I looked out there and sure enough, ladies were out there swimming in the nude. I yelled, "I'll stay here and watch your clothes so no one will steal them!" They didn't pay any attention to me. I thought then that there'd be an emergency. Oh, yes, it seemed like the tide was coming in, and I yelled: "Ladies the tide's coming in! Your lives are in danger! You must come in now!" They ignored me completely. I thought then if we did have an emergency we would need that horse. So I looked around to see if he was still there. Well, yes, he was standing exactly where I'd left him but S-O-U-N-D asleep! And there I was so concerned about someone stealing those ladies' clothing, and the possibility of them losing their lives. And all that time that horse was standing there sound asleep. I concluded my article, that there was still a difference between man and a horse! (Janssen and Beaty, STORYTELLING MARK TWAIN STYLE, 1988, p. 20)

* * * * *

ORION'S HOUSE

Janssen and Beaty were also excited to learn that Orion Clemens' actual house was still standing. Sam's older brother had eventually built a fine-looking house for himself, and then sent back home for his wife and daughter to join him during his term of office. They came and helped make his home a center for Carson City society, since Orion often served as Acting-Governor when the Governor went out of the Territory.

People in Carson City gave them directions and soon the authors were cruising the older residential streets, stopping now and again in front of the wonderful Victorian houses of early Carson City. Yes, there it was, just as the photo showed in Effie Mack's book MARK

TWAIN IN NEVADA. Orion's home had been restored as close as possible to its original condition. Its modern tenants were lawyers who took great pride in having law offices in one of Carson City's earliest homes: the dwelling place of Nevada's first Secretary and Acting-Governor, and of course, of his brother Mark Twain. Although Twain never lived permanently in Carson City, one of the upstairs rooms, they pointed out, was reserved for him whenever he was in town.

Twain's more permanent address in Nevada eventually came to be in nearby Virginia City which the authors would soon be visiting. But first they found themselves unexpectedly following the silver mining rush that had drawn Americans across the continent to Nevada in the first place.

* * * * *

REFERENCES

Janssen, Dale H. and Janice J. Beaty, STORYTELLING MARK TWAIN STYLE, Columbia, Missouri: Janssen Education Enterprise, Inc., 1988.
Mack, Effie Mona, MARK TWAIN IN NEVADA, New York: Charles Scribner's Sons, 1947.
Twain, Mark, ROUGHING IT, New York: Harper and Brothers, 1913.

* * * * *

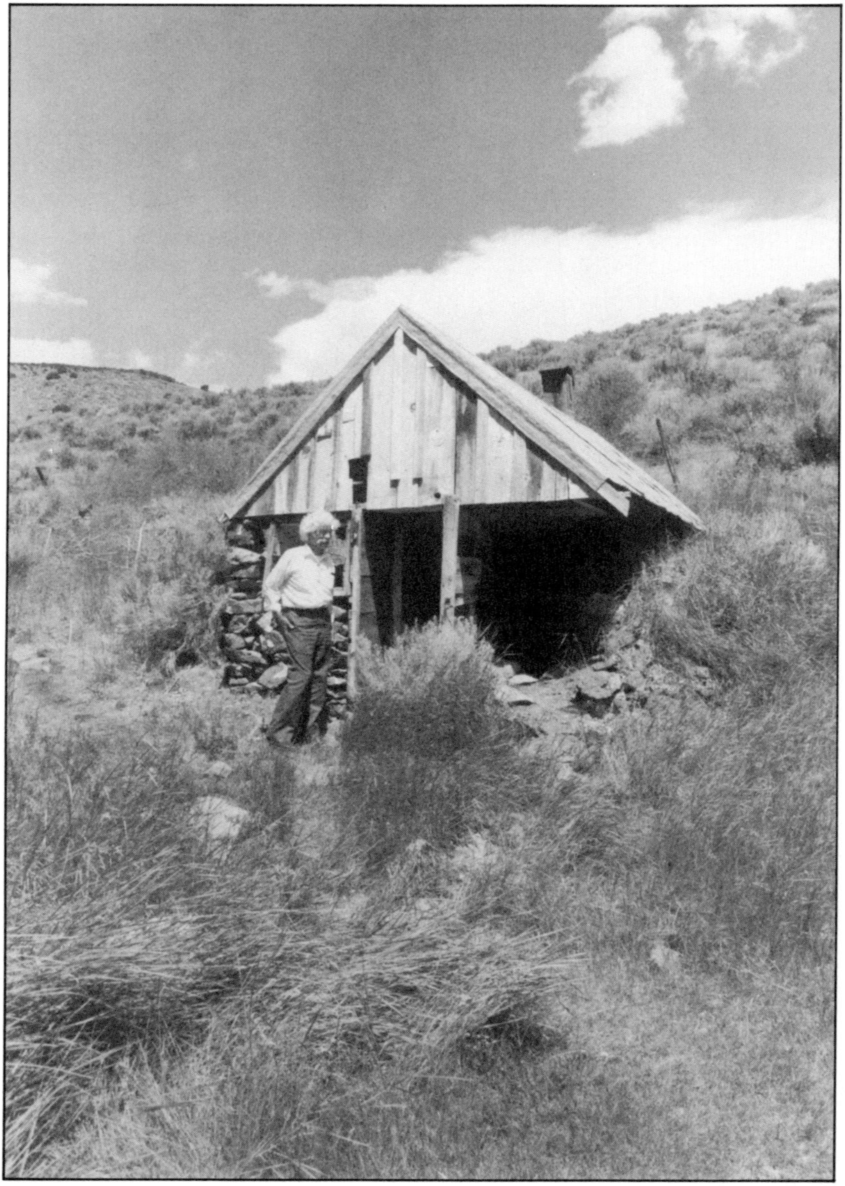

CHAPTER 10

MARK TWAIN'S NEVADA CABIN

NEWS OF THE CABIN

"Have you been to Mark Twain's cabin?"

This was the question posed to Janssen and Beaty as they stood watching the players at one of the Ormsby House's gaming tables.

"Not yet," was their reply. "We plan to visit his cabin at Jackass Hill in California after we've seen Virginia City."

"Oh, not that cabin. I mean Mark Twain's cabin in Nevada — his cabin at Unionville where he went mining for silver," was the response.

It was happening again! Janssen's striking resemblance to Mark Twain seemed to jog people's memories about Twain. Time and again someone would come up to Janssen with a story about a grandfather knowing Mark Twain, or some legend in their family concerning Samuel Clemens.

The authors pricked up their ears with interest. A Mark Twain cabin in Nevada? What was this about? Both authors knew about his famous Jackass Hill cabin near Angel's Camp gold-mining district in California. They planned to visit it soon. But a silver mining cabin in Nevada? They quickly wrote down the directions to Unionville and then went back to their thumb-worn copy of ROUGHING IT and other Mark Twain reference books.

"Yes, here it is. Samuel Clemens did have a cabin in Unionville during the silver rush days. He even built it himself!" declared Beaty. The more she read, the more excited she became.

"Oh, that was the cabin where everything fell through the roof!" she remembered from previous research. "But I didn't know that it was in Nevada — or that it would still be standing! Wonderful! Let's go!"

BACK ACROSS THE DESERT

So back they went across the "Forty-mile Desert;" but this time on Interstate 80 up toward Winnemucca and the Humboldt Range. Out on the open desert between the dots on the map marking Mills and Imlay, they looked for a turnoff on the right leading to Unionville. There it was: a road leading off into the desert straight as an arrow for

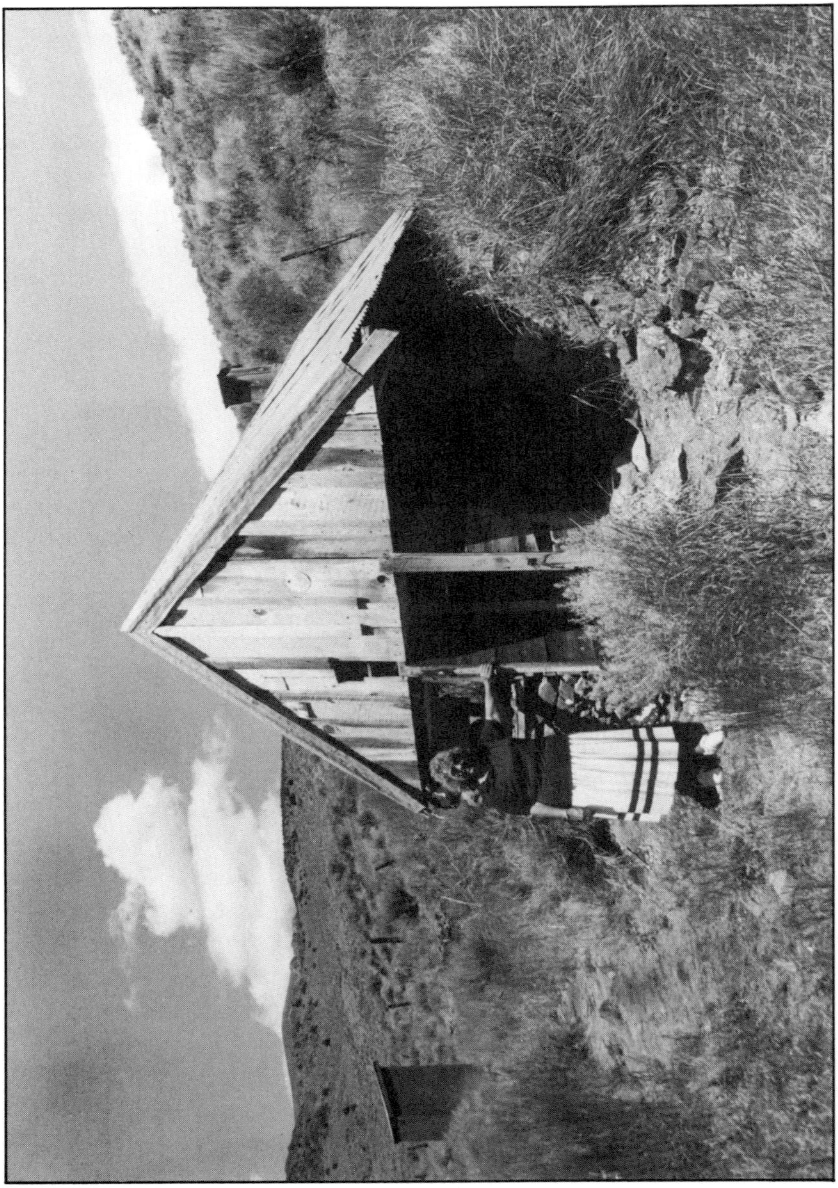

about 20 miles. Both authors kept their eyes peeled for a community of some kind off to the right of the road. Nothing. Only stark and barren mountains paralleling the road as far as the eye could see.

Finally they came to a historical marker describing Unionville as a once-prominent Humboldt mining town. A gravel road branched off to the right crossing the desert for two or three miles right up to the foot of the mountains. Could Unionville be somewhere up there?

As they approached the majestic but barren bulwark ahead, the authors wondered if the bit of greenery in a cleft at the base of the mountain could be trees that might mark a town. It did not seem as if there would be room enough for a town. But sure enough, as they drew nearer they could make out buildings on either side of the winding gravel road that seemed to disappear on up a canyon of some sort.

AT UNIONVILLE

A sign on a rail fence read: "Unionville, Best Little Ghost Town in Nevada." They drove on up the canyon between green poplar trees on either side of the gravel road, modest ranch houses that seemed to be occupied, an old school house off on a side road, a rock shop with a car parked in front, and an old corral with a split rail fence and stone ruins of buildings nearby. Deer were grazing along a tumbling creek to the left, and a peacock strutted across a yard near one house. What an interesting-looking community!

But where was Mark Twain's cabin? And how would they ever find it without help? Poplar trees in the desert, the authors had learned, were a sign that Mormons had been there — for the early Mormon pioneers planted poplars wherever they went as symbols of friendliness to those who would follow. Janssen and Beaty could only hope that some modern residents still lived by that code. At the end of the settled part of the canyon they turned back and decided to inquire at the rock shop with the car parked in front.

It was the right choice. The owners of the rock shop were at home right across the road. Not only did they know of the location of Mark Twain's cabin, but the husband took care of the grounds of the 4H building back of which the cabin was located.

MARK TWAIN'S CABIN

Back up the canyon road went the authors again to a pasture where palomino horses grazed, and sure enough, across the road was the 4H building where out in back up the sloping mountainside stood the remains of a three-sided stone cabin, the mountain being the fourth side. A historical marker in the yard confirmed it. Here was Mark Twain's Unionville cabin. A crumbling rock front with an open door space admitted the visitors to a rough interior and a further room back into the mountain with a stone fireplace. A wooden roof covered the structure.

Beaty got out ROUGHING IT and read what Mark Twain had to say: "We built a small, rude cabin in the side of the crevice and roofed it with canvas, leaving a corner open to serve as a chimney, through which the cattle used to tumble occasionally, at night, and mash our furniture and interrupt our sleep."

Yes, this was the place, all right — rebuilt a little more substantially than the original canvas lean-to.

The authors eventually learned that soon after he arrived in Carson City, Samuel Clemens had caught the mining fever that was infecting every other person, it seemed. As he tells it in ROUGHING IT:

"Discovery of a Brand-new Mining Region"

Every few days news would come of the discovery of a brand-new mining region; immediately the papers would teem with accounts of its richness, and away the surplus population would scamper to take possession. By the time I was fairly inoculated with the disease, "Esmeralda" had just had a run and "Humboldt" was begging to shriek for attention. "Humboldt! Humboldt!" was the new cry, and straightway Humboldt, the newest of the new, the richest of the rich, the most marvelous of the marvelous discoveries in silver land, was occupying two columns of the public press to "Esmeralda's" one. I was just on the point of starting to Esmeralda, but turned with the tide and got ready for Humboldt.

*****

Samuel Clemens and two young lawyer friends, together with an older miner he called Ballou and his dog Curney, acquired a wagon, two decrepit horses and 1800 pounds of provisions and mining gear. Although Twain described the trip in some detail in ROUGHING IT, a more abbreviated version with reference to the cabin also appeared in his first travel book, THE INNOCENTS ABROAD:

"Falling Down the Chimney"

Oliver was a young lawyer, fresh from the schools, who had gone out to the deserts of Nevada to begin life. He found that country, and our ways of life there, in those early days, different from life in New England or Paris. But he put on a woolen shirt and strapped a navy revolver to his person, took to the bacon and beans of the country and determined to do in Nevada as Nevada did. Oliver accepted the situation so completely that, although he must have sorrowed over many of his trials, he never complained — that is, he never complained but once. He, two others, and myself, started to the new silver-mines in the Humboldt Mountains — he to be the Probate Judge of Humboldt County, and we to mine. The distance was two hundred miles. It was dead of winter. We bought a two-horse wagon and put eighteen hundred pounds of bacon, flour, beans, blasting-powder, picks and shovels in it; we bought two sorry-looking Mexican "plugs," with their hair turned the wrong way and more corners on their bodies than there are on the mosque of Omar; we hitched up and started. It was a dreadful trip. But Oliver did not complain. The horses dragged the wagon two miles from town and then gave out. Then we three pushed the wagon seven miles, and Oliver moved ahead and pulled the horses after him by the bits. We complained, but Oliver did not. The ground was frozen; and it froze our backs while we slept; the wind swept across our faces and froze our noses. Oliver did not complain. Five days of pushing the wagon by day and freezing by night brought us to the bad part of the journey — the Forty Mile Desert . . . Still, this mildest-mannered man that ever was had not complained. We started across at eight in the morning, pushing through sand that had no bottom; toiling all day long by the wrecks of a thousand wagons, the skeletons of ten thousand oxen; by wagon-tires enough to girdle Long Island; by human graves; with our throats parched always with thirst; lips bleeding from the alkali dust; hungry, perspiring, and very, very weary — so

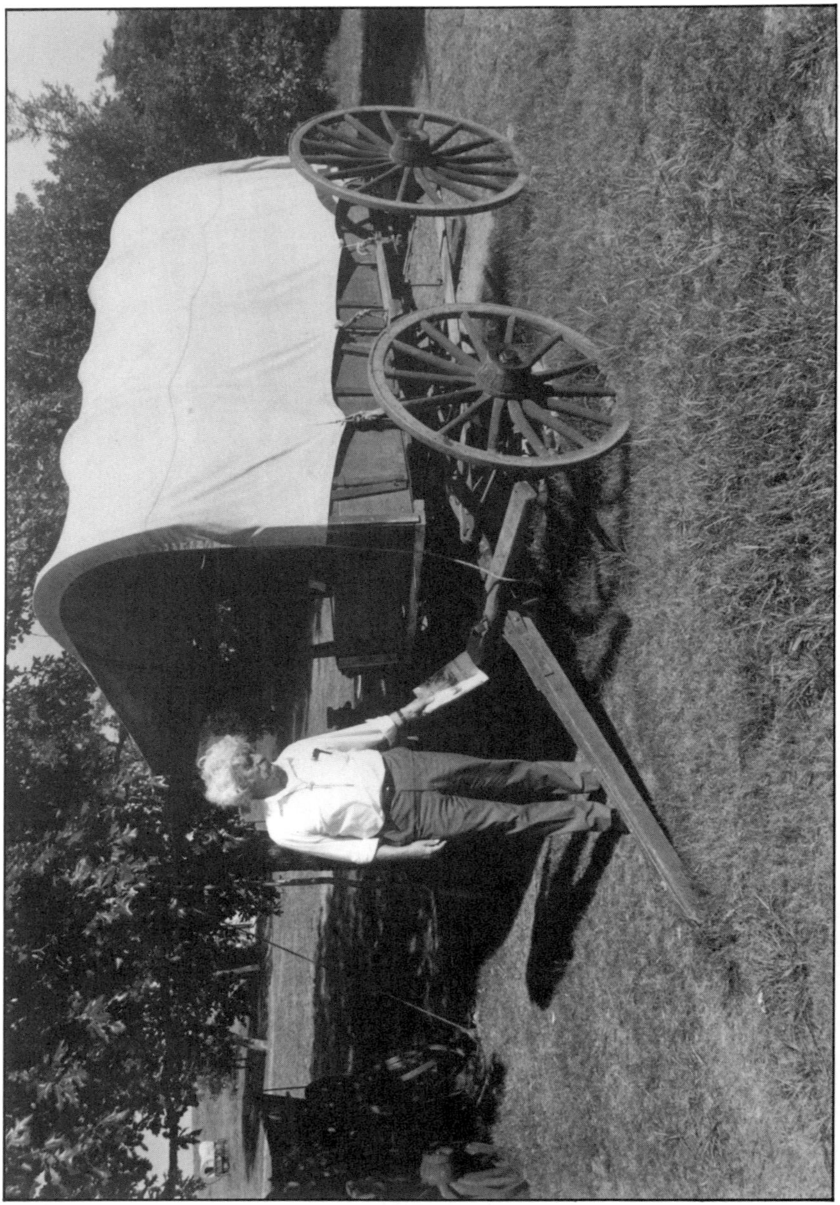

weary that when we dropped in sand every fifty yards to rest the horses, we could hardly keep from going to sleep — no complaints from Oliver; none the next morning at three o'clock, when we got across, tired to death. Awakened two or three nights afterward at midnight, in a narrow canyon, by the snow falling on our faces, and appalled at the imminent danger of being "snowed in," we harnessed up and pushed on till eight in the morning, passed the "Divide" and knew we were saved. No complaints. Fifteen days of hardship and fatigue brought us to the end of the two hundred miles, and the judge had not complained. We wondered if anything *could* exasperate him. We built a Humboldt house. It is done this way. You dig a square in the steep base of the mountain, and set up two uprights and top them with two joists. Then you stretch a great sheet of "cotton domestic" from the point where the joists join the hillside down over the joists to the ground; this makes the roof and the front of the mansion; the sides and back are the dirt walls your digging has left. A chimney is easily made by turning up one corner of the roof. Oliver was sitting alone in this dismal den, one night, by a sagebrush fire, writing poetry; he was very fond of digging poetry out of himself — or blasting it out when it came hard. He heard an animal's footsteps close to the roof; a stone or two and some dirt came through and fell by him. He grew uneasy and said: "Hi! — clear out from there, can't you!" — from time to time. But by and by he fell asleep where he sat, and pretty soon a mule fell down the chimney! The fire flew in every direction, and Oliver went over backward. About ten nights after that he recovered confidence enough to go to writing poetry again. Again he dozed off to sleep, and again a mule fell down the chimney. This time, about half of that side of the house came in with the mule. Struggling to get up, the mule kicked the candle out and smashed most of the kitchen furniture, and raised considerable dust. These violent awakenings must have been annoying to Oliver, but he never complained. He moved to a mansion on the opposite side of the canyon, because he had noticed the mules did not go there. One night about eight o'clock he was endeavoring to finish his poem, when a stone rolled in —

then a hoof appeared below the canvas — then part of a cow — the after part. He leaned back in dread, and shouted "Hooy! hooy! get out of this!" and the cow struggled manfully — lost ground steadily — dirt and dust streamed down, and before Oliver could get well away, the entire cow crashed through on to the table and made a shapeless wreck of everything!

Then for the first time in his life, I think, Oliver complained. He said:

"*This thing is growing monotonous!*"

Then he resigned his judgeship and left Humboldt County.

* * * * *

Samuel Clemens surely enjoyed dramatizing the hardships of his western adventures. But he also remembered the happy side. Through it all, he would never forget: "It was a hard, wearing, toilsome journey, but it had its bright side; for after each day was done and our wolfish hunger appeased with a hot supper of fried bacon, bread, molasses, and black coffee, the pipe-smoking, song-singing, and yarn-spinning around the evening campfire in the still solitude of the desert was a happy, carefree sort of recreation that seemed the very summit and culmination of earthly luxury. It is a kind of life that has a potent charm for all men, whether city- or country-bred. We are descended from desert-loving Arabs, and countless ages of growth toward perfect civilization have failed to root out of us the nomadic instinct. We all confess to a gratified thrill at the thought of "camping out." (ROUGHING IT, 1913)

SAMUEL CLEMENS' UNIONVILLE

The Unionville that Samuel Clemens found was a far cry from today's inhabited "ghost town." As he described it: "On the fifteenth day we completed our march of two hundred miles and entered Unionville, Humboldt County, in the midst of a driving snowstorm. Unionville consisted of eleven cabins and a liberty pole. Six of the cabins were strung along one side of the deep canyon; and the other five faced them. The rest of the landscape was made up of bleak mountain walls that rose so high into the sky from both sides of the canyon that the village was left, as it were, far down in the bottom of a crevice. It was always daylight on the mountaintops a long time before the darkness lifted and revealed Unionville."

Supposedly one of those cabins, or another one like it, eventually became the living quarters for Clemens and his three mining friends — at least this is the type of cabin that remains today as "Mark Twain's cabin," rather than a canvas lean-to.

But what about the silver mining? Were the four men successful? Did they come away with anything of value for all their long travels and sufferings?

MINING

Samuel Clemens' mining ventures are classics in themselves. They are all the more real because he experienced them. And he always came away with treasure, but seldom the kind he sought. Sometimes the treasure he found was a character sketch he invented about someone he associated with; more often it was other people's stories — yarns or tales spun around the fire at night; and then again it was the method of telling a story by building up the details almost carelessly, and then springing a surprise or "snapper" before his audience even realized they had been "taken," or "sold" as he called it.

Some of his best stories, though, involved himself as the main character, because they actually happened to him. So perhaps the principal treasure he mined out of the unyielding Unionville rock was his own experience that he could later bring to the surface in writing such stories as the following mining classic:

"All that Glitters . . ."

I confess, without shame, that I expected to find masses of silver lying all about the ground. I expected to see it glittering in the sun on the mountain summits. I said nothing about this, for some instinct told me that I might possibly have an exaggerated idea about it, and so if I betrayed my thought I might bring derision upon myself. Yet I was as perfectly satisfied in my own mind, as I could be of anything that I was going to gather up, in a day or two, or at furthest a week or two, silver enough to make me satisfactorily wealthy — and so my fancy was already busy with plans for spending this money. The first opportunity that offered, I sauntered carelessly away from the cabin, keeping an eye on the other boys, and stopping and contemplating the sky when they seemed to be observing me; but as soon as the coast was manifestly clear, I fled away as guiltily as a thief might have done and never halted till I was far beyond sight and call. Then I began my search with a feverish excitement that was brimful of expectation — almost of certainty. I crawled about the ground, seizing and examining bits of stone, blowing the dust from them or rubbing them on my clothes, and then peering at them with anxious hope. Presently I found a bright fragment and my heart bounded! I hid behind a boulder and polished it and scrutinized it with a nervous eagerness and a delight that was more pronounced than absolute certainty itself could have afforded. The more I examined the fragment, the more I was convinced that I had found the door to fortune. I marked the spot and carried away my specimen. Up and down the rugged mountainside I searched, with always increasing interest and always augmenting gratitude that I had come to Humboldt and come in time. Of all the experiences of my life, this secret search among the hidden treasures of silver land was the nearest to unmarred ecstacy. It was a delirious revel. By and by, in the bed of a shallow rivulet, I found a deposit of shining yellow scales, and my breath almost forsook me! A gold mine, and in my simplicity I had been content with vulgar silver! I was so excited that I half believed my overwrought imagination was deceiving me. Then a fear came upon me that people might be observing me and would guess my secret. Moved by this thought, I made a circuit of the place, and ascended a knoll to reconnoiter. Solitude. No creature was near. Then I returned to my mine, fortifying myself against possible disappointment, but my fears were groundless — the shining scales were still there. I set about scooping them out, and for an hour I toiled down the windings of the stream and robbed its bed. But at last the descending sun warned me to give up the quest, and I turned homeward laden with wealth. As I walked along I could not help smiling at the thought of my being so excited over my fragment of silver when a nobler metal was almost under my nose. In this little time the former had so fallen in my estimating that once or twice I was on the point of throwing it away.

 The boys were hungry as usual, but I could eat nothing.

Neither could I talk. I was full of dreams and far away. Their conversation interrupted the flow of my fancy somewhat, and annoyed me a little, too. I despised the sordid and commonplace things they talked about. But as they proceeded, it began to amuse me. It grew to be a rare fun to hear them planning their poor little economies and sighing over possible privations and distresses when a gold mine, all our own, lay within sight of the cabin and I could point it out at any moment. Smothered hilarity began to oppress me, presently. It was hard to resist the impulse to burst out with exultation and reveal everything; but I did resist. I said within myself that I would filter the great news through my lips calmly and be serene as a summer morning while I watched its effect on their faces. I said:

"Where have you all been?"

"Prospecting."

"What did you find?"

"Nothing."

"Nothing? What do you think of the country?"

"Can't tell yet," said Mr. Ballou, who was an old gold miner and had likewise had considerable experience among the silver mines.

"Well, haven't you formed any sort of opinion?"

"Yes, a sort of a one. It's fair enough here, maybe, but overrated. Seven-thousand-dollar ledges are scarce, though. That Sheba may be rich enough, but we don't own it; and besides, the rock is so full of base metals that all the science in the world can't work it. We'll not starve, here, but we'll not get rich, I'm afraid."

"So you think the prospect is pretty poor?"

"No name for it!"

"Well, we'd better go back, hadn't we?"

"Oh, not yet — of course not. We'll try it a riffle, first."

"Suppose, now — this is merely a supposition, you know — suppose you could find a ledge that would yield, say, a hundred and fifty thousand dollars a ton — would that satisfy you?"

"Try us once!" from the whole party.

"Or suppose — merely a supposition, of course — suppose you were to find a ledge that would yield two thousand dollars a ton — would that satisfy you?"

"Here — what do you mean? What are you coming at? Is there some mystery behind all this?"

"Never mind. I am not saying anything. You know perfectly well there are no rich mines here — of course you do. Because you have been around and examined for yourselves. Anybody would know that, that had been around. But just for the sake of argument, suppose — in a kind of general way — suppose some person were to tell you that two-thousand dollar ledges were simply contemptible — contemptible, understand — and that right yonder in sight of this very cabin there were piles of pure gold and pure silver — oceans of it — enough to make you all rich in twenty-four hours! Come!"

"I should say he was as crazy as a loon!" said old Ballou, but wild with excitement, nevertheless.

"Gentlemen," said I, "I can't say anything — I haven't been around, you know, and of course don't know anything — but all I ask of you is to cast your eyes on *that*, for instance, and tell me what you think of it!" and I tossed my treasure before them.

There was an eager scramble for it, and a closing of heads together over it under the candlelight. Then old Ballou said:

"Think of it? I think it is nothing but a lot of granite rubbish and nasty glittering mica that isn't worth ten cents an acre!"

So vanished my dreams. So melted my wealth away. So toppled my airy castle to the earth and left me stricken and forlorn.

Moralizing, I observed, then, that "All that glitters is not gold."

Mr. Ballou said I could go further than that, and lay it up among my treasures of knowledge, that *nothing* that glitters is gold. So I learned then, once for all, that gold in its native state is but dull, unornamental stuff, and that only lowborn metals excite the admiration of the ignorant with an ostentatious glitter. However, like the rest of the world, I still go on underrating men of gold and glorifying men of mica. Commonplace human nature cannot rise above that.

* * * * *

Mr. Ballou eventually led them to a possible "ledge" of gold- and silver-bearing quartz, but they would have to sink a shaft perhaps a hundred feet down or burrow a tunnel perhaps nine hundred feet horizontally. They worked for days on one and then the other with picks, shovels, and blasting powder. But the rock was unyielding. After working a week on their tunnel, Mark Twain commented: "at the end of which time we had blasted a tunnel about deep enough to hide a hogshead in, and judged that about nine hundred feet more of it would reach the ledge."

They tried buying "feet" in other miner's claims, but that got them little but false hopes and empty pockets. They finally mounted their horses in disgust and rode back to Carson City.

UNIONVILLE ROCK SHOP

Meanwhile, Janssen and Beaty returned to the folks with the rock shop and talked more about the early days in Unionville and Mark Twain's mining ventures. They asked the couple whether they knew anything about the rock Mark Twain had found that he thought was gold. The wife excused herself, went into the shop and came back with a glittering piece of rock with golden scales of pyrite flaking off it. It was Mark Twain's "fool's gold" found up the canyon in the stream bed, possibly where he had found it all those many years ago! She handed the rock to Beaty as a gift.

Of all the souvenirs of that summer of 1988, that rock was among the most treasured ones, the authors agreed. It eventually came to serve as a paperweight holding open pages when quoting from ROUGHING IT during the writing of this book. The crumbling nature of the rock caused Beaty to blow "golddust" off ROUGHING IT before she could turn the pages! That was her treasure.

* * * * *

REFERENCES

Mack, Effie Mona, MARK TWAIN IN NEVADA, New York: Charles Scribner's Sons, 1947.
Twain, Mark, THE INNOCENTS ABROAD, New York: Harper and Brothers, 1911.
Twain, Mark, ROUGHING IT, New York: Harper and Brothers, 1913.

*****

ark Twain
ALOON
HOME OF 1¢ SLOTS
HOT DOGS
WELCOME
BUCKET BLOOD SALOON
TERRITORIAL ENTERPRISE
1869

CHAPTER 11
VIRGINIA CITY, NEVADA

VIRGINIA CITY TODAY

Most tourists to western Nevada — to Reno or Carson City — have a secondary goal in mind as they travel, and that is Virginia City. It is a "must" for anyone touring that part of the state. To have gone to western Nevada and not visited Virginia City is like going to Paris and not visiting the Eiffel Tower; or going to New York City and not visiting the Statue of Liberty; or going to St. Louis and not seeing the Gateway Arch.

Virginia City, in other words, stands out as something special to see — something head and shoulders above everything else, both literally and figuratively. It is more than a mountain town perched 6,200 feet up on Mt. Davidson. It is more than a mining town straddling the Comstock Lode, one of the world's richest silver mines. It is more than a ghost town with 800 hardy souls in residence all year round. It is a restored historical treasure of the first magnitude where people live, work and go to school, and a million and a half tourists a year flock in to visit during the day.

Great throngs of tourists tramp along the old covered boardwalks of C Street in the summer to visit restored restaurants, saloons, craft shops, and museums; or to boo the villain in an old fashioned melodrama at Piper's Opera House; or to peruse the books at the Fourth Ward School museum in what looks to be a handsome Victorian mansion; or to tour the Chollar Silver Mine two blocks below the school; or even to view the annual camel race.

MARK TWAIN'S MARK

It is in Virginia City that the traveling public first becomes aware that Mark Twain actually lived in the West; and not only lived there, but made his first literary mark there. The signs are everywhere: the "Mark Twain Museum" at the *Territorial Enterprise* building where Mark Twain first worked as a reporter; "Mark Twain's Museum of Memories" in the old Nevada Bank; or "Mark Twain Saloon" across C Street from the *Enterprise*. His book ROUGHING IT is suddenly as prominently displayed as the guide books to Virginia City and the

Comstock Lode.

And no wonder. Of his three years in Nevada, Mark Twain spent 1862-1864 in Virginia City working on the *Territorial Enterprise*, one of the first and most influential newspapers in the Nevada Territory.

When his silver mining at Unionville didn't pan out, and after further mining misadventures at Esmeralda failed to produce anything of substance, Samuel Clemens turned to writing humorous letters to the *Territorial Enterprise* with his typical gusto about the people and places he was encountering. He signed his letters with the pen name "Josh" in the style of the day. *Enterprise* editor, Joseph Goodman was so taken by Clemens' freshness and originality that he offered him the job of reporter and city editor at $25 a week. That was $25 more than Samuel Clemens was able to recoup from his mining. He accepted the job and hiked on foot all the way back to Virginia City from Esmeralda.

MARK TWAIN'S NAME

And so "Mark Twain" was born. He covered murders and marriages, stage robberies and funerals, hay wagons and wagon trains — and all in his own original style in which the facts of the article sometimes took on a life of their own. He was a smashing success in "wide open" Virginia City, where anything from a silver strike to a gun fight was likely to happen any day of the week — and if it didn't, his words could help it along.

He soon came to realize that his own name, Samuel Clemens, wouldn't do. Neither would the ineffectual "Josh" — even though it expressed the idea that maybe the author of the article was just "joshing." His colleague and best friend William Wright had changed his own name to the pen name "Dan DeQuille" and was never known by anything else. Names were meaningful to Samuel Clemens. Throughout his life he took great pleasure in choosing just the right name or nickname for friends, animal pets, or characters in his stories. He must have thought carefully before selecting what has come to be the perfect pen name for himself.

JANSSEN'S VERSION OF THE PEN NAME

Dale Janssen had also looked carefully into the origin of Samuel Clemens' pen name. When Janssen first came to realize in 1983 the impact that his incredible Twain resemblance in appearance, voice, and mannerisms had on people, he was determined to find out all he could about the man Samuel Clemens who had become Mark Twain (See book MARK TWAIN WALKING AMERICA AGAIN). Thus he researched material about Clemens in Missouri, Iowa, Illinois, Connecticut, and New York: visiting libraries and museums, reading books and articles, gathering oral history from people in Mark Twain locations, and soaking up the "feel" of the setting on riverboats and cabins and the Study where Mark Twain wrote his major books. He was determined to come as close as he could to Mark Twain factually and to Mr. and Mrs. Samuel Clemens and their family. Then when he was called upon to appear as Mark Twain, he could make those appearances with the confidence that he was truly representing Samuel Clemens and what he stood for.

Janssen found several versions of how Mark Twain acquired his pen name. This is the one he chooses to tell during his appearances as Mark Twain:

"My Pen Name, Mark Twain"

Growing up in the small town of Hannibal, Missouri, I enjoyed not only watching the riverboats go by — but a dream that all the boys had there in Hannibal was to be on one of those riverboats — and to become a PILOT — oh my, that was a wonderful feeling! Then being on the riverboats and later becoming a pilot on the Mississippi River, I realized that this leadsman on the riverboat would throw out a line and drag it alongside the boat to measure the depth of the water. When it was about twelve feet, that meant it was safe for the riverboat. And when he did that he would yell: "MA-A-A-A-R-K- TWA-A-A-IN!" When we heard that cry it made us all feel good. And that was one reason I chose the pen name of "Mark Twain" — because it made people feel good. (Janssen and Beaty, STORYTELLING MARK TWAIN STYLE, 1988, p. 89)

*****

The folks in Virginia City may not have understood the significance of such riverboat jargon, but they quickly accepted the name "Mark Twain" for the young editor and reporter, and rarely called him anything else.

Janice Beaty's research had made her realize how significant the exact meaning of a word or a name was to Samuel Clemens. He had once said that the difference between the right word and one that was not quite right was the difference between "lightning and a lightning bug." Now she wondered whether Clemens might not also have had a little of "Josh" in mind when he chose his new pen name. After all, "Mark Twain" could also mean "look twice" — or rather, "take a second look."

MARK TWAIN'S HOAXES

That's what the citizens of Virginia City should have done each time they read an article signed "Mark Twain" — that is, taken a second look. Clemens was not only a humorist in his approach to writing, but he was also a practical joker. In the *Territorial Enterprise* his jokes sometimes took the form of hoaxes. He wrote these hoaxes as factual articles, but he inserted strange incongruities in his descriptions with which to alert the reader that the story was a fabrication and not to be believed. Several times, though, his hoaxes backfired when his readers missed the planted "warnings" and accepted the story as true.

Such was the case in the discovery of "The Petrified Man," one of the earliest of Clemens' hoaxes. This time his warning device seemed perfectly clear and reasonable to him: he had included a description of the so-called "petrified man" thumbing his nose! How could the reader miss the joke, he probably wondered? Just to make it a bit more complicated, he scrambled the description of the "man" so that the reader would have to look carefully to decifer what his thumb and fingers were doing.

As Mark Twain later admitted: "From beginning to end the 'Petrified Man' squib was a string of roaring absurdities, albeit they were told with an unfair pretense of truth that even imposed upon me to some extent, and I was in some danger of believing in my own fraud. But I really had no desire to deceive anybody, and no expectation of doing it. I depended on the way the petrified man was *sitting* to explain to the public that he was a swindle. Yet I purposely mixed that up with other things, hoping to make it obscure — and I did. I would describe the position of one foot, and then say his right thumb was against the side of his nose; then talk about his other foot, and presently come back and say the fingers of his right hand were spread apart; then talk about the back of his head a little, and return and say the left thumb was hooked into the right little finger; then ramble off about something else, and by and by drift back again and remark that the fingers of the left hand were spread like those of the right. But I was too ingenious. I mixed it up rather too much; and so all that description of the attitude, as a key to the humbuggery of the article, was entirely lost, for nobody but me ever discovered and comprehended the peculiar and suggestive position of the petrified man's hands." (Twain, *The Jumping Frog and 18 Other Stories*, 1931, p. 125)

Tricks like this when played on some of the residents of town sometimes got the young reporter into hot water. It reminded Dale Janssen of the story he liked to tell about Samuel Clemens' work in his brother's printing office:

"Stupid Story"

Before I was a pilot on the Mississippi River I remember going up to Keokuk, Iowa. That's where my brother Orion had a news printing office. One day we left for lunch and locked the door. When we came back someone had tacked a piece of paper on the door with the word STUPID written on it. When I looked at that word I remembered the many people who had written articles for the newspaper but wouldn't sign their names to them. Now here was someone who signed his name but forgot to write the article! (Janssen and Beaty, STORYTELLING MARK TWAIN STYLE, 1988, p. 72.)

*****

JANSSEN AND BEATY IN VIRGINIA CITY

Meanwhile the authors began their winding drive up a mountain canyon to Virginia City. They progressed through the little mining communities of Silver City and Gold Hill, and at last came out in the open, high above the desert on C Street of Virginia City. Beaty turned to ROUGHING IT to see what Mark Twain had to say about this second "birthplace" city of his:

"The 'City' of Virginia"

The "city" of Virginia roosted royally midway up the steep side of Mount Davidson, seven thousand two hundred feet above the level of the sea, and in the clear Nevada atmosphere was visible from a distance of fifty miles! It

MARK TWAIN
Was Robbed Here

This "Divide" Between Gold Hill and Virginia City Was Once Densely Populated. It Was Also A Favored Spot For Footpads and Murderers. Mineshafts Here Have Produced Many Skeletons Whose Wrists and Ankles Were Bound with Wire.

One Night in 1866 Mark Twain, Once A Reporter For The Territorial Enterprise, Was Held Up at this Spot and Robbed of His Watch and Money.

The Divide Was Destroyed in a Fierce Fire on Friday 13-1942. A Fascinating True History of the Old West. Visit The Territorial Enterprise, Home of MARK TWAIN Museum claimed a population of fifteen thousand to eighteen thousand, and all day long half of this little army swarmed the streets like bees and the other half swarmed among the drifts and tunnels of the "Comstock," hundreds of feet down in the earth directly under those same streets. Often we felt our chairs jar, and heard the faint boom of a blast down in the bowels of the earth under the office.

The mountainside was so steep that the entire town had a slant to it like a roof. Each street was a terrace, and from each to the next street below the descent was forty to fifty feet. The fronts of the houses were level with the street they faced, but their rear first floors were propped on lofty stilts; a man could stand at a rear first-floor window of a C Street house and look down the chimneys of the row of houses below him facing D Street.

*****

Yes, the authors could certainly recognize the mountainside community. What was left of its old buildings had been refurbished and now stood as living monuments to a wild and wonderful past. Tourists thronged the covered boardwalks of C Street just as residents did in Samuel Clemens' day. But the backs of today's buildings stood solidly above basements rather than on stilts.

MARK TWAIN'S ROBBERY

Taking a motel up on the open "Divide" between Gold Hill and Virginia City, Janssen and Beaty were startled by a nearby signboard that proclaimed: "Mark Twain was Robbed Here." Then they remembered reading the story of the fake robbery perpetrated on Samuel Clemens by his buddies from the *Territorial Enterprise* as a sort of "welcome back, Sam" joke on the occasion of his return from the Hawaiian Islands and San Francisco in 1866. He was in town to give one of his early humorous lectures on "Our Fellow Savages of the Sandwich Islands" at the Piper Opera House. But first he was to lecture down the road at Gold Hill and then walk up to his rooms in Virginia City.

His friends lay for him with masks and guns in the pitch black and cold night at the "Divide" and made him keep his hands raised above

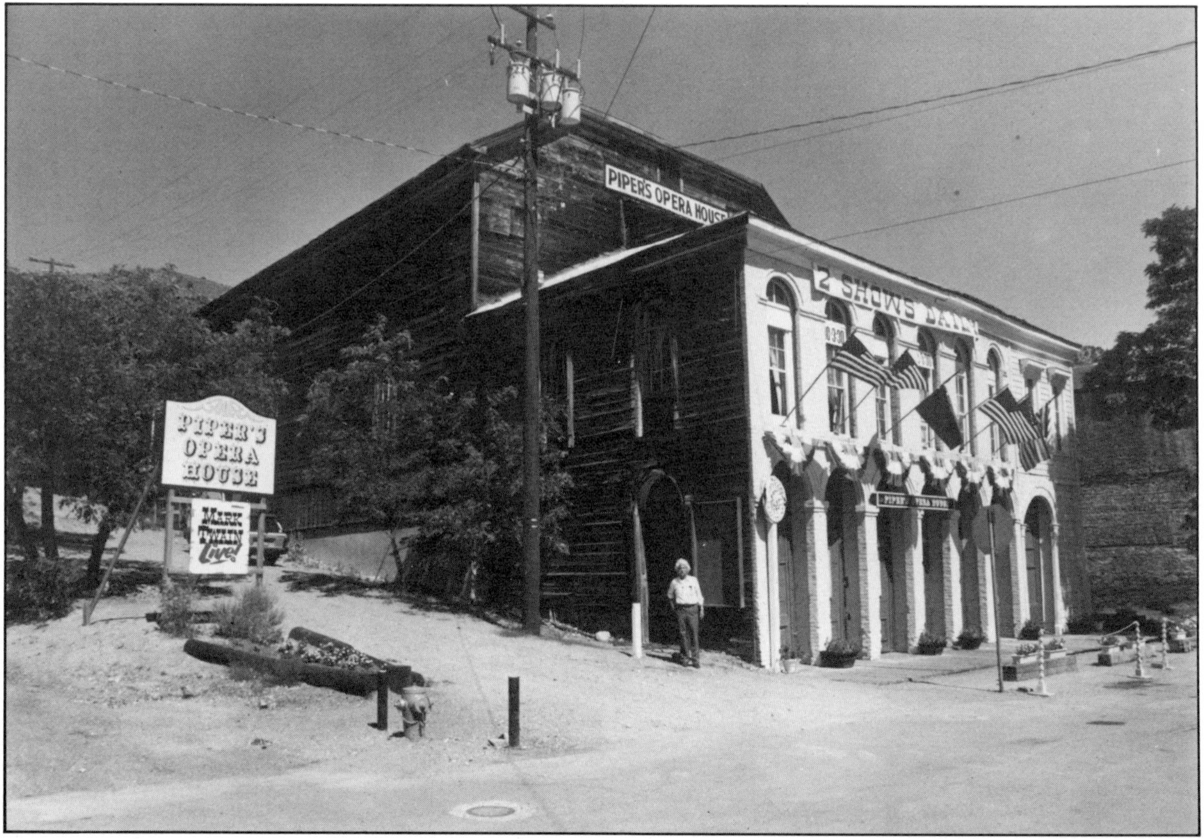
PIPER'S OPERA HOUSE
2 SHOWS DAILY
PIPER'S OPERA HOUSE
MARK TWAIN Live!

his head while they demanded he reach in his pockets for his watch and money: "Gentlemen, listen to reason. You see how I am situated — now *don't* put those pistols so close — I smell the powder. You see how I am situated. If I had four hands — so that I could hold up two and —" (ROUGHING IT, 1913)

Finally, they departed with his watch and money, which were eventually returned to him. But the joke backfired when several of them caught cold from exposure, since he was two hours late!

PIPER'S OPERA HOUSE

Janssen and Beaty were delighted to find that the Piper's Opera House where Mark Twain had eventually lectured still stood next to the courthouse on B Street. Not only had it survived in tact, but it flourished in the summer with two shows daily in addition to its theater museum. These particular performances featured a local actor doing "Mark Twain Live" much to Janssen's delight. It was a fascinating experience for him to watch a young man don the makeup necessary to convert himself into Mark Twain in his later years. It was just as meaningful for the young actor to meet a natural Mark Twain look-alike such as Dale Janssen who was focusing on Mr. and Mrs. Samuel Clemens and the family.

TERRITORIAL ENTERPRISE

The *Territorial Enterprise* building presently housed a clothing and souvenir store on its main floor and a Mark Twain museum in its basement. The newspaper had been sold but had not been printed since a 1986 issue. Sam Clemens would have done something about that were he here today, the authors decided. His was the voice that made the paper first in Nevada and a force to be reckoned with on the Pacific coast. Although his was a carefree spirit, Clemens was not afraid to speak out on issues and people that concerned him, no matter how controversial the issue. One such controversy led to a near duel. Since duels were illegal at that time, he was advised to leave town instead; or as Dale Janssen puts it in one of his Mark Twain monologues:

"Leaving Town in a Hurry"

I moved to Virginia City, Nevada. Worked for a newspaper there. One day someone said that it might be necessary for me to leave town because they didn't agree with what I was writing. I thought this over, and the very next morning, I decided to leave town — I decided to leave town in a hurry — without a forwarding address! (Janssen and Beaty, STORYTELLING MARK TWAIN STYLE, 1988, p. 82)

It was time for the author's departure as well. They would not be heading over the mountains by stagecoach to San Francisco. Instead, they would take their own trail west into California Mother Lode country where Samuel Clemens had mined for gold and discovered a treasure far more valuable.

* * * * *

REFERENCES

Crandall, Jim, "Virginia City: Life Among the Legends," *Nevada*, Aug. 1988, pp. 52-66.
Drury, Wells, AN EDITOR ON THE COMSTOCK LODE, Reno: University of Nevada Press, 1984.
Hillyer, Katharine, YOUNG REPORTER MARK TWAIN IN VIRGINIA CITY, Sparks, Nevada: Western Printing & Publishing Co., 1964.
Janssen, Dale H. and Janice J. Beaty, MARK TWAIN WALKING AMERICA AGAIN, Columbia, Missouri: Janssen Education Enterprise, Inc., 1987.
Janssen, Dale H. and Janice J. Beaty, STORYTELLING MARK TWAIN STYLE, Columbia, Missouri: Janssen Education Enterprise, Inc., 1988.
Mack, Effie Mona, MARK TWAIN IN NEVADA, New York: Charles Scribner's Sons, 1947.
McDonald, Douglas, VIRGINIA CITY AND THE SILVER REGION OF THE COMSTOCK LODE, Las Vegas: Nevada Publications, 1982.
Twain, Mark, THE JUMPING FROG AND 18 OTHER STORIES, New York: Boblin Sales Co., 1931.
Twain, Mark, ROUGHING IT, New York: Harper and Brothers, 1913.

* * * * *

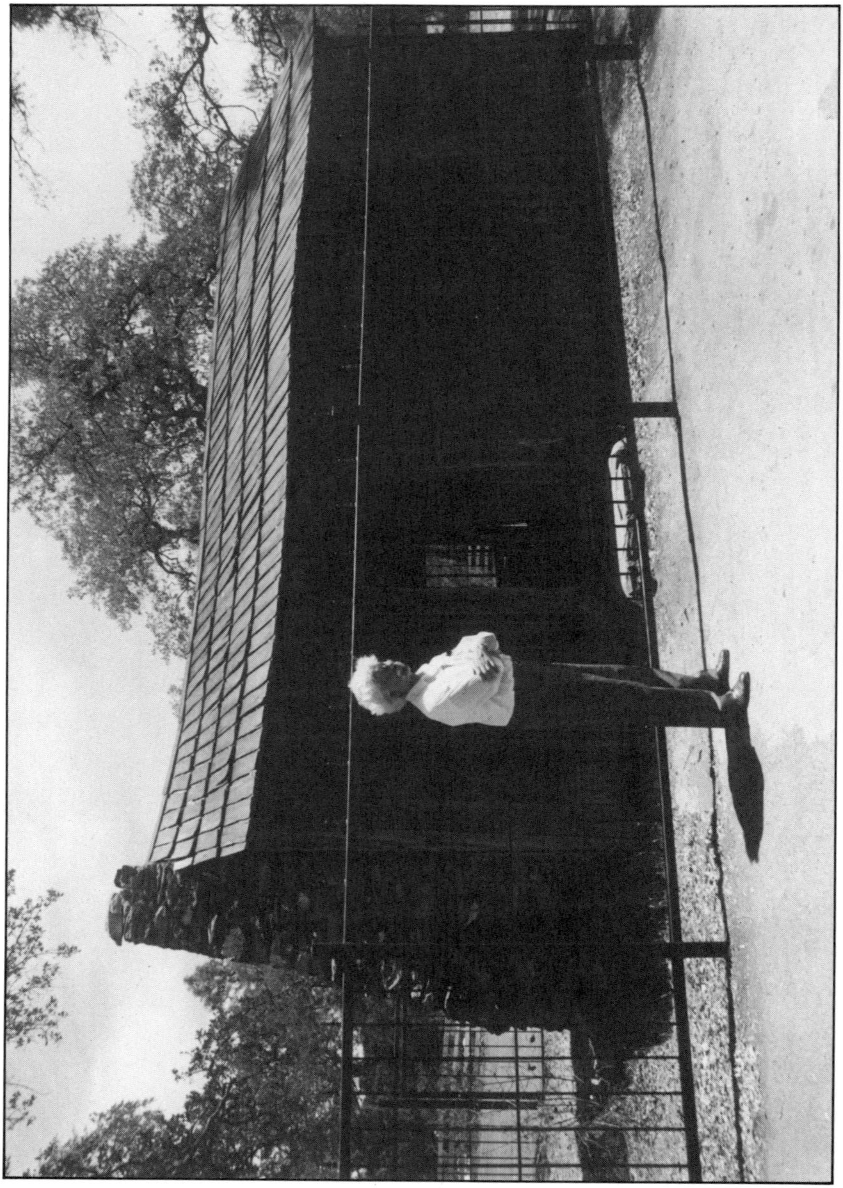

CHAPTER 12
CALIFORNIA GOLD

Up, up into the Sierra Nevada Mountains drove the authors following U.S.50 around the southern end of beautiful Lake Tahoe and then down the western slope of the mountains to Placerville at the edge of the foothills. They realized that they were following the first leg of the old stage and Pony Express route from Carson City to Sacramento. They realized further that Samuel Clemens had taken this route numerous times in his journeyings back and forth from Virginia City to San Francisco. Thirteen times, he said in ROUGHING IT; but we must take this with a grain of salt, since he often used the number "thirteen" for effect rather than accuracy.

PLACERVILLE/SACRAMENTO

Placerville was the key location here. The old stage road and U.S.50 itself continued on to Sacramento, where a traveler in Samuel Clemens' day then transferred to a steamboat for the final leg of the trip over to San Francisco. The steamer *Antelope* was the vessel Clemens traveled aboard, many and many a time. The *Delta King* and *Delta Queen* later plied the same ship canal from Sacramento to San Francisco. Today the *Delta King* is still in tact, although docked permanently at a wharf in Old Sacramento historical site. About a block away stands another monument to past glory: a bronze statue of the Pony Express rider just across the street from his final destination, the historic Wells Fargo Office.

Placerville eventually boasted a stellar array of names in the development of the young nation. Mark Hopkins started out there, opening a grocery store with a single wagonload of supplies for the miners. He threw in with Collis Huntington who was selling shovels, and ended up owning the Central Pacific Railroad. Phillip Armour started a butcher shop selling meat to the miners, and went on to become the great American meat packing baron. John Studebaker gave up making Conestoga wagons in Indiana and followed the emigrants out to Placerville where he forged wheel barrows for miners. Taking his grubstake back to Indiana, he parlayed it into developing the Studebaker Automobile Company.

North of Placerville up at Nevada City a young Herbert Hoover came with an engineering degree out of Stanford, and eventually went on to become a President of the United States. Another soon-to-be-famous Californian, George Hearst, started his fortune there that eventually became a newspaper empire. Then there was Samuel Clemens, a young newspaper reporter known for his wild humor, who settled into a cabin one winter south of Placerville down by Angels Camp . . . Venturesome country, indeed, this Western Slope of the nation!

Placerville even had a hand in the development of Virginia City, Nevada. When silver was discovered there in 1858, Placerville became the chief outfitting point for the California rush to the Comstock Lode. The hills surrounding Placerville soon were piled high with boxes awaiting shipment over the Sierras. Booking a stagecoach to Virginia City or back to Placerville was not all that simple during the rush to the Comstock when teams, wagons, and mule trains clogged the road twenty-four hours a day. Of course Horace Greeley, the famous newspaper editor, made it to Placerville — and on time, too — we have learned ever so many times!

The authors turned south in Placerville onto State 49, the "Golden Chain Highway," and soon found themselves winding through the rounded foothills, yellow with wild oats and dotted with dark oak trees. Their destination: the town of Angels Camp, a former mining camp in the foothills 80 miles north of Yosemite National Park. This was the town where Samuel Clemens discovered a treasure greater than gold: a story — a story that would gain him instant fame across the country, and change the course of his life forever.

CLEMENS IN SAN FRANCISCO

When Mark Twain "left town in a hurry" from Virginia City early one morning, he continued over the mountains to Sacramento and by steamer to San Francisco. There he found a job as reporter for the San Franciso *Call*. He and his companion Steve Gillis (his "second" in the duel that never happened and a compositor for the *Territorial Enterprise*), had a grand life in the city after work, playing Twain's favorite of all games: billiards. The two of them explored the city on foot, locating every pool table that could be found and then spending the night playing.

Dale Janssen recognized this great love of Samuel Clemens in his own modern version of the story:

"Left-handed Pool Player"

I had this appearance one evening in San Francisco, and the night before that, playing a game of pool with some of the men, they said: "Well, Mr. Clemens, you're new in town." I said, "Yes, I am." "Do you enjoy a game of pool?" they asked. I said, "I sure do." "Well, Mr. Clemens, since you're new in town" — this one man said that he would play me a game of pool, and he would play me left-handed. So there I was chalking my cue stick and waiting to get a shot. Well, I never got a shot. He made all the balls on the table. I said, "My, you're a very good pool player left-handed. Do you know how good you'd be playing right-handed?" "No, Mr. Clemens, I don't," he said. "You see, I'm a left-handed pool player!"

*****

But feisty Steve Gillis enjoyed a scrap as much as a game, and could not resist jumping into a fight whenever one occurred — any fight. When he ended up in jail after one particular altercation, Samuel Clemens had to put up his bail. Both men then decided they needed a rest from San Francisco for the time being. Gillis went back to Virginia City. Clemens accepted an invitation from Steve Gillis's brother Jim to spend some time at his mining cabin in the Tuolumne foothills near Angels Camp.

JACKASS HILL

On December 4, 1865 Samuel Clemens took up residence with Jim Gillis in his cabin on Jackass Hill, a deserted mining settlement near the town of Angels Camp. With them were Gillis's mining companion Dick Stoker and Jim's youngest brother, Billy Gillis. Mark Twain describes the area in ROUGHING IT:

"We Lived in a Small Cabin"

We lived in a small cabin on a verdant hillside, and there were not five other cabins in view over the wide expanse of hill and forest. Yet a flourishing city of two or three thousand population had occupied this grassy dead solitude during the flush times of twelve or fifteen years before, and where our cabin stood had once been the heart of the teeming hive, the center of the city. When the mines gave out the town fell into decay, and in a few years wholly disappeared — streets, dwellings, shops, everything — and left no sign. The grassy slopes were as green and smooth and desolate of life as if they had never been disturbed.

*****

POCKET MINING

There was still gold in the ground, but it was not easy to come by. The miners who stayed behind to pick over the leavings from former years had developed a particular technique for tracing down the elusive yellow metal: pocket mining. This was a special form of panning for gold used in this particular area of California. Since Samuel Clemens had still not overcome his "gold fever" of earlier years, it was not difficult to involve him in the excitement of the pocket mining that the other three were engaged in. He described it in ROUGHING IT:

"Pocket-hunting"

Pocket-hunting is an ingenious process. You take a spadeful of earth from the hillside and put it in a large tin pan and dissolve and wash it gradually away till nothing is left but a teaspoonful of fine sediment. Whatever gold was in that earth has remained, because, being the heaviest, it has sought the bottom. Among the sediment you will find half a dozen yellow particles no larger than pinheads. You are delighted. You move off to one side and wash another pan. If you find gold again, you move to one side further, and wash a third pan. If you find *no* gold this time, you are delighted again, because you know you are on the right scent. You lay an imaginery plan, shaped like a fan, with its handle up the hill — for just where the end of the handle is, you argue that the rich deposit lies hidden, whose vagrant grains of gold have escaped and been washed down the hill, spread farther and farther apart as they wandered. And so you proceed up the hill, washing the earth and narrowing your lines every time the absence of gold in the pan shows that you are outside the spread of the fan; and at last, twenty yards up the hill your lines have converged to a point — a single foot from that point you cannot find any gold. Your breath comes short and quick, you are feverish with excitement; the dinner-bell may ring its clapper off, you pay no attention; friends may die, weddings transpire, houses burn down, they are nothing to you; you sweat and dig and delve with a frantic interest — and all at once you strike it! Up comes a spadeful of earth and quartz that is all lovely with soiled lumps and leaves and sprays of gold. Sometimes that one spadeful is all — $500. Sometimes the nest contains $10,000, and it takes you three or four days to get it all out. The pocket-miners tell of one nest that yielded $60,000 and two men exhausted it in two weeks, and then sold the ground for $10,000 to a party who never got $300 out of it afterward.

*****

Samuel Clemens joined the miners on the hillsides around the cabin during December. It was hard, monotonous work with Gillis digging and washing the dirt and Clemens carrying buckets of water up the hill from a distant stream. Physical labor of this nature had little appeal for Clemens. The few specks of gold they turned up, however, kept them going, and the good companionship made up for other lacks. At the end of the day they would retire to their cabin, light up a fire in the fireplace, cook their meal, and enjoy an evening of smoking and yarning, in which Jim Gillis related outlandish tall tales about his partner Dick Stoker, who never blinked an eye.

Clemens with his prodigious riverboat pilot's memory, began storing up these tales — pehaps without even realizing it. He would use them again and again throughout his life as a writer. But at the moment he was more interested in relaxing, enjoying the companionship, and possibly making a gold strike in the daytime.

A LUNAR RAINBOW

They eventually worked their way over to the town of Vallecito in Calaveras County by New Years, 1865. On New Years night Clemens saw a magnificent lunar rainbow that appeared about 8 P.M. in a very light drizzle of rain. Such a rare sighting seemed to him an auspicious omen of good fortune. Undoubtedly he had a gold strike in mind.

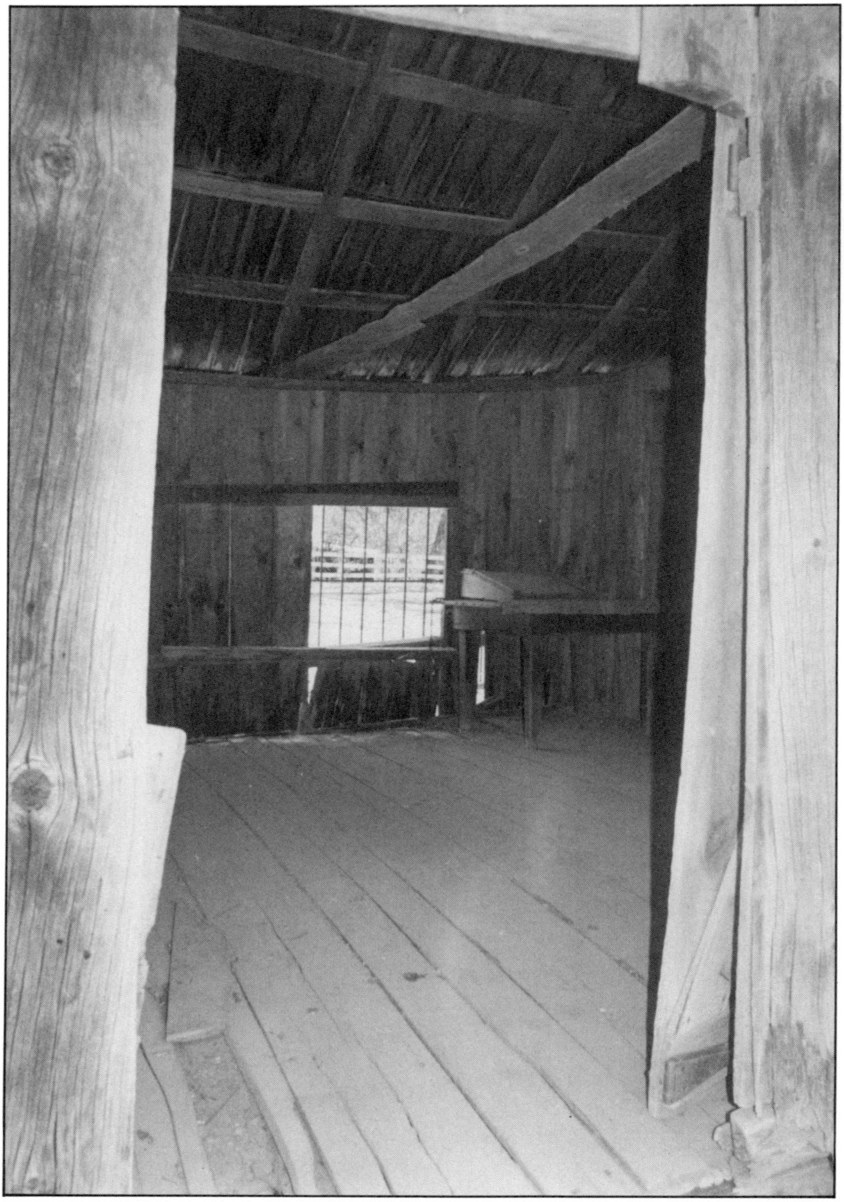

Never could he have guessed the form that the good fortune eventually would take! He began keeping a notebook as he had as a pilot on the Mississippi River. Into this notebook he recorded the dates and places that he traveled, dreams, fragments of stories, names that appealed to him, and things that happened to people he knew, often with his own abbreviations. Items from this particular notebook would be used by Mark Twain in his literary work for the rest of his life.

BACK TO THE CABIN

On January 3, 1865 Clemens and the miners returned to the cabin on Jackass Hill by way of Angels Camp and the ferry over the Stanislaus River. Their evening storytelling sessions became as rich and hilarious as ever. One story that Clemens especially relished was Jim Gillis's rendition of a Shakerspearian burlesque, "The Tragedy of the Burning Shame" featuring Dick Stoker as Rinaldo. (Mark Twain would later convert that story to "The King's Camelopard" or "The Royal Nonesuch" performed by the king and the duke in HUCKLEBERRY FINN.) The cabin had old bunks and no planking on the floor, but a wealth of first class literature: books by Byron, Shakespeare, Bacon, and Dickens.

Clemens loved the mining stories just as much. Jim Gillis often told them in dialect, and once again, Clemens' pilot's memory stored them away, seemingly word for word. Six years later Mark Twain would record in ROUGHING IT;

> "Tom Quartz, Gold Mine Cat"
>
> One of my comrades there — another of those victims of eighteen years of unrequited toil and blighted hopes — was one of the gentlest spirits that ever bore its patient cross in a weary exile; grave and simple Dick Baker, pocket-miner of Dead-Horse Gulch. He was forty-six, gray as a rat, earnest, thoughtful, slenderly educated, slouchily dressed, and clay-soiled, but his heart was finer metal than any gold his shovel ever brought to light — than any, indeed, that ever was mined or minted.
>
> Whenever he was out of luck and a little down-hearted, he would fall to mourning over the loss of a wonderful cat he used to own (for where women and children are not, men of kindly impulses take up with pets, for they must love

something). And he always spoke of the strange sagacity of that cat with the air of a man who believed in his secret heart that there was something human about it — maybe even supernatural.

I heard him talking about this animal once. He said:

"Gentlemen, I used to have a cat here, by the name of Tom Quartz, which you'd 'a' took an interest in, I reckon — most anybody would. I had him here eight year — and he was the remarkablest cat *I* ever see. He was a large gray one of the Tom specie, an' he had more hard, natchral sense than anyone in this camp — 'n' a *power* of dignity — he wouldn't let the Gov'ner of Californy be familiar with him. He never ketched a rat in his life — 'peared to be above it. He never cared for nothing but mining. He knowed more about mining, that cat did, than any man *I* ever, ever see. You couldn't tell *him* noth'n' 'bout placer-diggin's — 'n' as for pocket-mining, why he was just born for it. He would dig out after me an' Jim when we went over the hills prospect'n', and he would trot along behind us for as much as five mile, if we went so fur. An' he had the best judgment bout mining-ground — why you never see anything like it. When we went to work, he'd scatter a glance around, 'n' if he didn't think much of the indications, he would give a look as much as to say, 'Well, I'll have to get you to excuse *me*,' 'n' shove for home. But if the ground suited him, he would lay low 'n' keep dark till the first pan was washed, 'n' then he would sidle up 'n' take a look, an' if there was about six or seven grains of gold, *he* was satisfied — he didn't want no better prospect 'n' that — 'n' then he would lay down on our coats and snore like a steamboat till we'd struck the pocket, an' then get up 'n' superintend. He was nearly lightnin' on superintending.

"Well, by an' by, up comes this yer quartz excitement. Everybody was into it — everybody was pick'n' 'n' blast'n instead of shovelin' dirt on the hillside — everybody was put'n' down a shaft instead of scrapin' the surface. Noth'n' would do Jim, but *we* must tackle the ledges, too, 'n' so we did. We commenced put'n' down a shaft, 'n' Tom Quartz he began to wonder what in the Dickens it was all about. *He* hadn't ever seen any mining like that before, 'n' he was all upset, as you may say — he couldn't come to a right understanding of it no way — it was too many for *him*. He was down on it, too, you bet you — he was down on it powerful — 'n' always appeared to consider it the cussedest foolishness out. But that cat, you know, was *always* agin new-fangled arrangements — somehow he never could abide 'em. *You* know how it is with old habits. But by an' by Tom Quartz begin to git sort of reconciled a little, though he never *could* altogether understand that eternal sinkin' of a shaft an' never pannin' out anything. At last he got to comin' down in the shaft hisself, to try to cipher it out. An' when he'd git the blues, 'n' feel kind o' scruffy, 'n' aggravated 'n' disgusted — knowin' as he did, that the bills was running' up all the time an' we warn't makin' a cent — he would curl up on a gunny-sack in the corner an' go to sleep.

"Well, one day when the shaft was down about eight foot, the rock got so hard that we had to put in a blast — the first blast'n' we'd ever done since Tom Quartz was born. An' then we lit the fuse 'n' climb out 'n' got off 'bout fifty yards — 'n' forgot 'n' left Tom Quartz sound asleep on the gunny-sack. In 'bout a minute we seen a puff of smoke bust up out of the hole 'n' then everything let go with an awful crash, 'n' about four million ton of rocks 'n' dirt 'n' smoke 'n' splinters shot up 'bout a mile an' a half into the air, an' by George, right in the dead center of it was old Tom Quartz a-goin' end over end, an' a-snortin' an' a-sneez'n', an' a-clawin' an' a-reachin' for things like all possessed. But it warn't no use, you know, it warn't no use. An' that was the last we seen of *him* for about two minutes 'n' a half, an' then all of a sudden it begin to rain rocks and rubbage, an' directly he come down ker-whop about ten foot off f'm where we stood. Well, I reckon he was p'raps the orneriest-lookin' beast you ever see. One ear was sot back on his neck, 'n' his tail was stove up, 'n' his eye-whiskers was singed off, 'n' he was all blacked up with powder an' smoke, and all sloppy with mud 'n' slush f'm one end to the other. Well, sir, it warn't no use to try to apologize — we couldn't say a word. He took a sort of a disgusted look at hisself, 'n' then he looked at us — an' it was just exactly the same as if he had said — 'Gents, maybe *you* think it's smart to take advantage of a cat that ain't had no experience of quartz-minin', but *I* think *different*' — an' then turned on his heel 'n' marched off home without ever saying another word.

"That was jest his style. An' maybe you won't believe it, but after that you never see a cat so prejudiced agin quartz-mining as what he was. An' by an' by when he *did* get to goin' down in the shaft ag'in, you'd 'a' been astonished at his sagacity. The minute we'd tetch off a blast 'n' the fuse'd begin to sizzle, he'd give a look as much to say, "Well, I'll have to git you to excuse *me*, an' it was surpris'n' the way he'd shin out of that hole 'n' go f'r a tree. Sagacity? It ain't no name for it. 'Twas *inspiration*!

I said, "Well, Mr. Baker, his prejudice against quartz-mining *was* remarkable, considering how he came by it. Couldn't you ever cure him of it?"

"*Cure him*! No! When Tom Quartz was sot once, he was *always* sot — and you might 'a' blowed him up as much as three million times 'n' you'd never 'a' broken him of his cussed prejudice ag'in quartz mining."

The affection and the pride that lit up Baker's face when he delivered this tribute to the firmness of his humble friend of other days, will always be a vivid memory with me.

* * * * *

Some of the best of Mark Twain's short stories came from that cabin on Jackass Hill. For years afterwards he told them on the lecture platform to great acclaim, or inserted them in his books when he wanted to make a point. "Jim Baker's Blue-jay Yarn" about a bird who stored hundreds of acorns in a hole that never seemed to fill up because it was a knothole in a cabin, is one of the funniest sketches in his book A TRAMP ABROAD. He used it as an illustration that "animals talk to each other, of course." And as for his most famous animal story of all — but that was yet to come.

* * * * *

REFERENCES

Anderson, Frederick, Michael B. Frank, and Kenneth M. Sanderson (eds.), MARK TWAIN'S NOTEBOOK & JOURNALS, VOL. I, Berkeley: University of California Press, 1975.

Bowker, Michael, "Jumping Back to the Gold Rush," *Westways*, April, 1988, pp. 33-36.

Lennon, Nigley, MARK TWAIN IN CALIFORNIA, San Francisco: Chronicle Books, 1982.

Janssen, Dale H. and Janice J. Beaty, STORYTELLING MARK TWAIN STYLE, Columbia, Missouri: Janssen Education Enterprise, Inc., 1988.

Twain, Mark, ROUGHING IT, New York: Harper and Brothers, 1913.

Twain, Mark, A TRAMP ABROAD, New York: Harper and Brothers, 1907.

Zainer, Phyllis, and Lou Zainer, CALIFORNIA GOLD: THE STORY OF THE RUSH TO RICHES, Tahoe Paradise, California: Zanel Publications, 1980.

*****

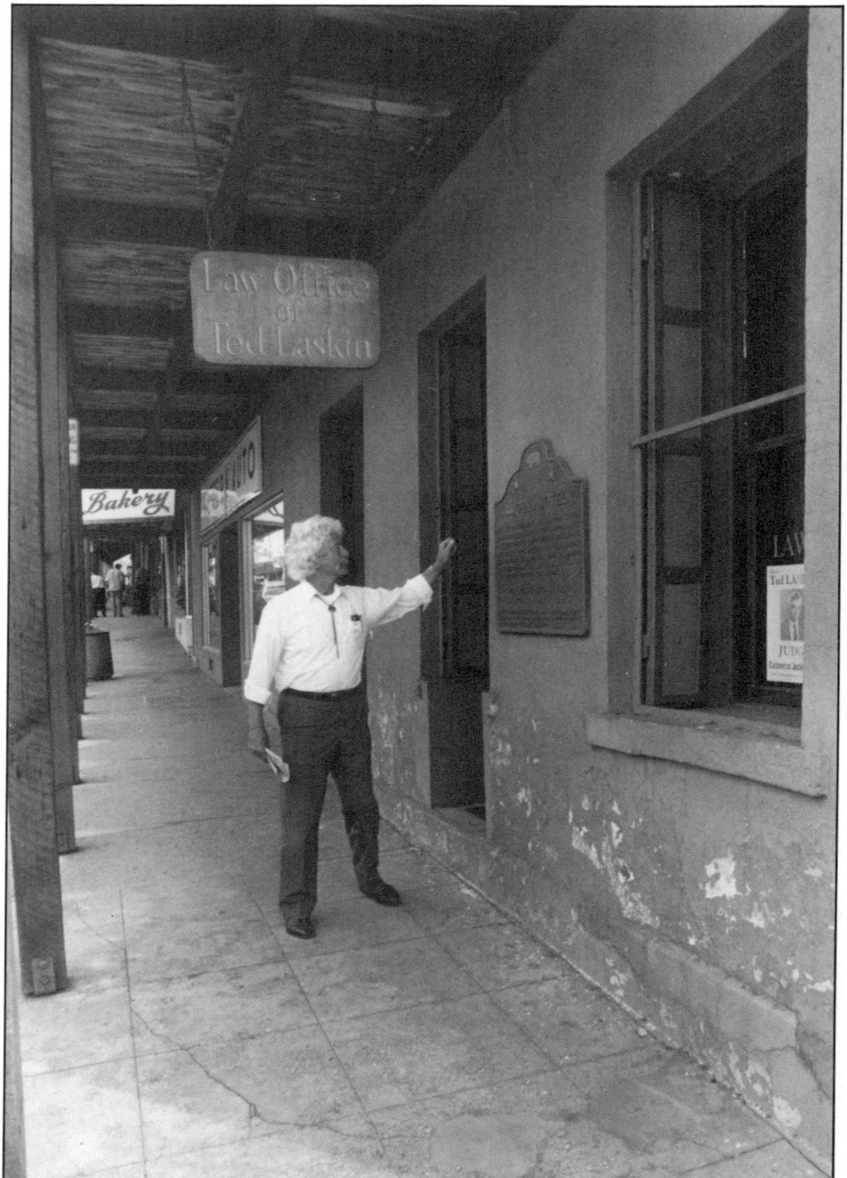
Law Office
of
Ted Laskin
Bakery

CHAPTER 13

THE CELEBRATED JUMPING FROG

TO ANGELS CAMP

By January 23, 1865 Clemens and Jim Gillis were back in Calaveras County again, this time prospecting near the town of Angels Camp. During good weather they slept out under the stars, but this time it rained — and rained — and rained. So they took a room at the Angels Hotel and ate their meals in the tavern there run by a Frenchman. "Beans and dishwater" (coffee) were the only items on the menu, remembered Samuel Clemens.

Every time the rain let up, out they went again to the slopes. Jim Gillis was bound and determined to make this trip pay off. Samuel Clemens was not so enthusiastic. As Albert Bigelow Paine records in MARK TWAIN: A BIOGRAPHY:

"Then the rain would come again and interfere with their work. One afternoon, when Clemens and Gillis were following certain tiny sprayed specks of gold that were leading to a pocket somewhere up the long slope, the chill downpour set in. Gillis, as usual, was washing, and Clemens carrying the water. The 'color' was getting better with every pan, and Jim Gillis believed that now, after their long waiting, they were to be rewarded. Possessed with the miner's passion, he would have gone on washing and climbing toward the precious pocket, regardless of everything. Clemens, however, shivering and disgusted, swore that each pail of water was his last. His teeth were chattering and he was wet through. Finally he said, in his deliberate way:

"Jim, I won't carry any more water. This work is too disagreeable."

Gillis had just taken out a panful of dirt.

"Bring one more pail, Sam," he pleaded.

"Oh, h--l, Jim, I won't do it; I'm freezing."

"Just one more pail, Sam," he pleaded.

"No, sir, not a drop, not if I knew there were a million dollars in that pan." (Paine, p. 272, 1912)

So Gillis posted a thirty-day claim by the pan of dirt and returned with Clemens to Angels Camp. They never did get back to their pan, but in later years the rest of the story was confirmed by Joe Goodman and Steve Gillis: the rain finally washed the dirt off naturally, revealing a handful of gold nuggets. Two Austrian miners came along, found it, and sat down to wait for the thirty days to be up. Then they staked their own claim, followed the lead further up, and took maybe ten or twenty thousand dollars worth of gold out of the pocket!

THE JUMPING FROG

Meanwhile, back at the Angels Hotel the exhausted miners recuperated by playing pool on a dilapidated old table in the saloon, or by listening to the yarn-spinning by some of the older patrons. One was Ben Coon, a former Illinois River pilot who told long-winded stories that seemed to have no point to them. One of his stories that caught Samuel Clemens' fancy was about a fellow who had a jumping frog that he liked to bet on.

Clemens recorded the bare-bones outline of the story in his notebook:

> Coleman with his jumping frog — bet stranger $50 — stranger had no frog, and C. got him one — in the mean time stranger filled C.'s frog full of shot and he couldn't jump. The stranger's frog won. (Paine, p. 273, 1912)

Clemens and Gillis had fun mimicking the teller of the story later on because they thought that not only was the tale absurd but also the teller who droned on without ever smiling or reaching his point. "I don't see no p'ints about that frog that's any better'n any other frog," they would drone to each other in a monotone, and then double over with laughter.

Dick Stoker joined them at the end of January. On February 20 the three of them finally left Angels Camp and walked back to their cabin on Jackass Hill in a snow storm. Clemens continued on to San Francisco on February 26. When he went through his mail he found a letter from Artemus Ward, the well-known humorist he had met during his lecture tour in Virginia City. Ward had been impressed with Mark Twain's writing and now wanted a story from him to include in a book he was publishing. But the letter had been delayed so it seemed too late to send anything. Ward later persisted, until Clemens eventually decided to put the jumping frog story into his own words. He changed the name of the betting man from Coleman to Jim Smiley, stretched the story out to include all kinds of betting, and then wrote: (in part)

"Jim Smiley and his Jumping Frog"

. . . there was a feller here once by the name of Jim Smiley, in the winter of '49 — or maybe it was the spring of '50 — I don't recollect exactly, somehow, though what makes me think it was one or the other is because I remember the big flume warn't finished when he first come to the camp; but anyway, he was the curiousest man about always betting on anything that turned up you ever see, if he could get anybody to bet on the other side; and if he couldn't he'd change sides. Any way that suited the other man would suit *him* — any way just so's he got a bet, *he* was satisfied. But still he was lucky; uncommon lucky; he most always come out winner. He was always ready and laying for a chance; there couldn't be no solitr'y thing mentioned but that feller'd offer to bet on it, and take ary side you please, as I was just telling you. If there was a horserace, you'd find him flush or you'd find him busted at the end of it; if there was a dog-fight, he'd bet on it; if there was a cat-fight, he'd bet on it; if there was a chicken-fight, he'd bet on it; why, if there was two birds setting on a fence, he would bet you which one would fly first . . .

Thish-yer Smiley had a mare — the boys called her the fifteen-minute nag, but that was only in fun, you know, because of course she was so slow and always had the asthma or the distemper, or the consumption, or something of that kind. They used to give her two or three hundred yards' start, and then pass her under way; but always at the fag end of the race she'd get excited and desperate like, and come cavorting and straddling up, and scattering her legs around limber, sometimes in the air, and sometimes out to one side among the fences, and kicking up m-o-r-e dust and raising m-o-r-e racket with her coughing and sneezing and blowing her nose — and *always* fetch up at the stand just about a neck ahead, as near as you could cipher it down.

And he had a little small bull-pup, that to look at him you'd think he warn't worth a cent but to set around and look ornery and lay for a chance to steal something. But as soon as money was up on him he was a different dog; his under-jaw'd begin to stick out like the fo'castle of a steamboat, and his teeth would uncover and shine like the furnaces. And a dog might tackle him and bully-rag him, and bite him, and throw him over his shoulder two or three times, and Andrew Jackson — which was the name of the pup — Andrew Jackson would never let on but what *he* was satisfied, and hadn't expected nothing else — and the bets being doubled and doubled on the other side all the time, till the money was all up; and then all of a sudden he would grab that other dog jest by the j'int of his hind leg and freeze to it — not chaw, you understand, but only just grip and hang on till they throwed up the sponge, if it was a year. Smiley always come out winner on that pup, till he harnessed a dog once that didn't have no hind legs, because they'd been sawed off in a circular saw, and when the thing had gone along far enough, and the money was all up, and he come to make a snatch for his pet holt, he see in a minute how he'd been imposed on, and how the other dog had him in the door, so to speak, and he 'peared surprised, and then he looked sorter discouraged-like, and didn't try no more to win the fight, and so he got shucked out bad. He give Smiley a look, as much to say his heart was broke, and it was *his* fault for putting up a dog that hadn't no hind legs for him to take holt of, which was his main dependence in a fight, and then he limped off a piece and laid down and died. It was a good pup, that Andrew Jackson, and would have made a name for hisself if he'd lived, for the stuff was in him and he had genius — I know it, because he hadn't no opportunities to speak of, and it don't stand to reason that a dog could make such a fight as he could under them circumstances if he hadn't no talent. It always makes me feel sorry when I think of that last fight of his'n, and the way it turned out.

Well, thish-yer Smiley had rat-tarriers, and chicken cocks, and tomcats and all them kind of things, till you couldn't rest, and you couldn't fetch nothing for him to bet on but he'd match you. He ketched a frog one day, and took him home, and said he cal'lated to educate him; and so he never done nothing for three months but set in his back yard and learn that frog to jump. And you bet you he *did* learn him, too. He'd give him a little punch behind, and the next minute you'd see that frog whirling in the air like a doughnut — see him turn one summerset, or maybe a couple, if he got a good start, and come down flat-footed all right, like a cat. He got him up so in the matter of ketching flies, and kep' him in practice so constant, that he'd nail a fly every time as fur as he could see him. Smiley said all a frog wanted was education, and he could do 'most anything — and I believe him. Why, I've seen him set Dan'l Webster down here on this floor — Dan'l Webster was the name of the frog — and sing out, "Flies, Dan'l, flies!" and quicker'n you could wink he'd spring straight up and snake a fly off'n the counter there, and flop down on the floor ag'in as solid as a gob of mud, and fall to scratching the side of his head with his hind foot as indifferent as if he hadn't no idea he'd been doin' any more'n any frog might do. You never see a frog so modest and straightfor'ard as he was, for all he was so gifted. And when it come to fair and square jumping on the dead level, he could get over more ground at one straddle than any animal of his breed you ever see. Jumping on a dead level was his strong suit, you understand; and when it come to that, Smiley was monstrous proud of his frog, and well he might be, for fellers that had traveled and been everywhere all said he laid over any frog that ever *they* see.

Well, Smiley kep' the beast in a little lattice box, and he used to fetch him down-town sometimes and lay for a bet. One day a feller — a stranger in the camp, he was — come acrost him with his box, and says:

"What might it be that you've got in the box?"

And Smiley says, sorter indifferent-like, "It might be a parrot, or it might be a canary, maybe, but it ain't — it's only just a frog."

And the feller took it, and looked at it careful, and turned it round this way and that, and says "H'm — so 'tis. Well, what's he good for?"

Well, Smiley says easy and careless, "He's good enough for one thing, I should judge — he can outjump any frog in Calaveras County."

The feller took the box again, and took another long, particular look, and give it back to Smiley, and says, very deliberate, "Well," he says, "I don't see no p'ints about that frog that's any better'n any other frog."

"Maybe you don't," Smiley says. "Maybe you understand frogs and maybe you don't understand 'em; maybe you've had experience, and maybe you ain't only a amature, as it were. Anyways, I've got *my* opinion, and I'll resk forty dollars that he can outjump any frog in Calaveras County."

And the feller studied a minute, and then says, kinder sadlike, "Well, I'm only a stranger here, and I ain't got no frog, but if I had a frog, I'd bet you."

And then Smiley says, "That's all right — that's all right — if you'll hold my box a minute, I'll go and get you a frog." And so the feller took the box, and put up his forty dollars along with Smiley's, and set down to wait.

So he set there a good while thinking and thinking to himself, and then he got the frog out and prized his mouth open and took a teaspoon and filled him full of quail-shot — filled him pretty near up to his chin — and set him on the floor. Smiley he went to the swamp and slopped around in the mud for a long time, and finally he ketched a frog, and fetched him in, and give him to this feller, and says:

"Now, if you're ready, set him alongside of Dan'l, with his forepaws just even with Dan'l's, and I'll give the word." Then he says, "One — two — three — *git!*" and him and the feller touched up the frogs from behind, and the new frog hopped off lively, but Dan'l give a heave, and hysted up his shoulders — so — like a Frenchman, but it warn't no use — he couldn't budge; he was planted as solid as a church, and he couldn't no more stir than if he was anchored out. Smiley was a good deal surprised, and he was disgusted too, but he didn't have no idea what the matter was, of course.

The feller took the money and started away; and when he was going out at the door, he sorter jerked his thumb over his shoulder — so — at Dan'l, and says again, very deliberate, "Well," he says, "*I* don't see no p'ints about that frog that's any better'n any other frog."

Smiley he stood scratching his head and looking down at Dan'l a long time, and at last he says, "I do wonder what in the nation that frog thow'd off for — I wonder if there ain't something the matter with him — he 'pears to look mighty baggy, somehow." And he ketched Dan'l by the nap of the neck, and hefted him, and says, "Why blame my cats if he don't weigh five pound!" and turned him upside down and he belched out a double handful of shot. And then he see how it was, and he was the maddest man — he set the frog down and took out after the feller, but he never ketched him. And . . . (See Janssen and Beaty, STORYTELLING MARK TWAIN STYLE, p. 170, 1988)

*****

THE STORY

So that was the story. Pretty funny if the teller drags it out the right way in the manner of the old time yarn-spinners. Hilarious, in fact, when you come right down to it. And very Mark-Twainian in its phrasing when you compare it with his later tales. Just the kind of thing Twain himself would have done with a frog. No wonder the story appealed to him!

Unlike the pan of dirt Jim Gillis left on the hillside, Mark Twain had taken the raw ingredients of this unlikely yarn and washed them and refined them and read them aloud over and over until he had shaped them into a nugget of the purest gold. No one would ever be bored by Mark Twain's telling of this tale like they had been by Ben Coon's rendition.

And then he sent off the story to Artemus Ward's publisher in New York. But it really was too late for inclusion in Ward's book, so the publisher sent the story along to the New York *Saturday Press*, a popular national magazine. It appeared on November 8, 1865. New Yorkers had never read anything like it. It was the talk of the day. People laughed till they cried, and then passed the magazine along for others to enjoy. Who was this "Mark Twain" anyway? What else had he written?

As was the custom of the day, newspapers and magazines up and down the East Coast began copying the story for their own readers. The word finally reached the West Coast about the smashing success of their own "Wild Humorist of the Pacific Slope." A San Francisco newspaper, the *Alta California* noted: "Mark Twain's story in the *Saturday Press* of November 8 . . . has set New York in a roar, and he may be said to have made his mark . . . The papers are copying it far and near. It is voted the best thing of the day . . ." (Lennon, MARK

TWAIN IN CALIFORNIA, 1982, p. 84)

Mark Twain must have been pleased at such a reception. But he was sorry that his first story to appear in New York had to be such a "villainous backwoods sketch" as he called it — so he said. Why couldn't it have been one of the more serious or refined things he had written? (Doesn't the reader wonder, then, why he sent this one and not another story?)

But Samuel Clemens had always told tall tales. When a neighbor back in Hannibal, Missouri asked his mother if she ever believed anything that that son of hers said, she replied: "Oh, yes, I know his average. I discount him ninety per cent. The rest is pure gold." (Clemens, Cyril, MY COUSIN MARK TWAIN, 1939, p. 8). So it was that "The Celebrated Jumping Frog of Calaveras County," the tallest of Mark Twain's tall tales was also pure gold. And so it was that Mark Twain was now committed to following his reputation east.

JANSSEN AND BEATY AT ANGELS CAMP

The authors followed winding Route 49 through the foothills to the modern town of Angels Camp. They drove slowly through town with thoughts similar to those they had had about Jamestown, Tennessee, the starting point of their trip a month earlier. Would any old buildings or historical remains be preserved? Would the people of Angels Camp remember or share any of their Mark Twain heritage with the authors?

At first glance the name "Mark Twain" did not seem to appear in lights on motel or restaurant signs. But a closer look showed them that a few older buildings remained: three churches, the Odd Fellows Hall, and yes, there it was — the Angels Hotel, a block long building with a plaque on the wall to commemorate the rooms where Mark Twain had first heard the Jumping Frog story. And the town park also boasted a wonderful Mark Twain statue.

FROGTOWN

But the thing that captured a visitor's attention in Angels Camp was frogs. They came in all shapes and sizes as souvenirs. Even the bakery had a collection in its window. "Be sure to visit Frogtown" was the word townsfolks gave to the authors.

What was Frogtown, they wondered? Turning off Route 49 at the Frogtown sign just south of town, the authors pulled into an immense

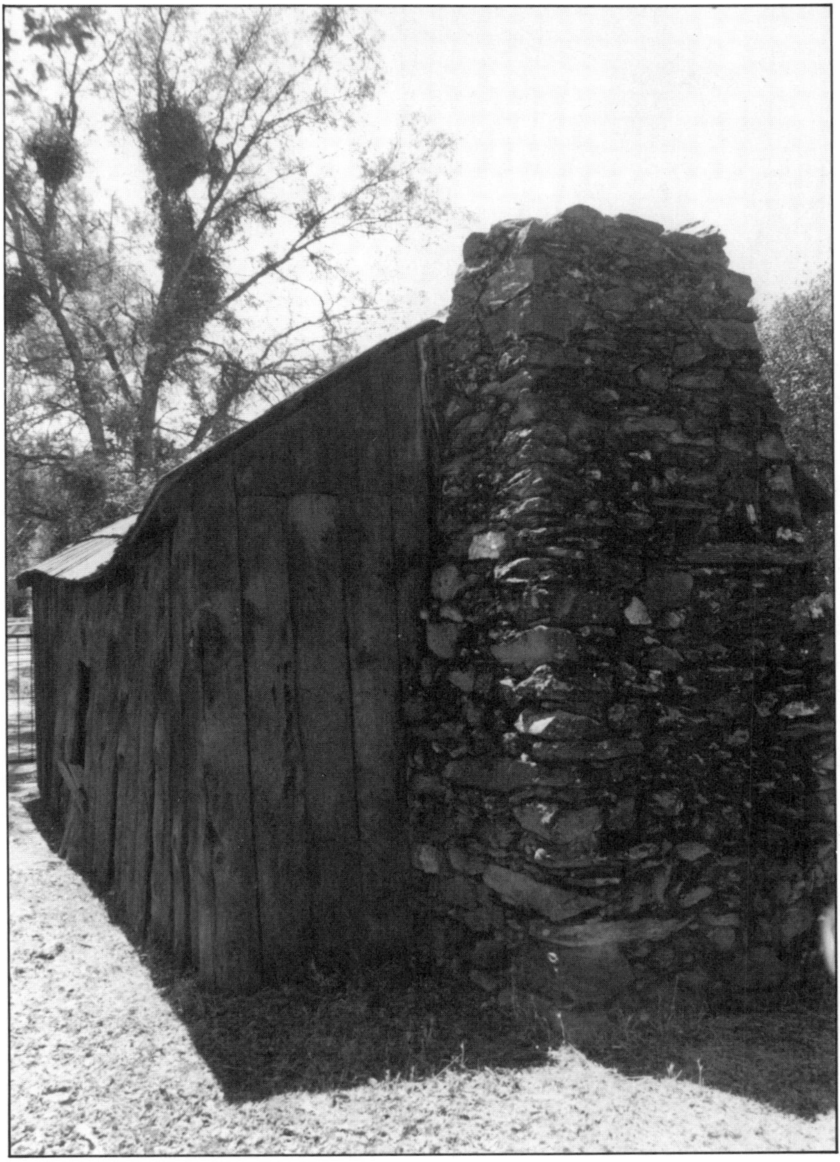

empty parking lot beside the multiple entry gates to a huge arena. This was Frogtown? Yes, they learned. It was the site of the annual International Frog Jumping Contest, attracting 3,000 contestants from around the world — plus their frogs — plus their trainers! Mark Twain would have loved it!

Janssen and Beaty soon learned the fascinating history of the contest, a cross between a historical celebration, a rodeo, and a county fair. It all started back in 1928 when the muddy ruts and chuck holes of Main Street were finally paved over. The townspeople decided to celebrate the paving of their street with a "Frog Jubilee and Days of Forty-nine Celebration." 15,000 people turned up that first year. Many came in the costumes of red-shirted miners, Mexicans, cowpunchers, gamblers, Chinese coolies, dancing girls, Indians, or pioneer women. They crowded around a one-ring jump area to watch a frog called "The Pride of San Joaquin" establish a world jumping record of three feet, six inches. There were 51 frog entries that first year.

This year the huge stadium accommodated 45,000 spectators. Besides frog jumping, the Calaveras County Fair and Jumping Frog Jubilee (May 19-22) featured cattle penning, sheep dog trials, calf branding, musical chairs, a Pony Express Relay Race, wild cow milking, professional arm wrestling, and storytelling. (Mark Twain would have been pleased at that last one!) But no frog entry beat the 1986 champion, Rosie the Ribeter, with an incredible jump of 21 feet 5.75 inches! Shades of Jim Smiley!

Dale Janssen came away with a tiny metallic lapel pin of a jumping frog. It was his "gold" treasure!

THE CABIN ON JACKASS HILL

Then on to Jackass Hill across the Stanislaus River on a spectacular bridge over a lake, traveled the authors, and finally up to the top of one of the hills. There was the cabin — old and weather-beaten but a reconstruction of the original cabin that had burned down many years ago. It was rebuilt around the sturdy stone fireplace that survived the fire. Today the cabin is surrounded by a high wrought iron fence for protection. Modern residences dot the hills, a lovely off-the-beaten path hideaway, you would think. Yet with all the car traffic up the dusty road, the residents must sometimes wish this pilgrimage spot for one of America's most beloved authors was not quite so popular.

Janssen and Beaty contemplated the cabin and what it meant in the life of Samuel Clemens: another beginning, it would seem. That was

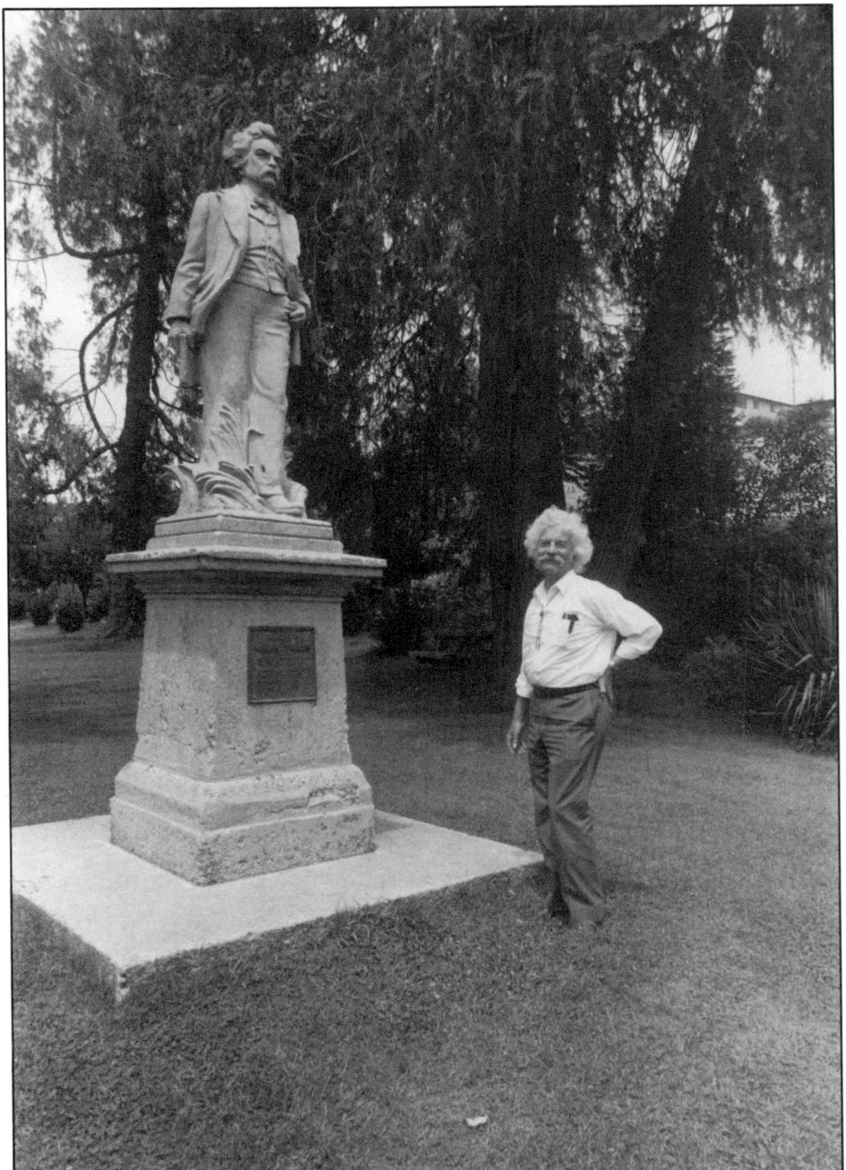

surprising to them; they had not really thought about Jackass Hill in those terms. It had originally seemed to them when they started their own pilgrimage, traveling west Mark Twain style, that his Jackass Hill cabin would have been more of a retreat from the world for Samuel Clemens. But it was so much more, they now realized. It was truly a beginning of vast importance for this man of thirty. Whether or not he realized it, this location would mark him forever as a writer — not a miner, not a riverboat pilot, nor even a newspaper man, but a story writer — and a great one.

And then the authors thought about what it meant in their own lives as well: this was not the end of their journey, as they might have originally intended. Was this another beginning?

END

REFERENCES

Calaveras Californian, (newspaper), Angels Camp, California: May 18, 1978.
Clemens, Cyril, MY COUSIN MARK TWAIN, Emmaus, Penna.: Rodale Press, 1939.
Janssen, Dale H., and Janice J. Beaty, STORYTELLING MARK TWAIN STYLE, Columbia, Missouri: Janssen Education Enterprise, Inc., 1988.
"Jump On Over," *Calaveras County Fair and Jumping Frog Jubilee*, 1988.
Lennon, Nigley, MARK TWAIN IN CALIFORNIA, San Francisco: Chronicle Books, 1982.
Paine, Albert Bigelow, MARK TWAIN: A BIOGRAPHY, New York: Harper and Brothers, 1912.
Twain, Mark, ROUGHING IT, New York: Harper and Brothers, 1913.

*****

DALE H. JANSSEN has lived in Missouri most of his life. After completing a B.S. degree in business and marketing at the University of Missouri, Columbia, he engaged in research and marketing, followed by becoming a transportation law practitioner. While successfully defending needed rail service in western Iowa, Janssen enjoyed playing singalong harmonica music at schools and nursing homes. This led to the completion of certificate courses in music therapy, nurse assistant and social services. Playing harmonica music in a nursing home eventually led to the discovery of Janssen as a Mark Twain look-alike. His own researching of Mark Twain in libraries and communities across the nation and in Germany supported his appearances as Mark Twain in Missouri, Iowa, Illinois, New York and Connecticut, highlighted by his appearance as Mark Twain on the national television "Real People" program. Recent accomplishments include the production of a documentary videotape "Mark Twain Remembers," the co-authoring of the books MARK TWAIN WALKING AMERICA AGAIN, STORYTELLING MARK TWAIN STYLE, and TRAVELING WEST MARK TWAIN STYLE, plus the co-teaching of a college course and workshop "Storytelling Mark Twain Style."

JANICE J. BEATY, Ph.D., a Professor in Human Services at Elmira College, Elmira, New York is an Elmira native who has traveled widely in Europe, the Middle East, Southeast Asia, the Caribbean and Mexico, living for a number of years on Guam in the Pacific, before returning home to teach and write. Dr. Beaty teaches courses in Early Childhood Education, Children's Literature, Folklore, and Storytelling Mark Twain Style. She is a Mark Twain researcher and writer ("Mark Twain's Cats at Quarry Farm," MARK TWAIN WALKING AMERICA AGAIN, STORYTELLING MARK TWAIN STYLE), as well as an author of children's books (NUFU AND THE TURKEYFISH, SEEKER OF SEAWAYS) and teacher-training textbooks (SKILLS FOR PRESCHOOL TEACHERS, OBSERVING DEVELOPMENT OF THE YOUNG CHILD). Dr. Beaty has done Mark Twain research at libraries and historical sites across the United States and in Bermuda. TRAVELING WEST MARK TWAIN STYLE (as a co-author) is her twelfth book. Her hobbies include photography which she often uses to illustrate her books.